CADILLAC

SALMIERI

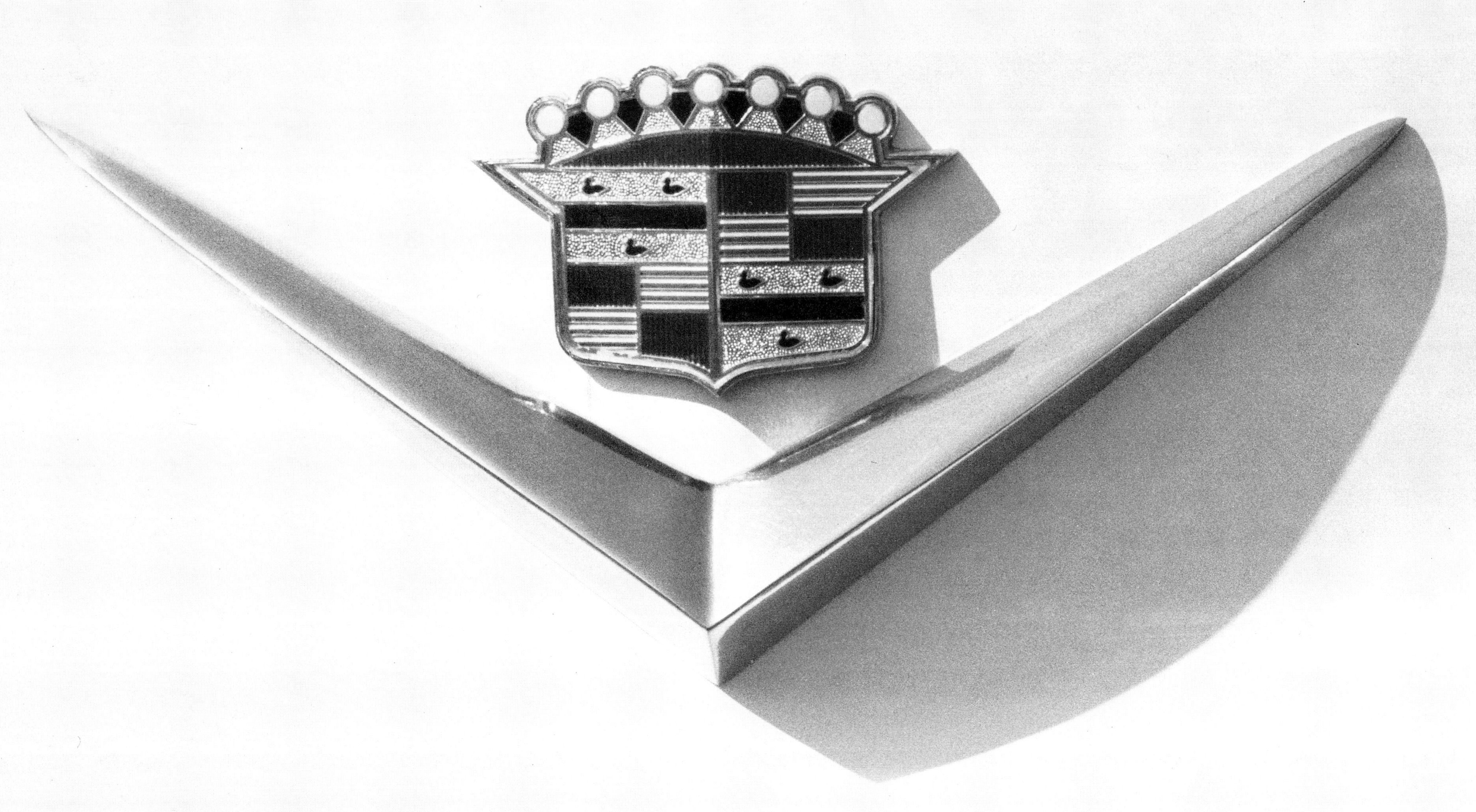

C A D I L L A C

PHOTOGRAPHS BY STEPHEN SALMIERI
HAND-PAINTED BY SYDNIE MICHELE SALMIERI

TEXT BY OWEN EDWARDS

TABARD
PRESS

Tabard Press
27 West 20th Street
New York, N.Y. 10011

First published in the United States of America in 1985 by
Rizzoli International Publications, Inc.

ISBN: 0-914427-39-3

Printed and bound in Singapore.

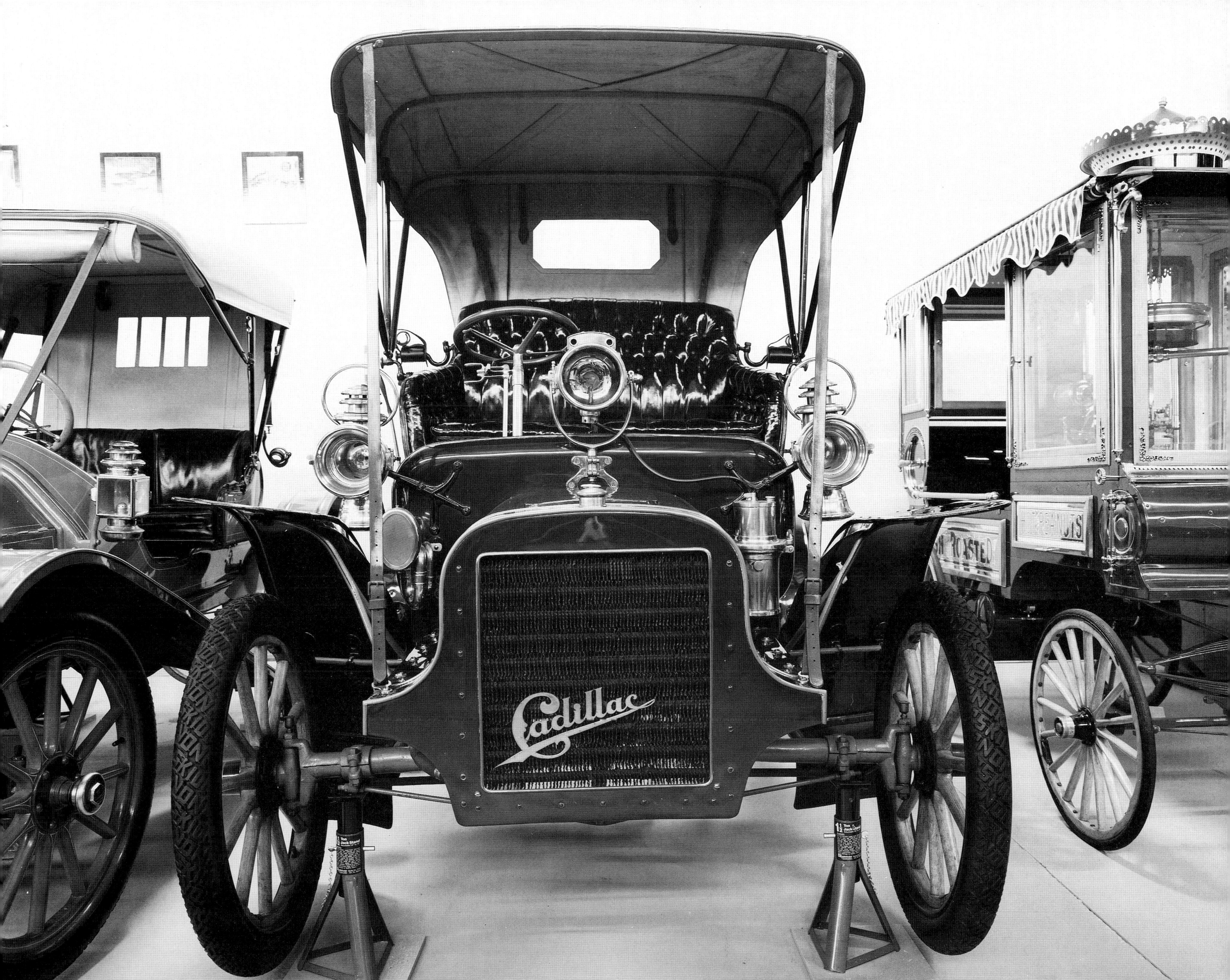
Cadillac

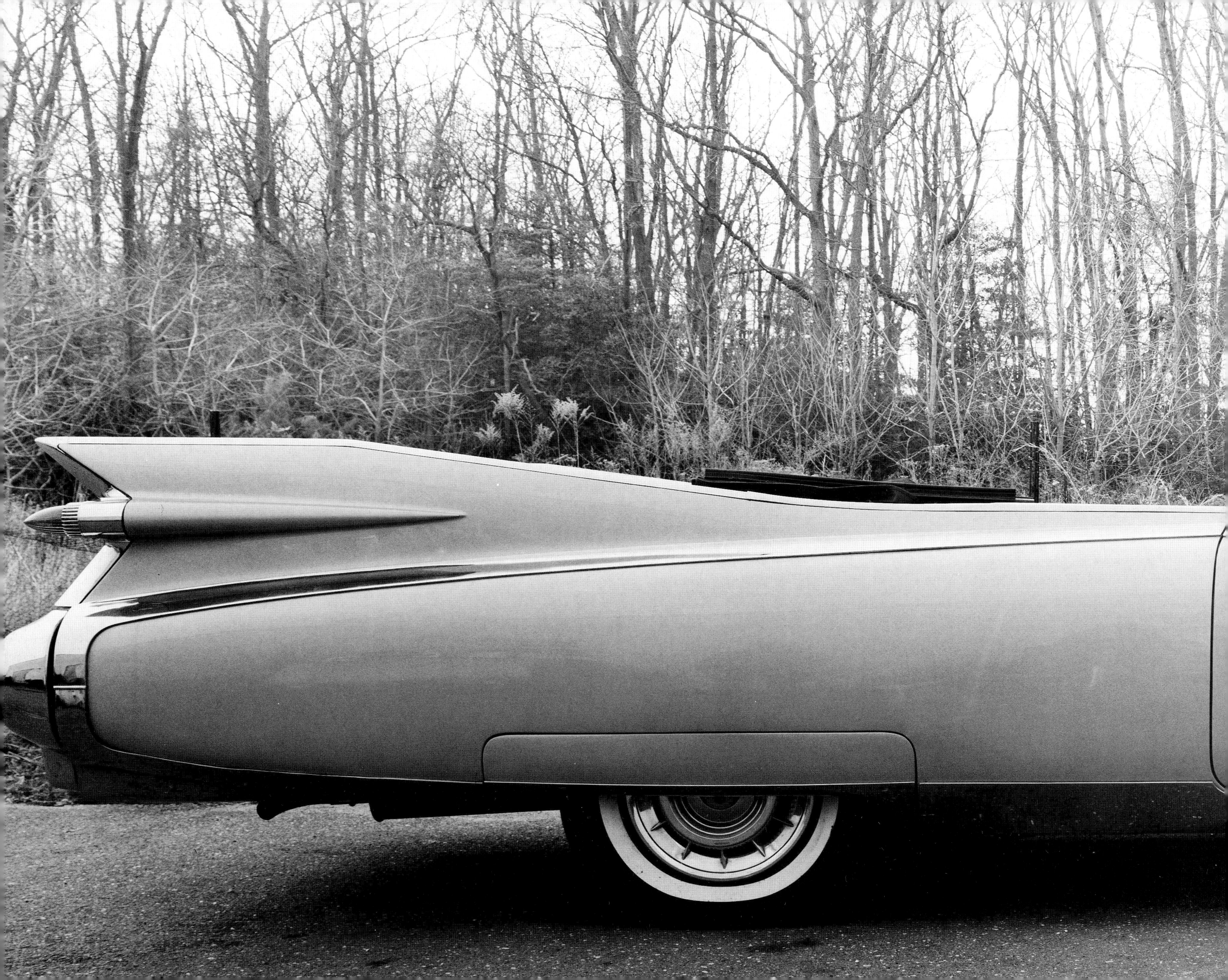

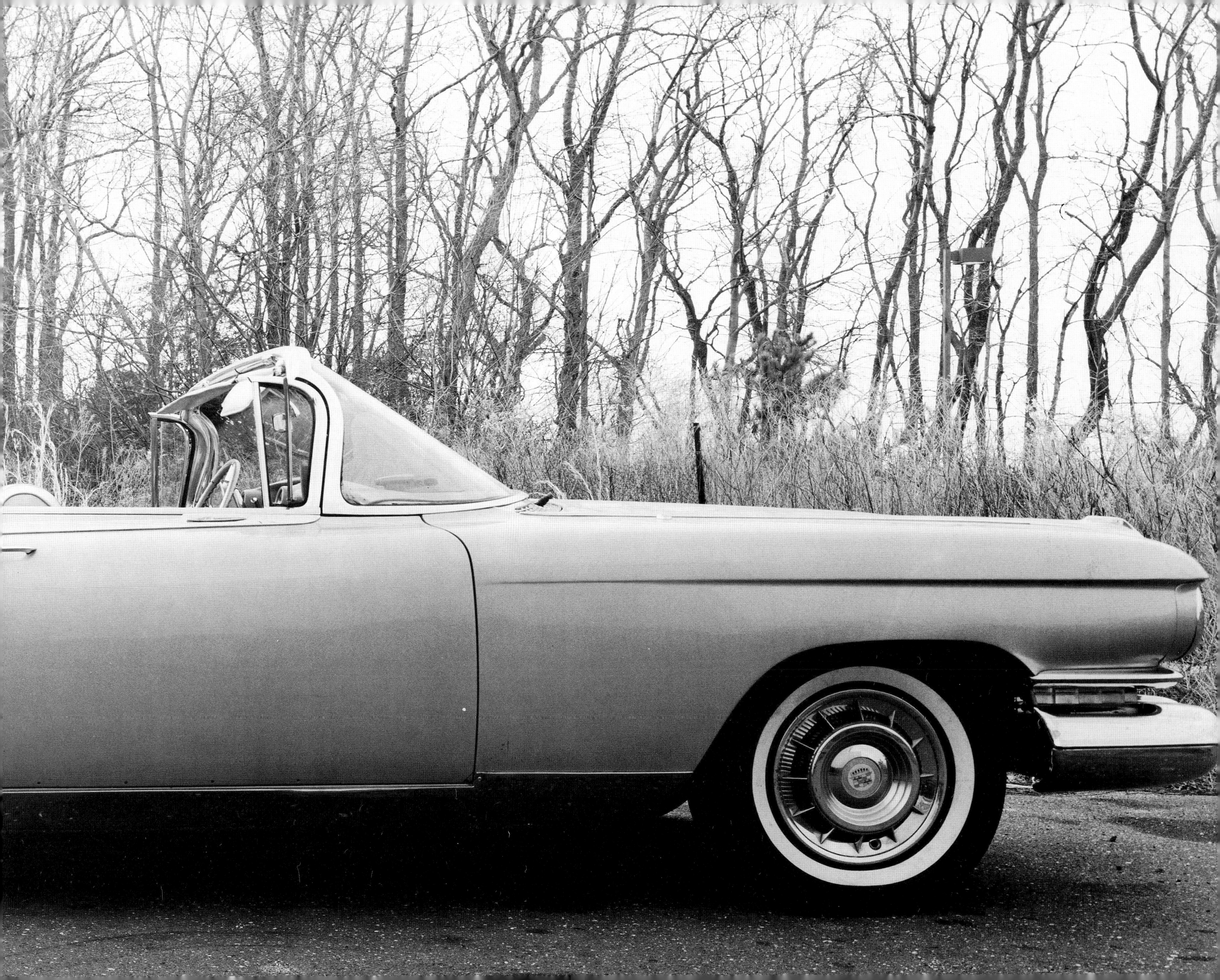

AN AMERICAN ICON

My father never had a Cadillac. In one way or another it marked him, and us, since the symbolic power of that particular car was such that not having one—in the fifties, in a town of green lawns and elm-lined streets forty-five minutes from Wall Street—meant as much as having one. Among my friends, knowing whose family had a Cadillac and whose didn't was essential information, like knowing who was Catholic.

We were prosperous enough to own a Cadillac, or at least optimistic for a future of limitless possibilities, which was a kind of prosperity. The act of going into debt to buy even the most far-fetched car was an expression of hope and a commitment to a country that had weathered depression and war and ended up owning the bright horizon; to drive home in a new Cadillac was as righteous as tithing the church, and as patriotic as saluting the flag. What was good for General Motors was good for America, said our Secretary of Defense, and few doubted he was right.

We did, once, veer close to making what was for American car buyers the ultimate choice. Toward the end of the war, we owned a black four-door La Salle, a '36 or '37, its rear window decorated with our A gasoline ration card. As a reward for good behavior, I was sometimes allowed to ride into town standing on the running board, G-Man style, my arm crooked around the post of the wing window. Those were days when there were giants in the driveway. More than anything else about the car, its great pachyderm mass stays in my memory. Like our quiet, boundless neighborhood, like my father, the machine was reassuringly large, and magisterially protective. The La Salle, though produced throughout its fourteen-year

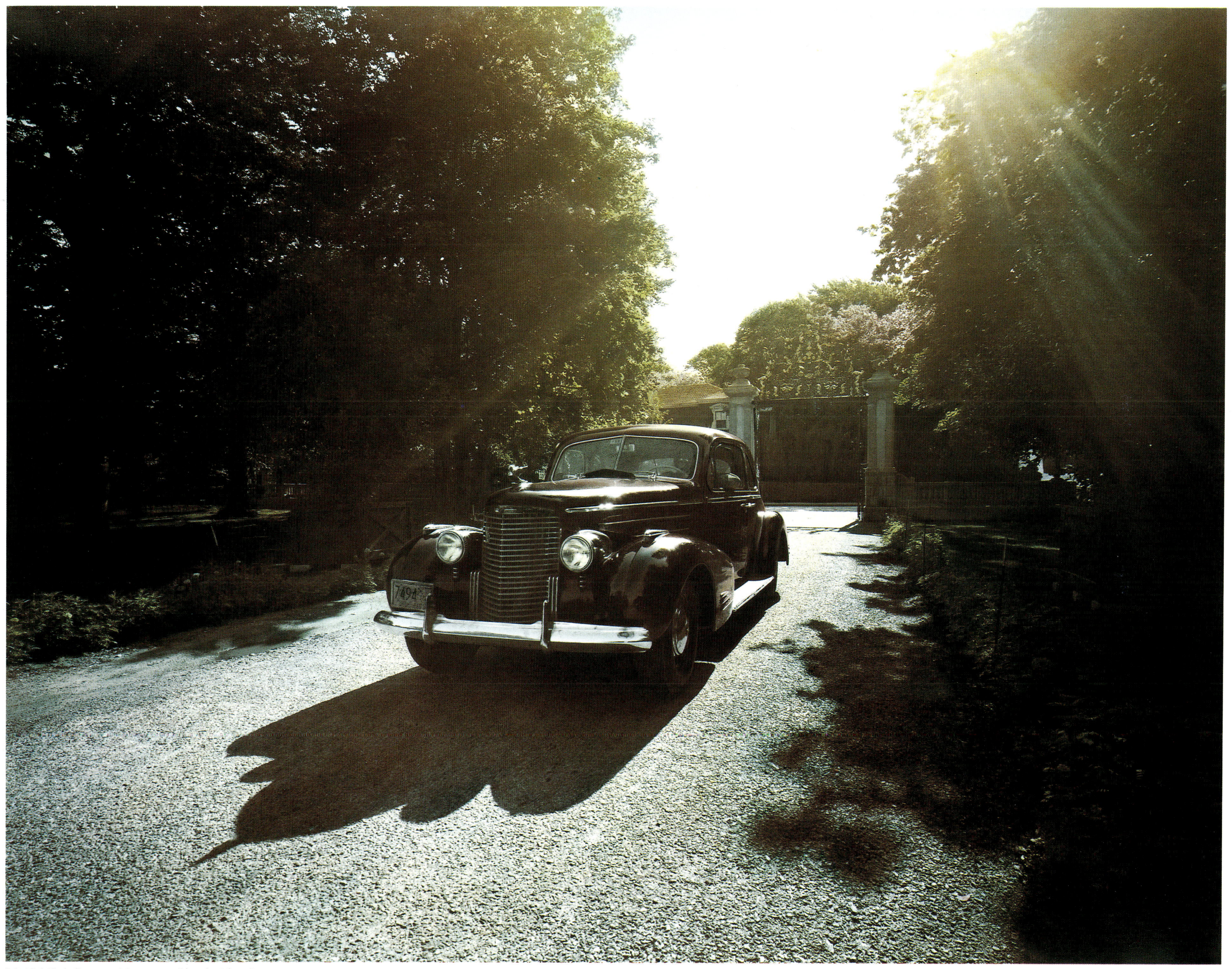

1940 V.16 Coupe; Newport, Rhode Island

history by Cadillac Motors, always kept a separate identity. Auto historians consider this a contributing factor to its mysterious lack of success, but it may well have been the reason my father bought one. No matter what its heritage, it was *not* a Cadillac. (How my father could afford the car, even used, I can't understand; the Depression years had been a movable famine for him, and his credit can't have been much good; but he had managed to buy it, and I suspect that what the car was *not* meant more to him than what it was.

The La Salle was not reintroduced after the war, and in 1947 or so my father embarked on his determined path of non-Cadillac ownership, driving home one bright spring day in a dark blue Chrysler. Then came a Mercury convertible, and a series of Buick convertibles reaching its dramatic crescendo in a lumbering green Dynaflow Roadmaster.

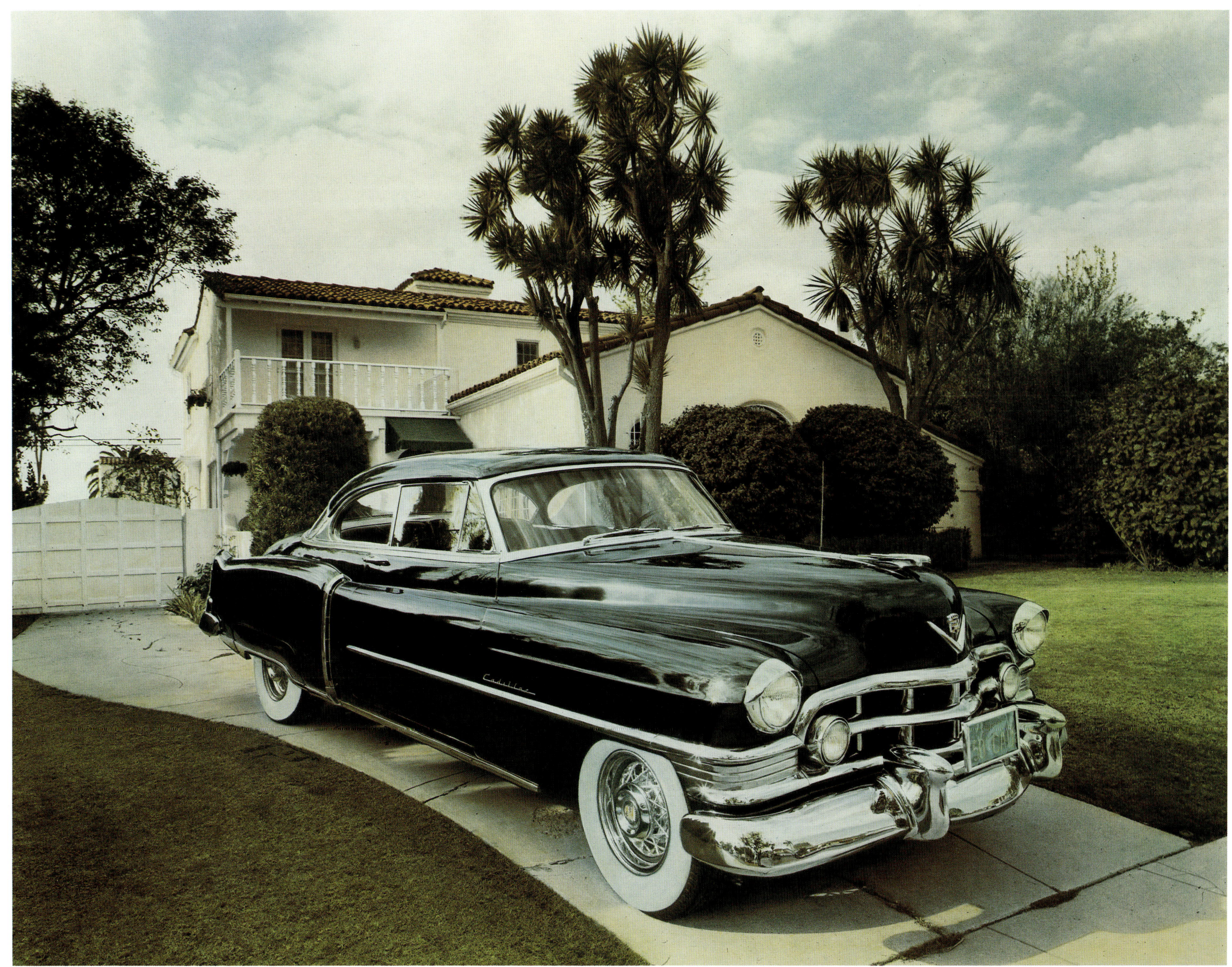

1950 Coupe de Ville; Santa Monica, California

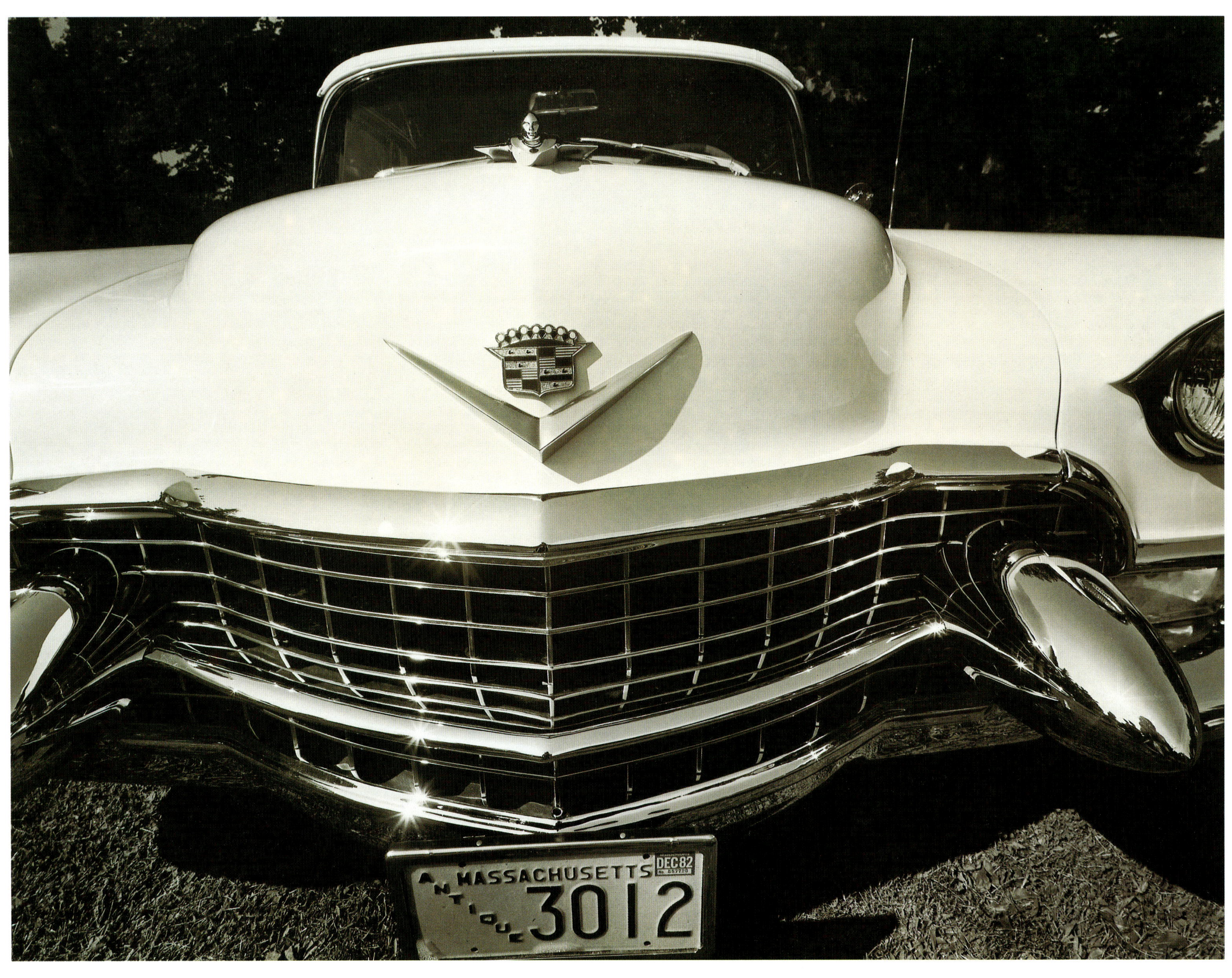

1955 Coupe de Ville; Amherst, Massachusetts

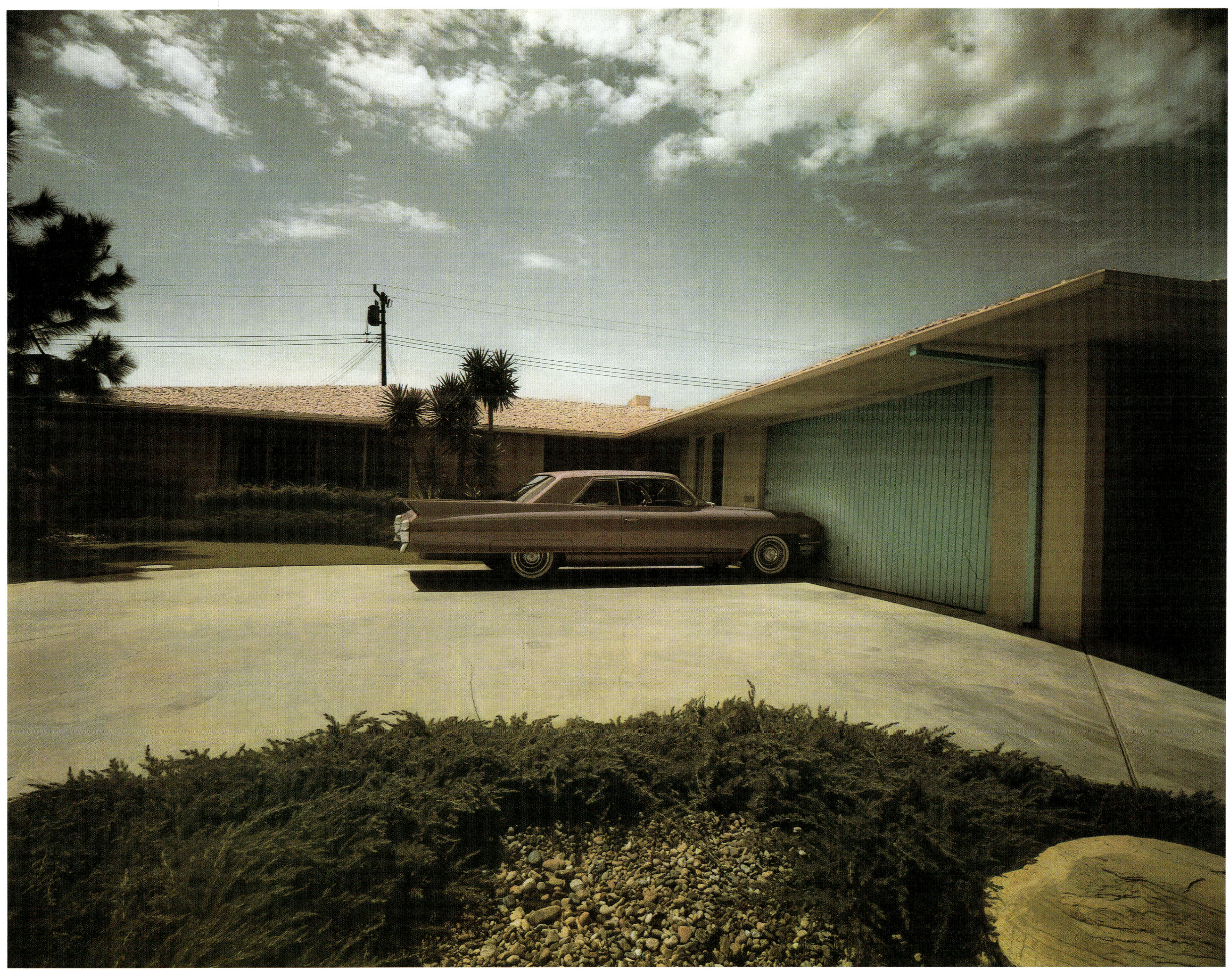

1962 Coupe de Ville; Beverly Hills, California

It's too late to ask my father why we didn't have a Cadillac, but I think I can guess. For him, there must have been only two kinds of people who owned Cadillacs: those who were well-off, as the cozy suburban saying had it, and those who wanted to look better off than they were. To be the former might be a matter of time, and luck. To be the latter was unthinkable, contemptible, "typical" (a word which invariably expressed disapproval when uttered with a short shake of the head and upturned eyes). So we fell into a family lifetime of letting the rest of America lust after the car called—by the company that made it and the company it kept—the Standard of the World. To make exaggerated claims for a product is probably the oldest tradition in merchandising. Anything from motor oil to snake oil can be called the standard of the world—it is the kind of fundamentally ambiguous term

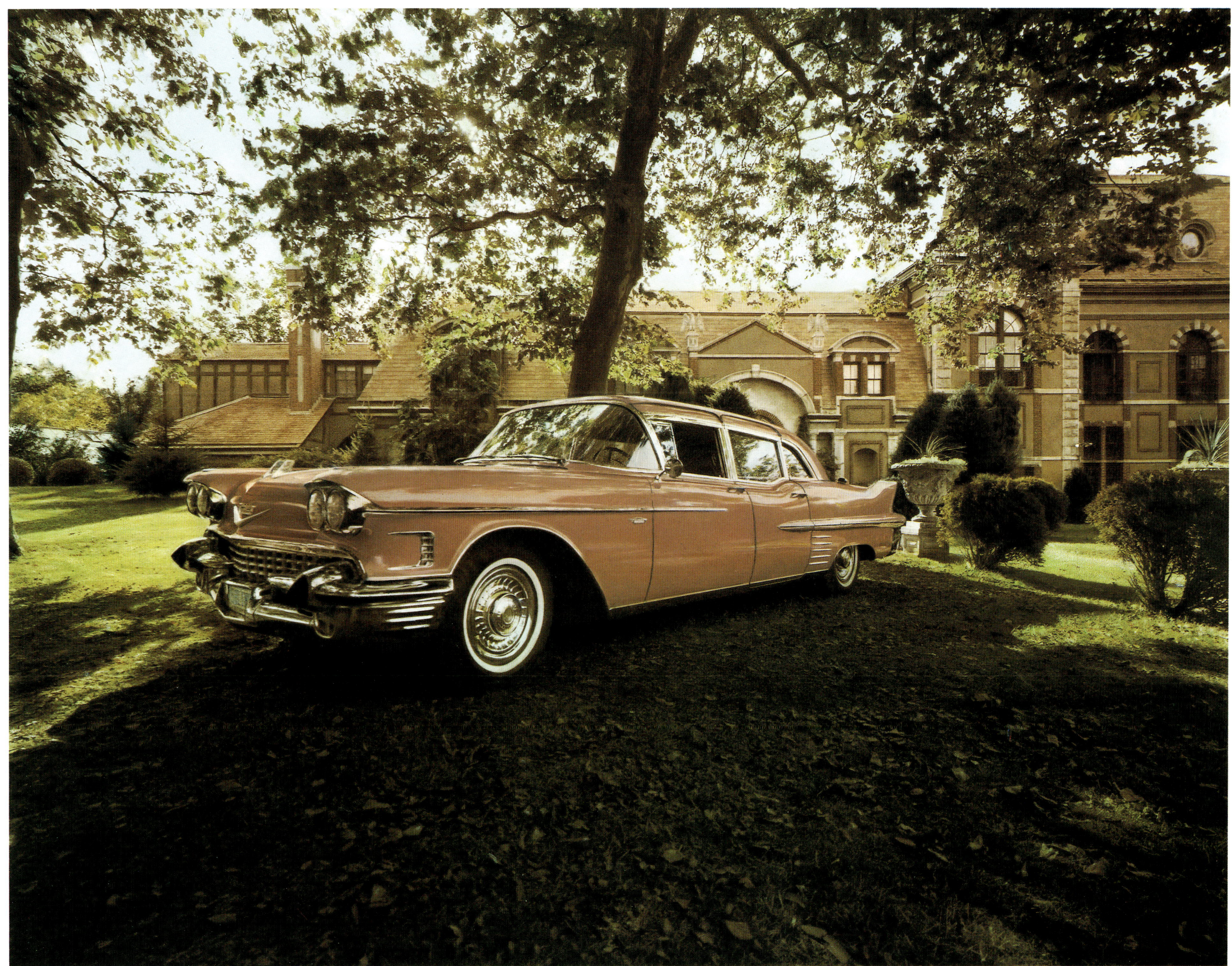

1958 Fleetwood Seventy-Five Sedan; Newport, Rhode Island

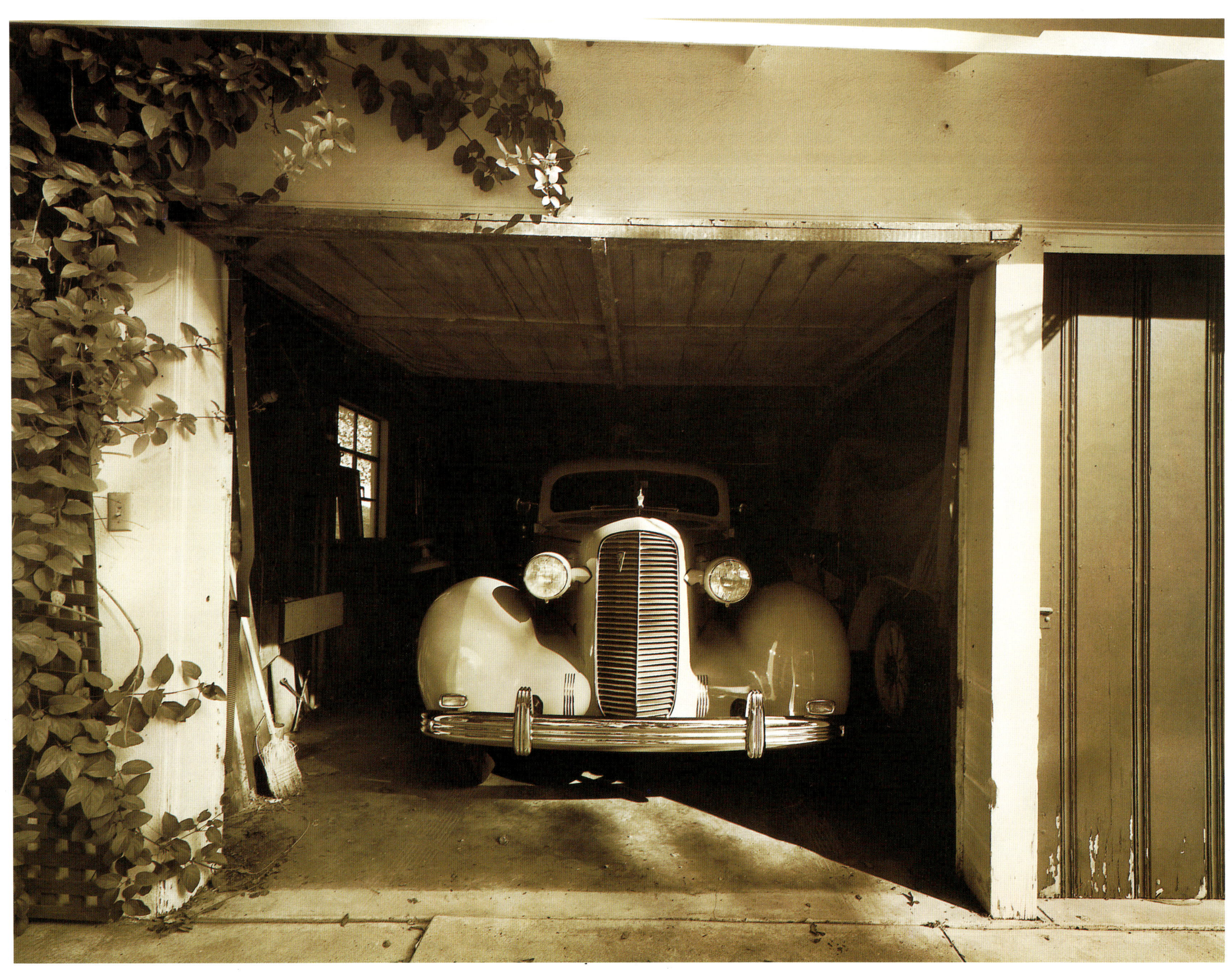

1936 Coupe; Beverly Hills, California

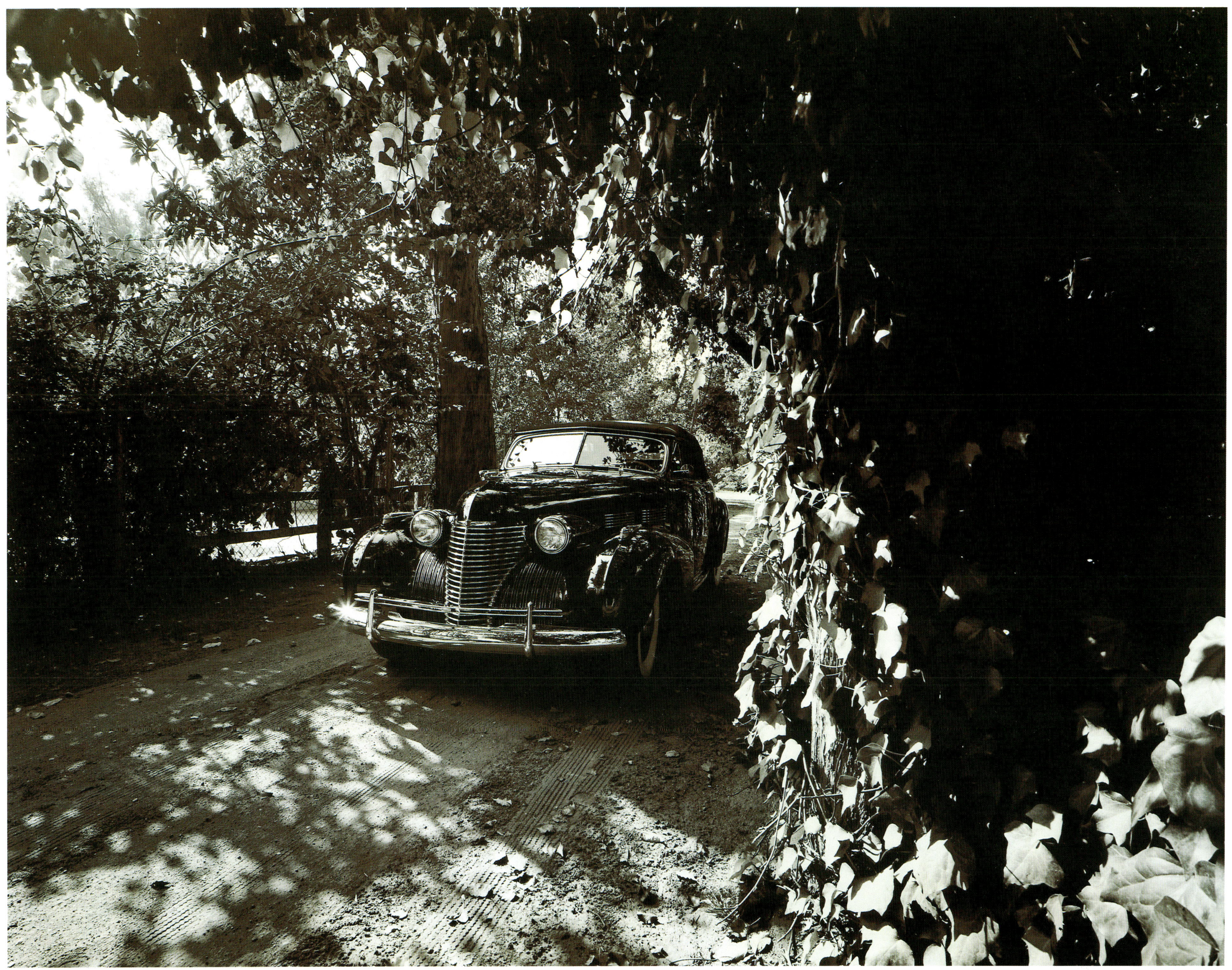

1940 Convertible; Beverly Hills, California

beloved of advertising copywriters. But for the claim to have any weight at all, a manufacturer must do one of two things: either create a product that truly is the best, or assemble resources of size and strength sufficient to outlast or overwhelm the competition and become the standard by default. From time to time, by one or the other of these strategies, combined with an unwritten and mysterious recipe of ingredients that represents the witches' brew of the manufacturing process, a given product does, in fact, become undeniably the standard.

On rare occasions, it may even become something that represents far more than than the fact of its existence or the range of its usefulness, evolving into a touchstone, a near-magical thing that serves our psyches as admirably as our practical needs. It is then that a product becomes not just the standard of the world, but the standard by which we judge our well-being. All manufacturers dream of this unexplainable

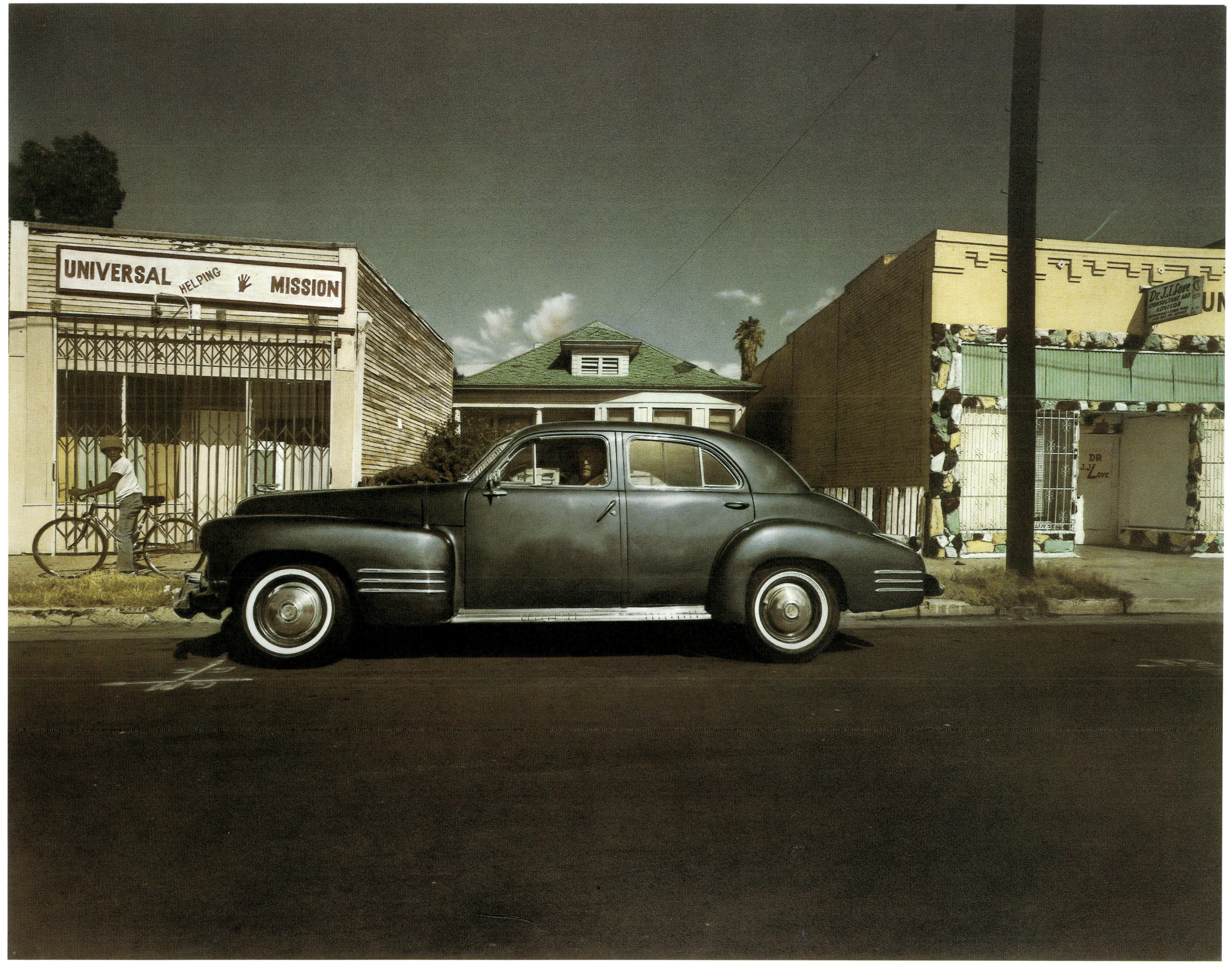

1941 Sedan; Watts, California

consecration; the best companies work with that goal in mind, if only as an unspoken hope. But no one has ever figured out how to make it happen, and when it does, no one can ever quite understand the reason why.

Whatever its merits or flaws as an automobile, the Cadillac is one of these material touchstones, perhaps the most potent that American industry has ever produced. Much has been written about the symbolism of the car in America, and even the most blatantly rhapsodic tracts are not completely implausible. Uniquely, the automobile is both the charger on which we ride in search of the grail, and the grail itself: conveyance and destination at the same time.

In cars we seek, and sometimes find, ourselves. Even in these utilitarian times, to know a person's car is to know a surprising amount about that person. If it can no

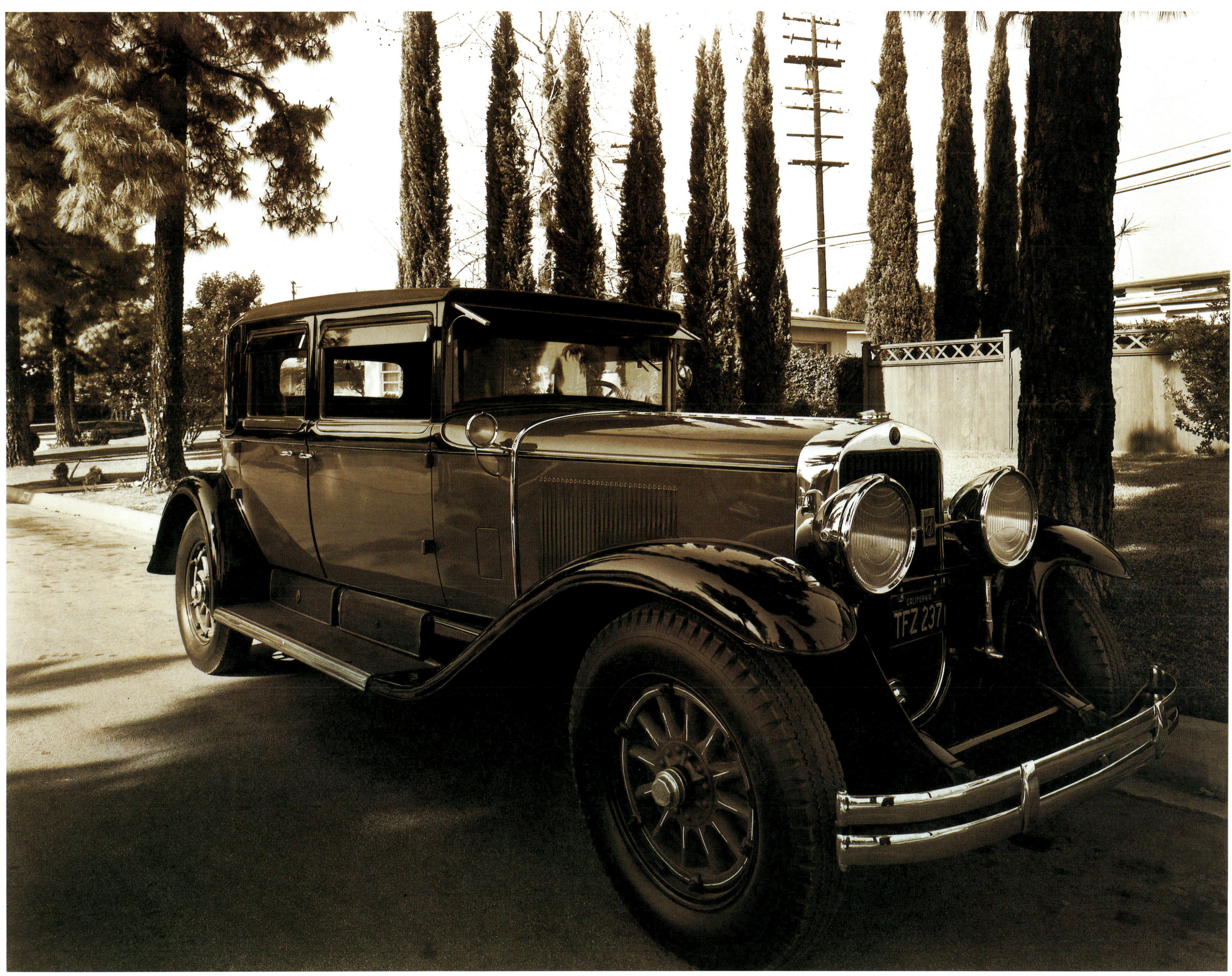

1928 Fleetwood; Los Angeles, California

longer invariably be said that we are what we drive (as it might have been in the fifties), nevertheless, not even the most utility-minded driver buys a car without some self-revealing emotion figuring in the final decision. Even now, when the id and the ego are sternly subjugated to the dour exigencies of economy and high-minded efficiency, the American man or woman who has absolutely no feeling one way or another about what he or she drives is as eccentric and unlikely as an heiress living in rags or a poor man with fifty cats.

Yet perhaps that particular idea is just the wishful thinking of a man brought up to believe that to love cars was part of what it was to *be* a man, that it was nearly on a par with loving women, and was in fact closely connected to that love. In fact, current reality is drabber. Most cars now are low-profile creatures, in body and spirit. It is their morality we celebrate, not their dash and arrogance. Chastened by Arabs and Japanese,

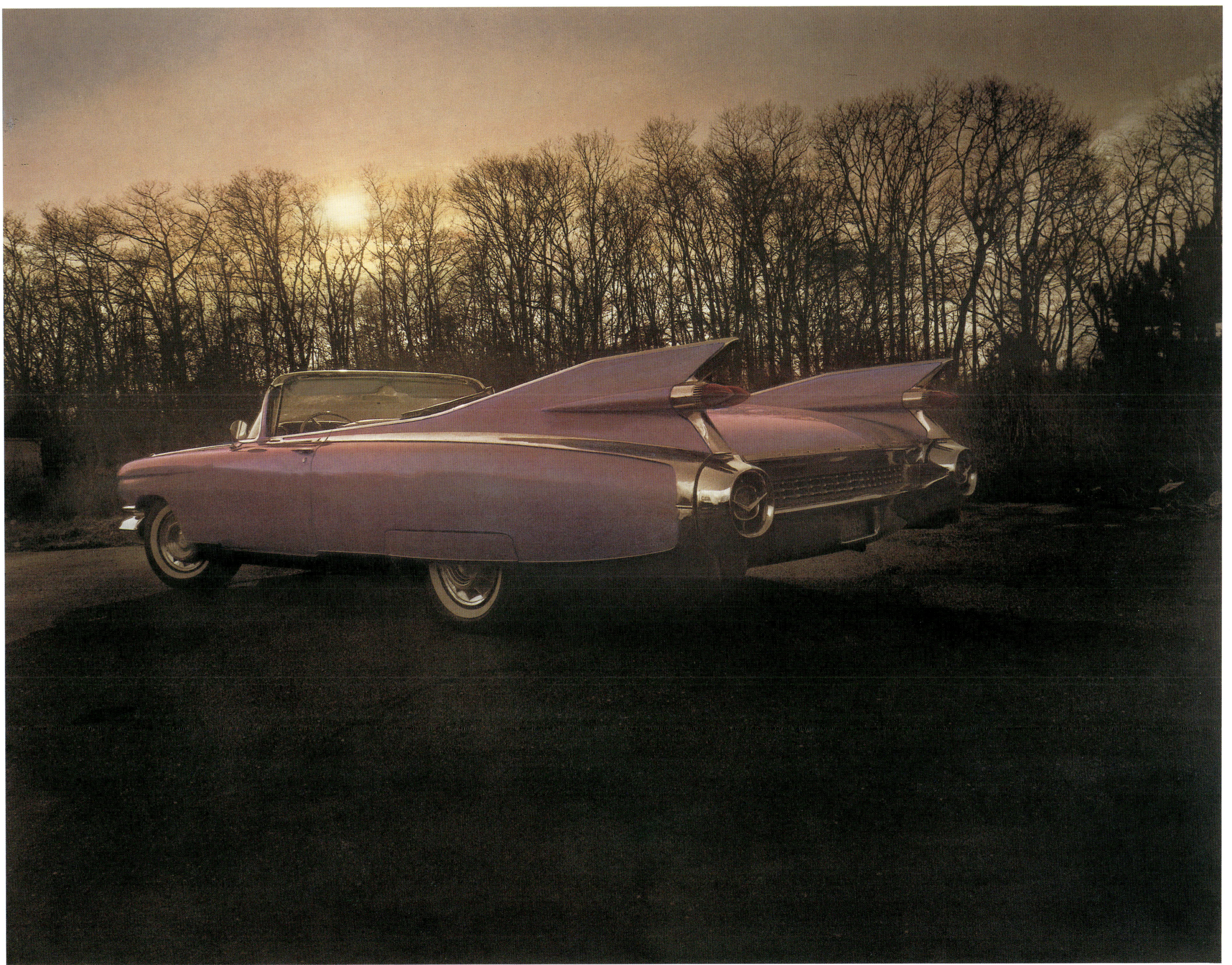

1959 Eldorado Convertible; Asbury Park, New Jersey

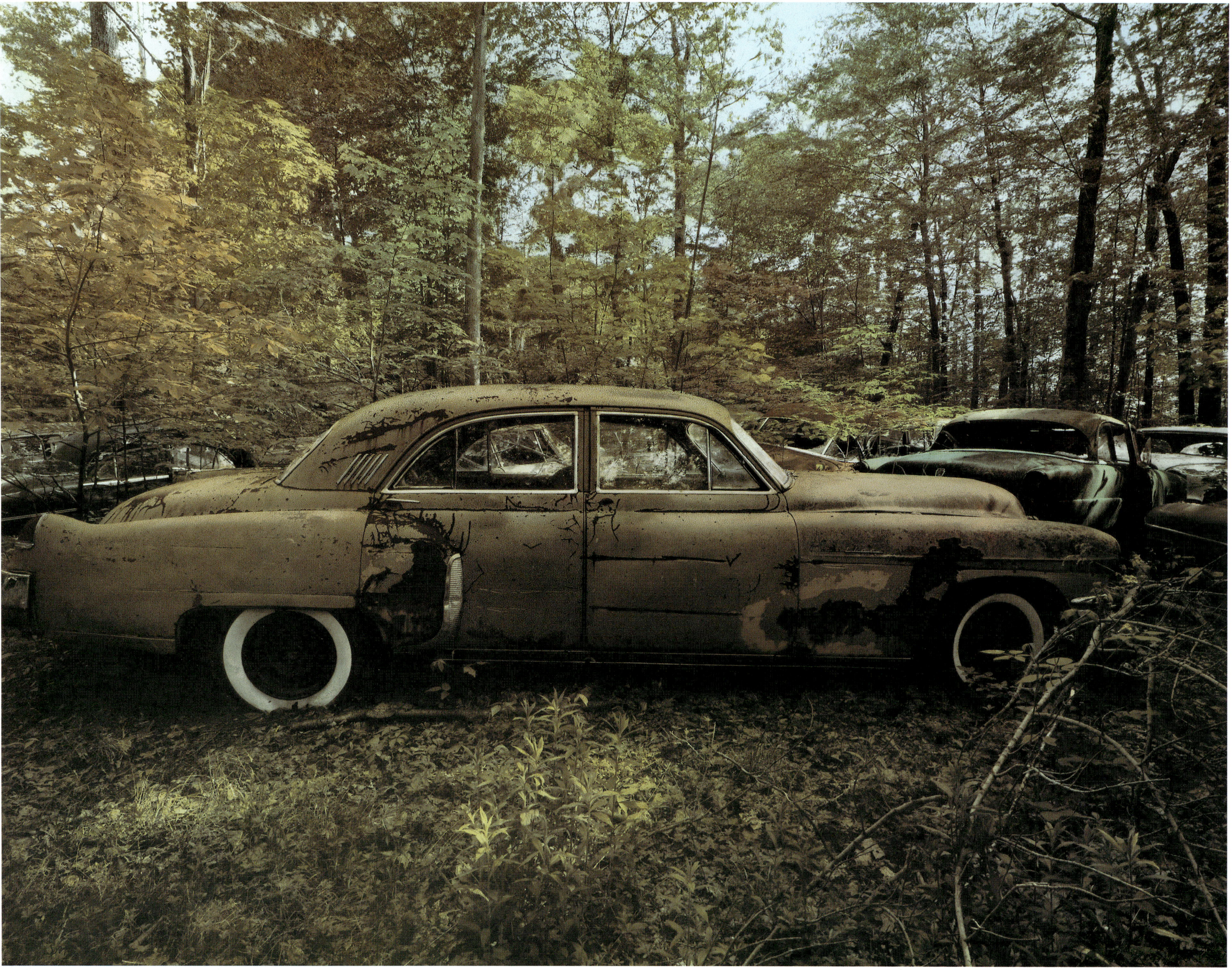

1949 Fleetwood Special: Woodstock, New York

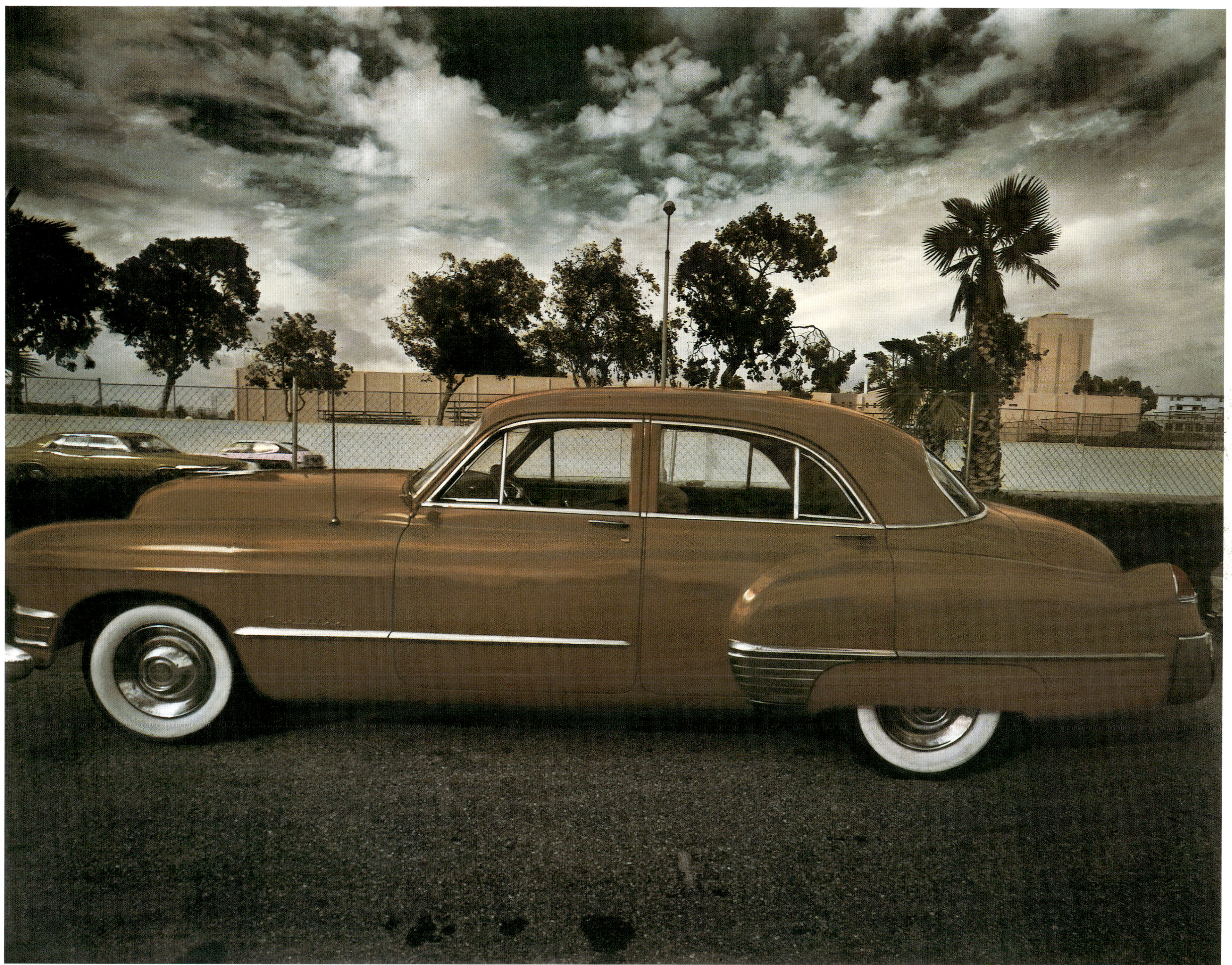

1949 Sedan; Santa Monica, California

undermined by those cardinal capitalist sins of sloth and greed, our automotive wellspring of upward and outward mobility has gone into a born-again retreat. The result has been an end, probably forever, of Detroit's giddy golden age, and the onset of a four-wheeled puritanism that has pushed the car away from its once central place in our hearts and minds.

If this change has not been completely recognized yet, if the automobile still seems stubbornly central to our romantic fantasies, it is due to the extraordinary power of the great crescendo of car love that both energized and characterized the fifties. Whatever passion we feel toward cars today is in large part a form of residual radiation from Detroit's "big bang" of that limitless decade. Always an integral part of the American Dream, the car in the fifties became the ultimate symbol of that dream. Its forms grew symphonic, the most

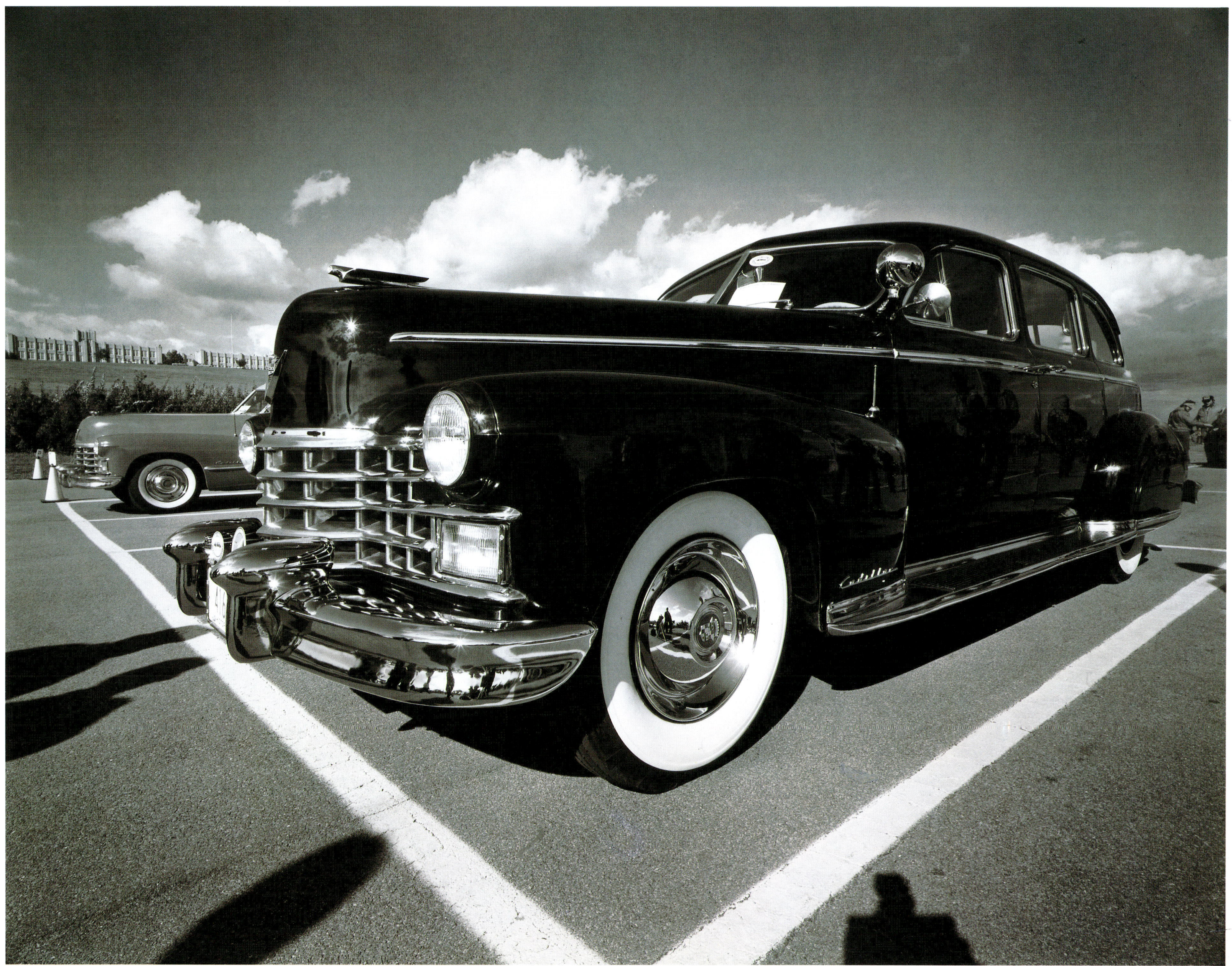

1946 Fleetwood; Hershey, Pennsylvania

astonishing heights of flamboyance were bought and extolled, and the art of the designer became a game of how far the shapes of steel could be taken before losing touch with the yearning human soul.

Nothing exemplified this period more fully than the Cadillac, the biggest bang of all. So dominant was its position, by the end of the fifties, as the definitive luxury touring car, that it attained a charismatic state that remains even today, when the car itself has settled into the conservative anti-drama of late middle age.

Since the early part of the twentieth century, Cadillac Motors had sought success for its products as the cars of aspiration and wealth. Competition at this Olympian level was fierce throughout the years. Packard, Deusenberg, Pierce, Lincoln, and other makes produced regal models that vied for the title of America's greatest and most elegant cars. For the 1933 World's Fair

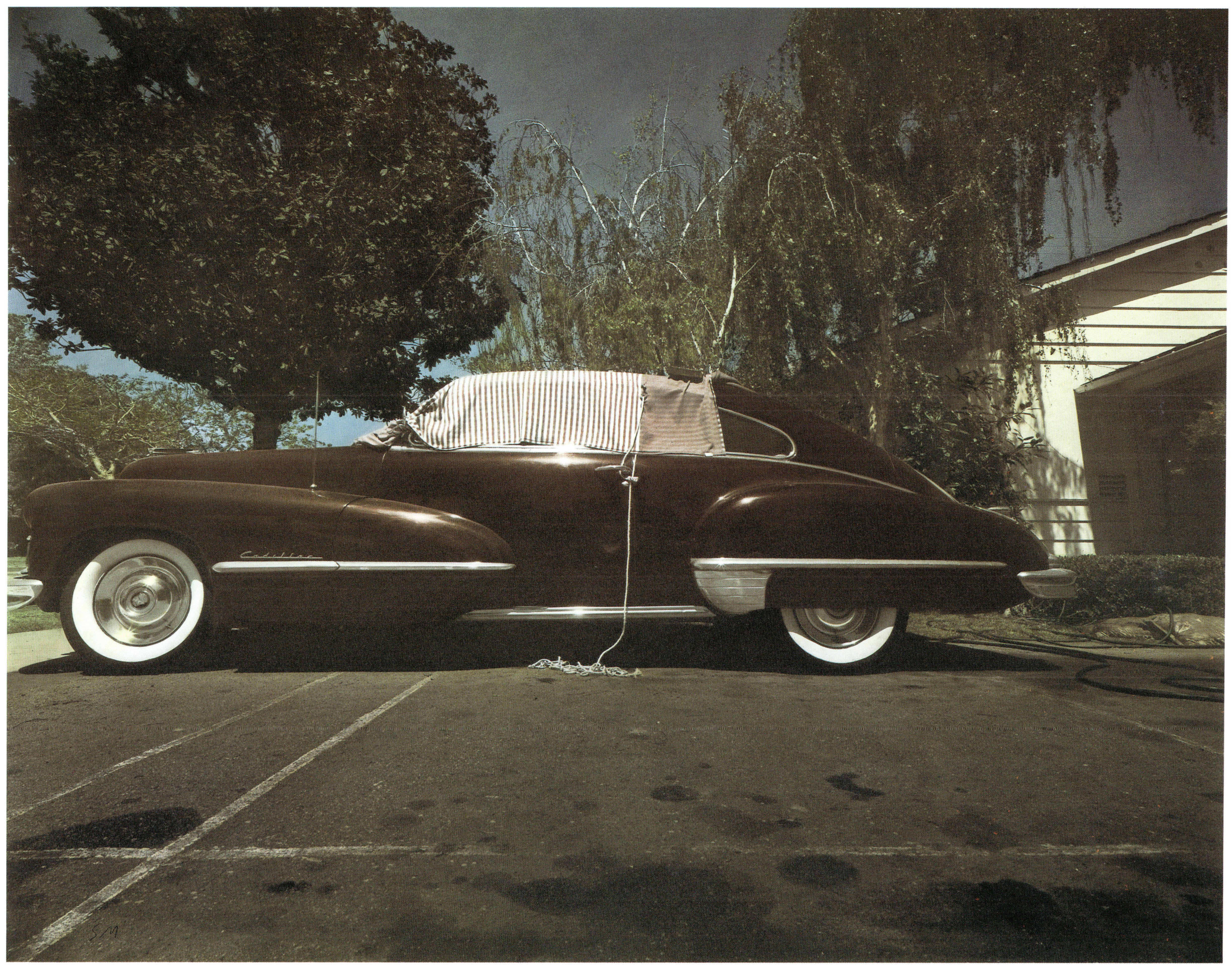

1947 Coupe; Beverly Hills, California

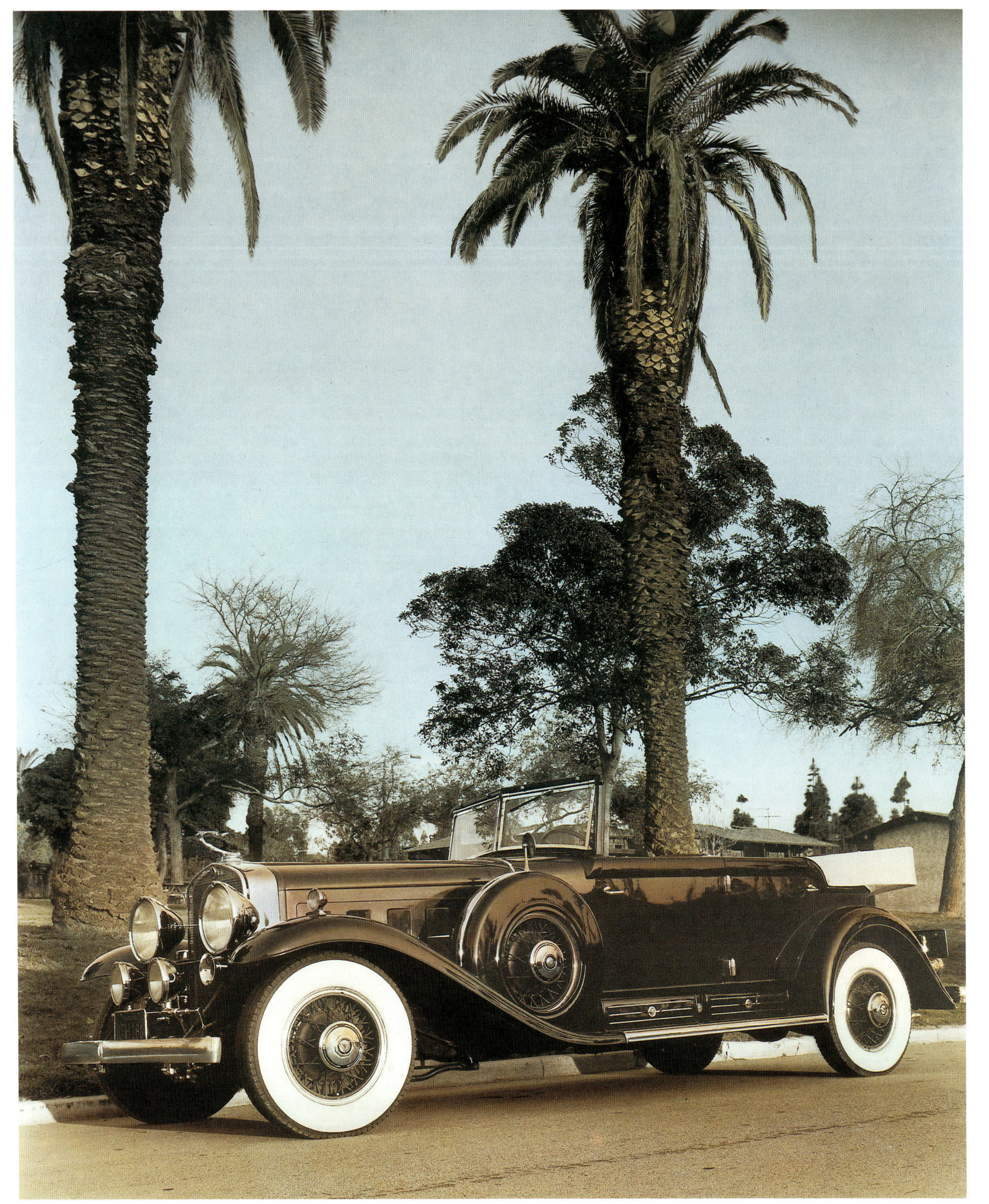

1930 Convertible Sedan; Long Beach, California

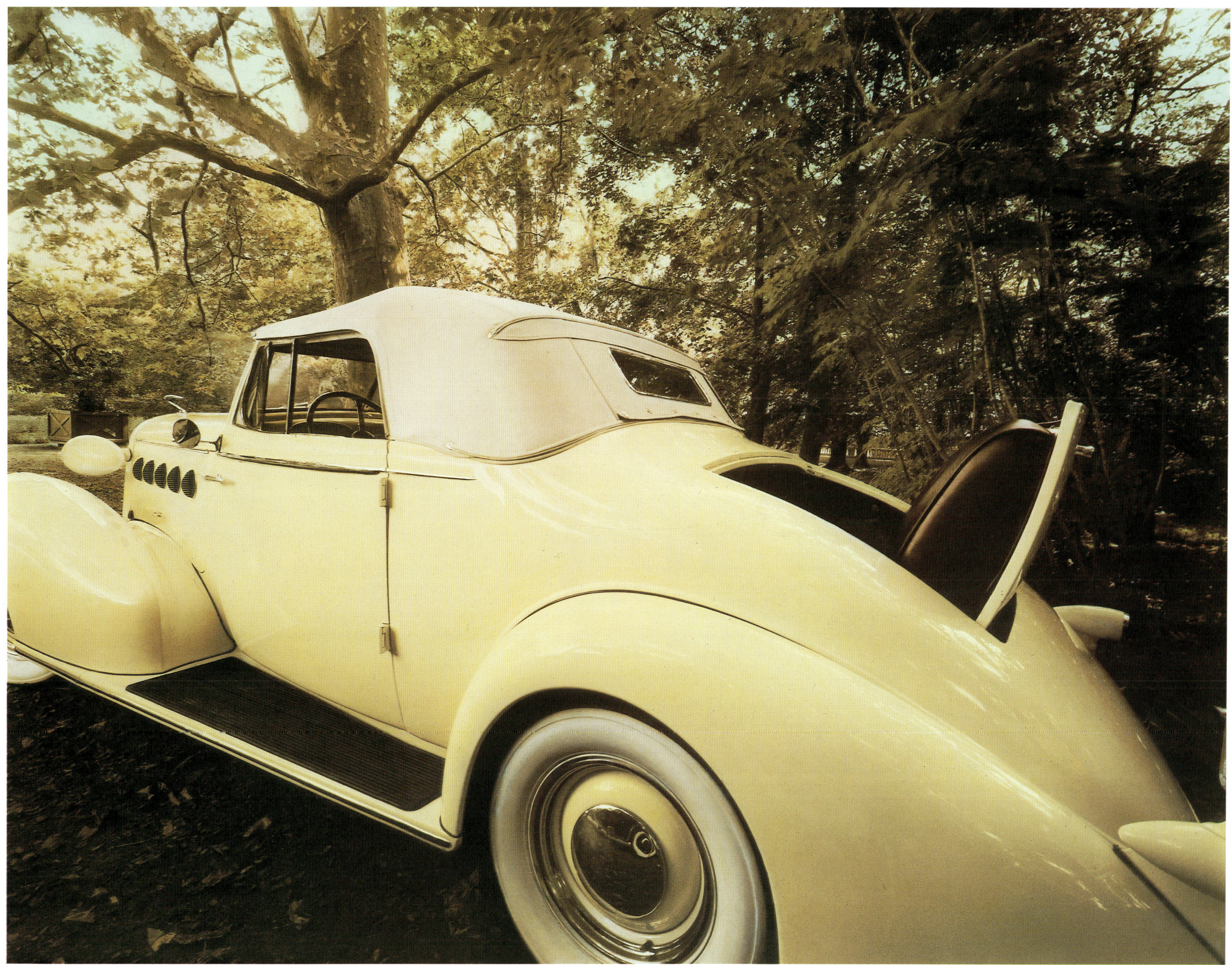

1935 La Salle Convertible; Atlanta, Georgia

in Chicago, Cadillac built a splendid V-16 fastback coupe with powerful, modern lines and a revolutionary hidden spare tire, but the racy model didn't upstage the even more daring Pierce Silver Arrow. A trend toward luxury and solid engineering was established, though, that would mark Cadillacs even when the demise of most of their major competitors gave them breathing room at the top.

The St. Laurent to Cadillac's Dior was a man named Harley Earl, a successful customizer in Los Angeles (where even in the early twenties the automobile reigned supreme) who was contracted to design the 1927 La Salle and went on to become the chief stylist for General Motors until his retirement in the sixties. In a sense, the whole idea of designing a car as a single entity was Earl's invention, and the classic method of creating models in sculpted clay was an approach that

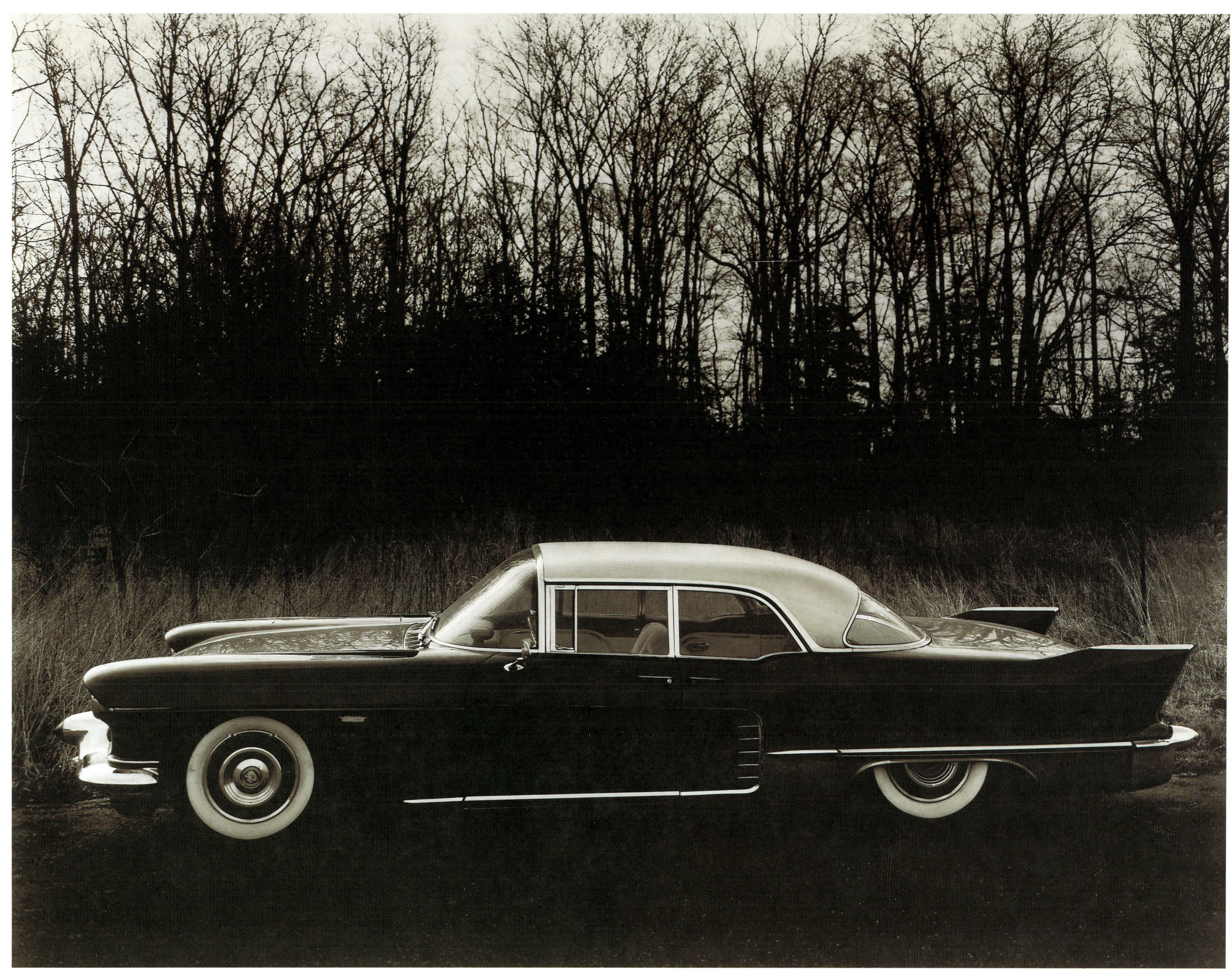

1957 Eldorado Brougham; Point Pleasant, New Jersey

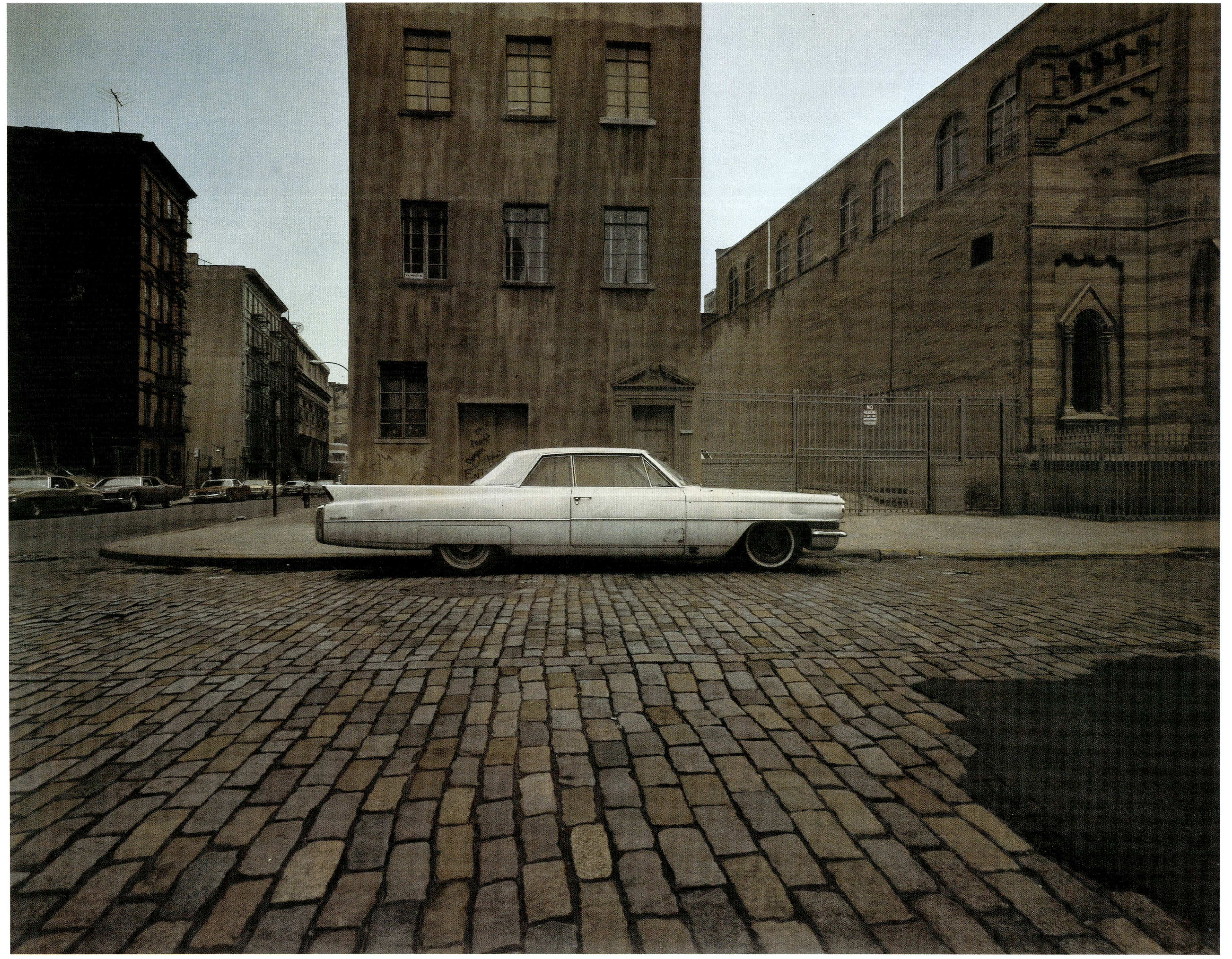

1963 Coupe de Ville; New York City

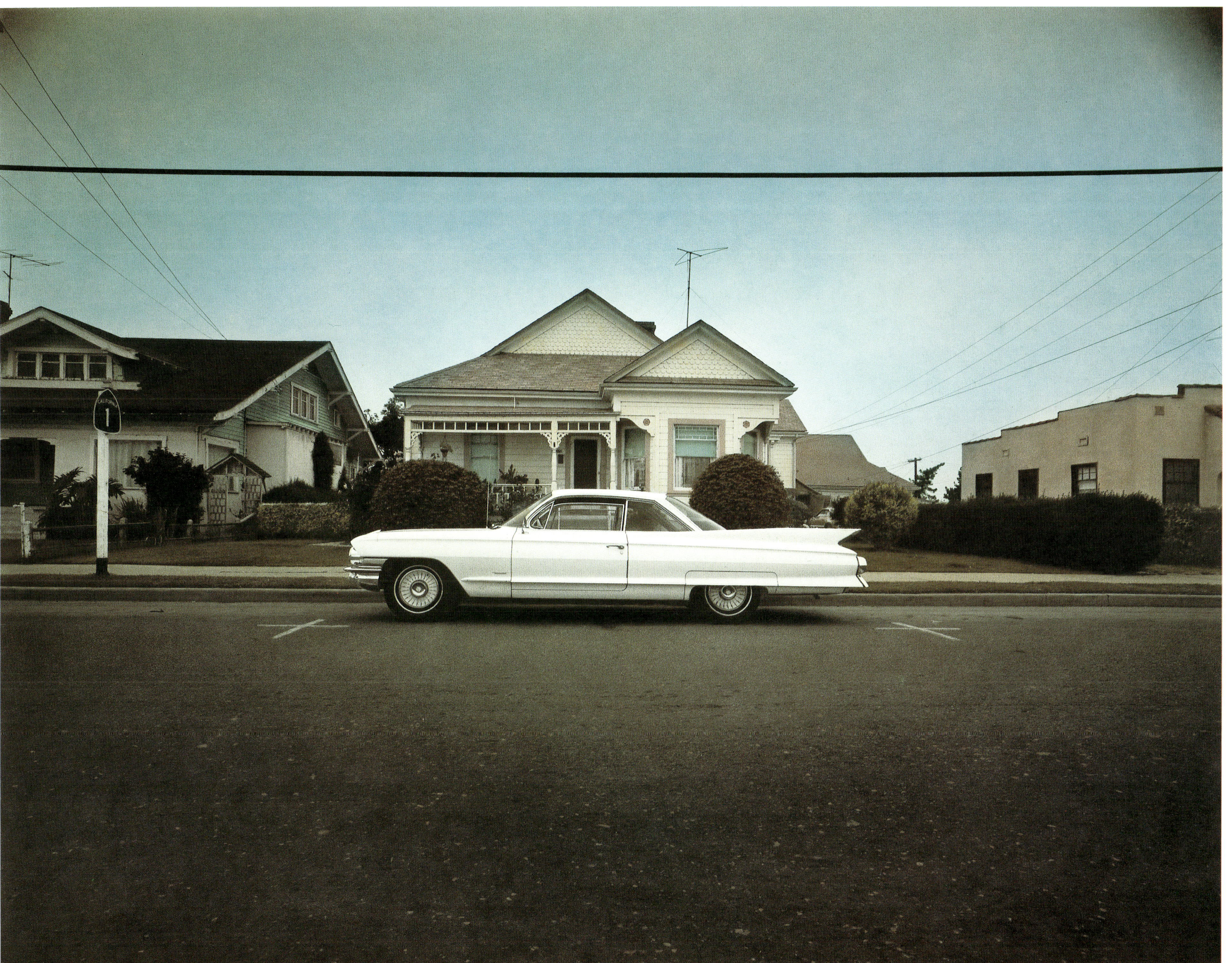

1961 Coupe de Ville; Route 1, California

he pioneered. Henry Ford may have given the American car a democratic appeal, but Harley Earl made it an art form everyone could understand, criticize, influence (by buying, or not buying), and collect, ecstatically, year after year.

Earl's background as a custom coachbuilder inclined him to think of a car as a personal statement, for both the designer and the buyer. As a result, many of his designs—from racy La Salles to bucktoothed Buicks to the smooth '55 Chevy—exerted a powerful hold on American imaginations. But despite his considerable successes with other GM makes, Earl's great daring and élan reached their most eloquent level with the Cadillac, his magnum opus.

At the end of the Second World War, two factors combined to raise the Cadillac to mythic eminence. The ebullience over life beginning again, after years of

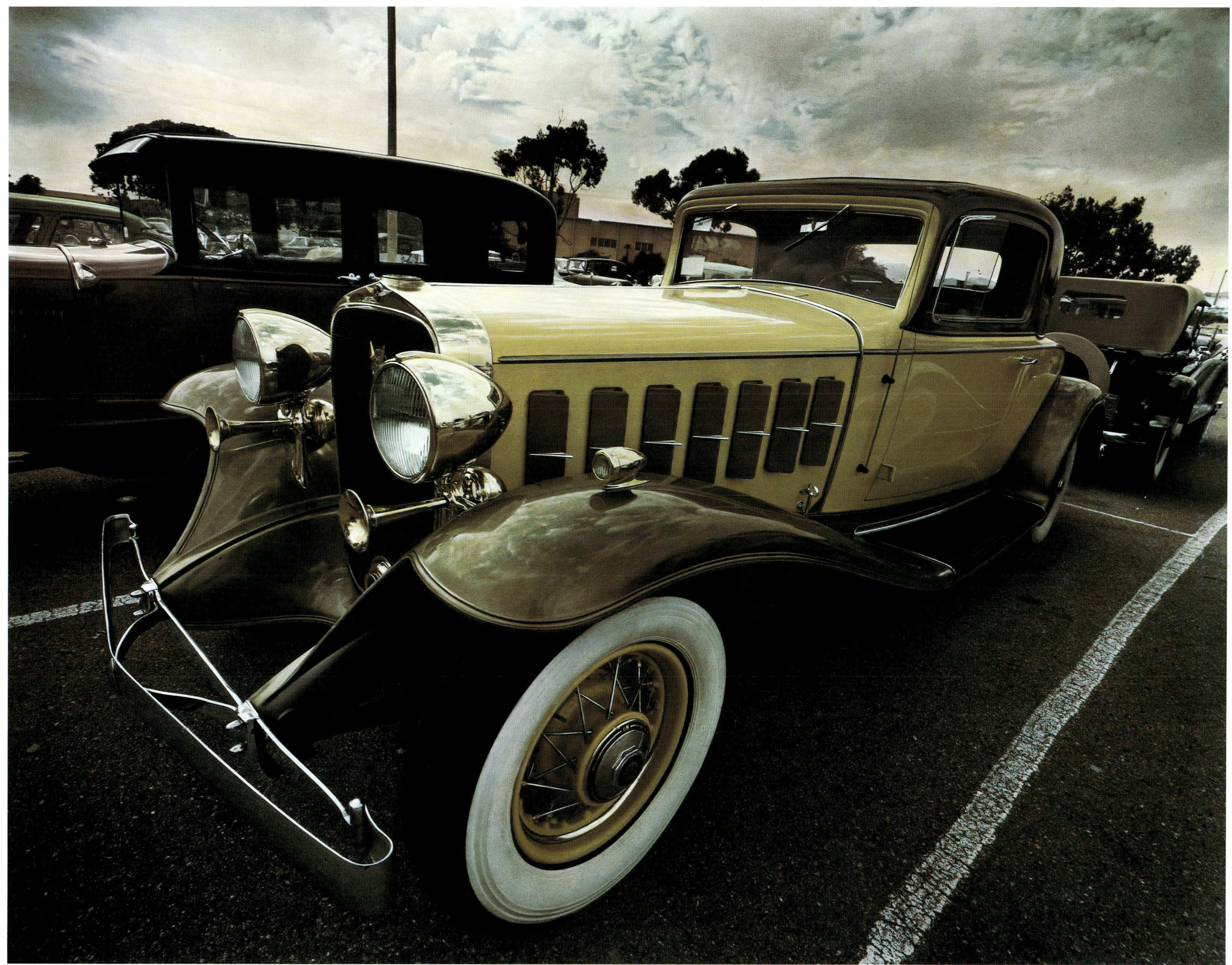

1932 Coupe; Santa Monica, California

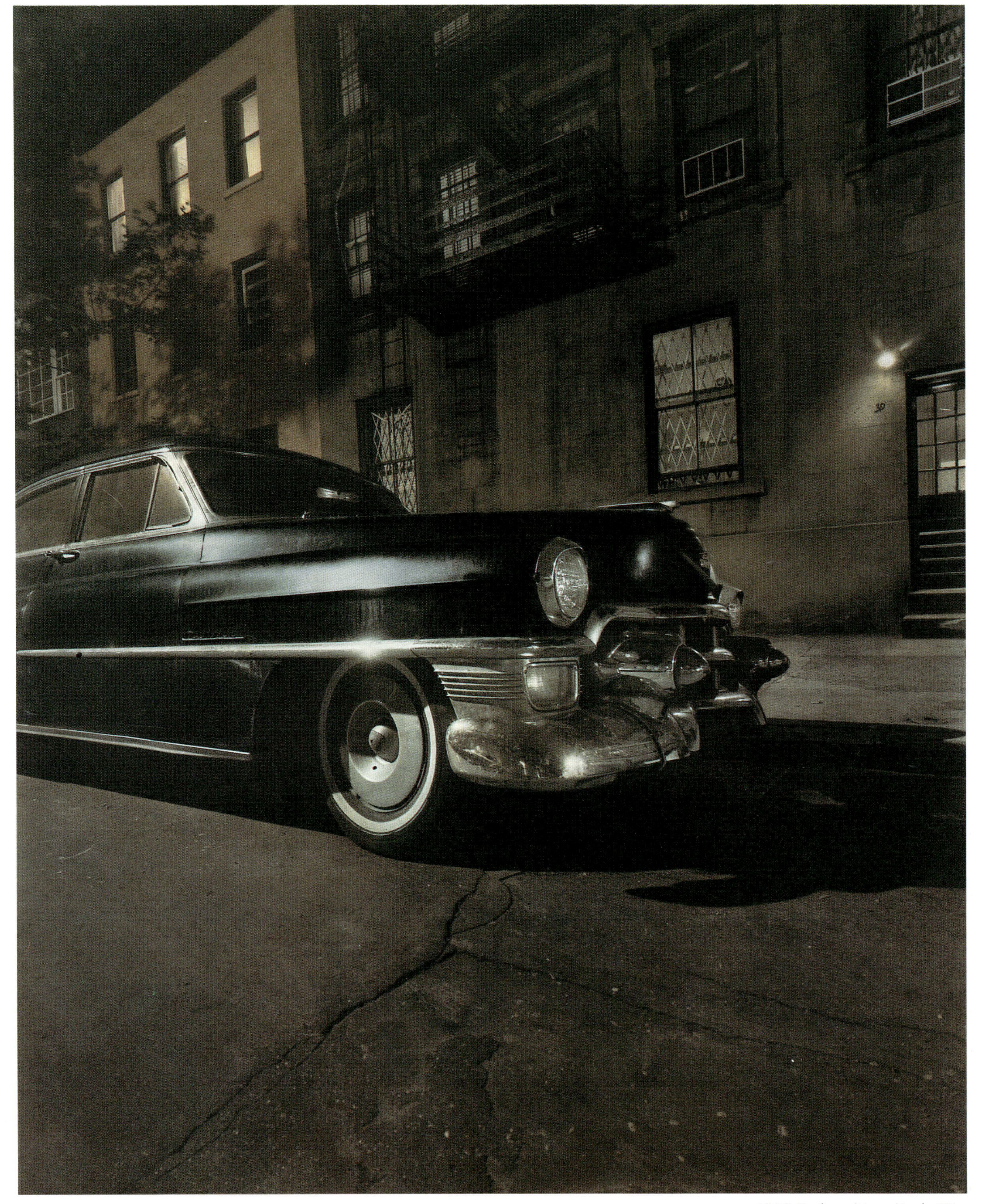

1953 Sedan; New York City

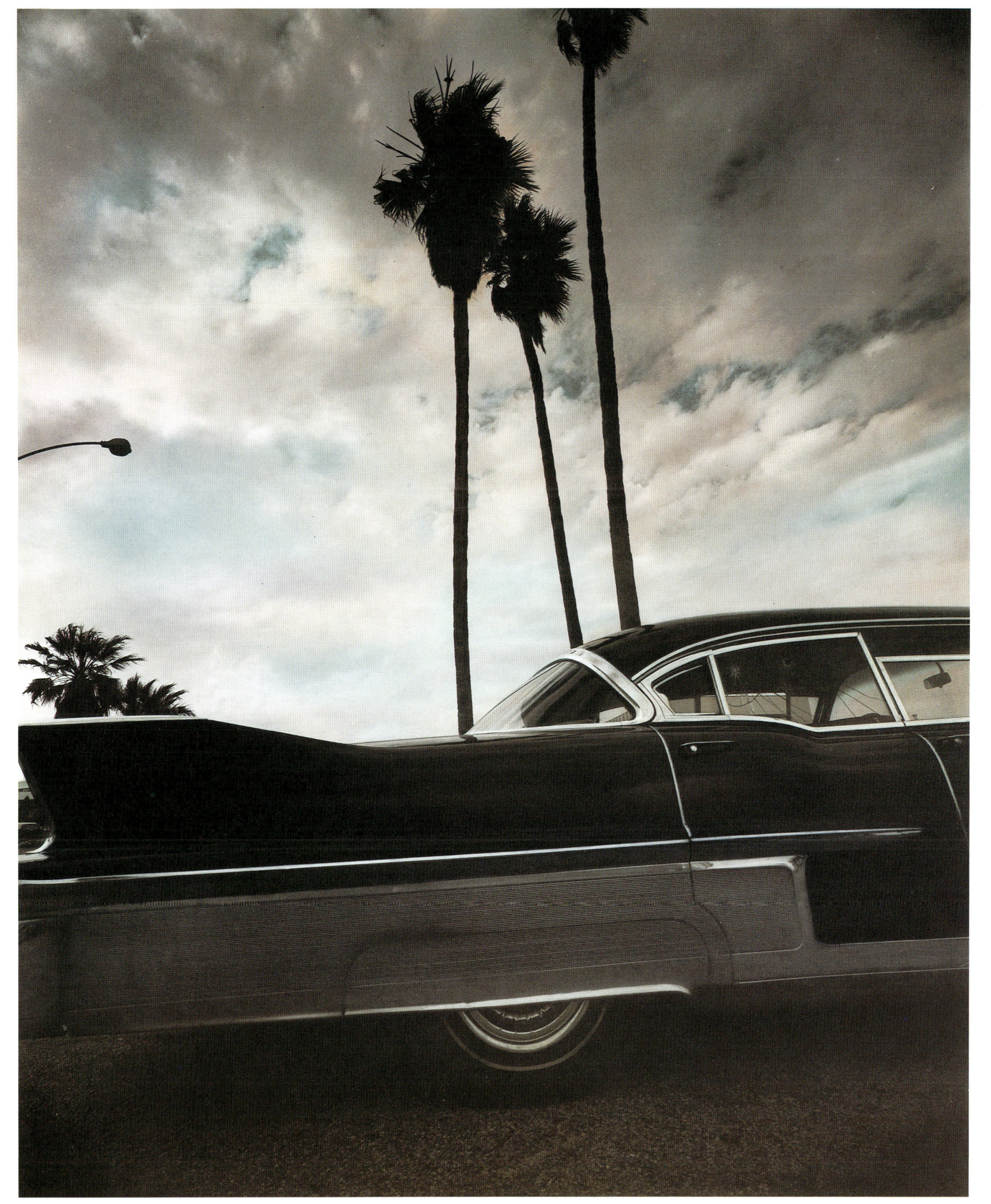

1958 Fleetwood Special; Santa Barbara, California

uncertainty and upheaval, created a demand for a return to opulence which Cadillac had survived to fill. When, in 1947, 96,000 orders for Cadillacs went unfilled, General Motors decided to give their most profitable division the largest share of limited steel supplies, plus the budget to make the car even more lavishly irresistible.

In the history of automotive design, this show of confidence in the car's future was akin to Pope Julius II giving Michelangelo the Sistine ceiling for a canvas. Earl was being given a car to express his own vision of paradise, and for the next twelve years he worked with the passion of the true believer.

Just before Pearl Harbor, at an airfield near Detroit, Earl had happened to see an early production model of the Lockheed P-38, a revolutionary fighter plane designed by Clarence Johnson. The P-38 looked like no other aircraft, with its streamlined engine mounts and twin tail booms, and for Earl it was clearly an epiphany.

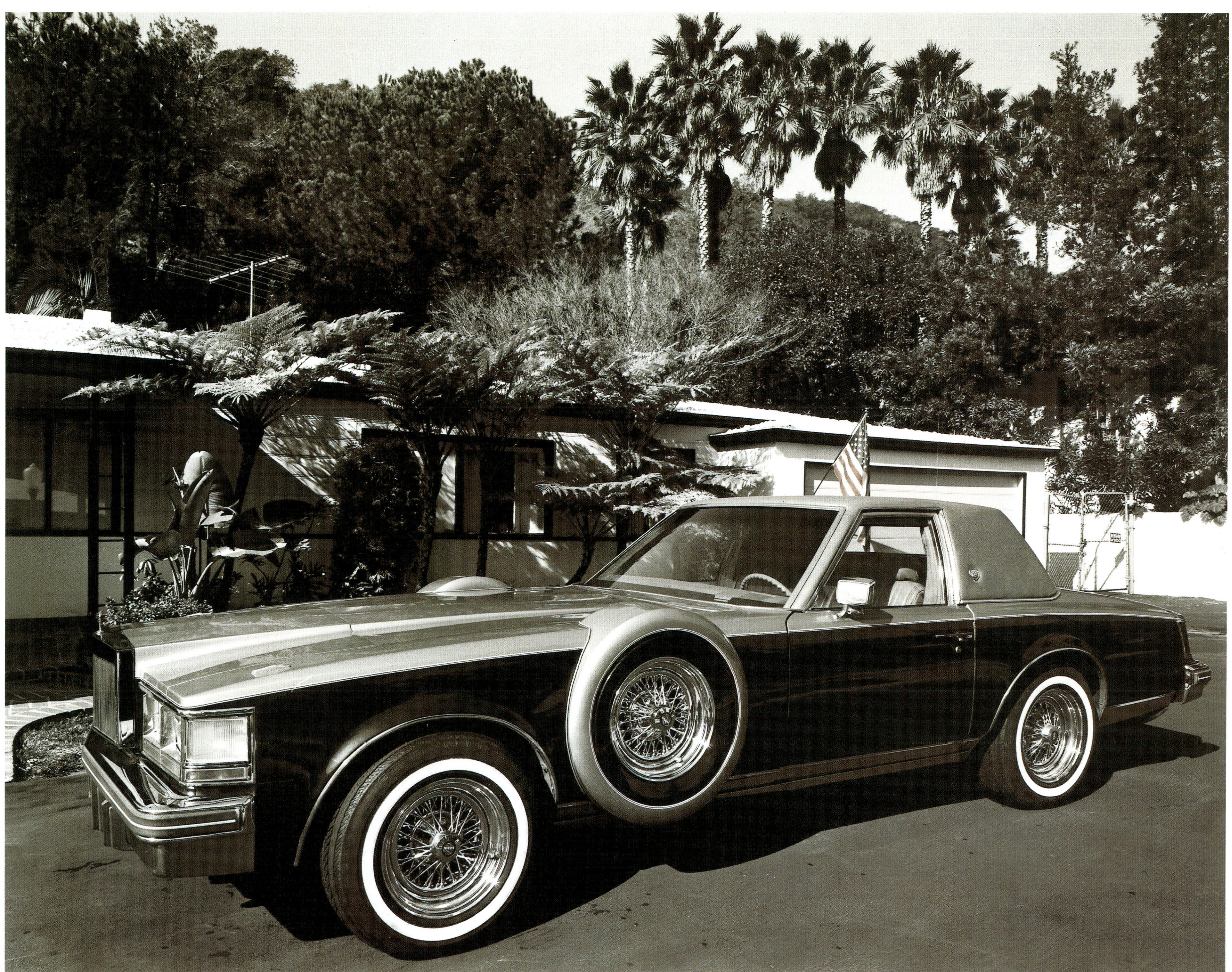

1978 Grandeur Opera Coupe; Beverly Hills, California

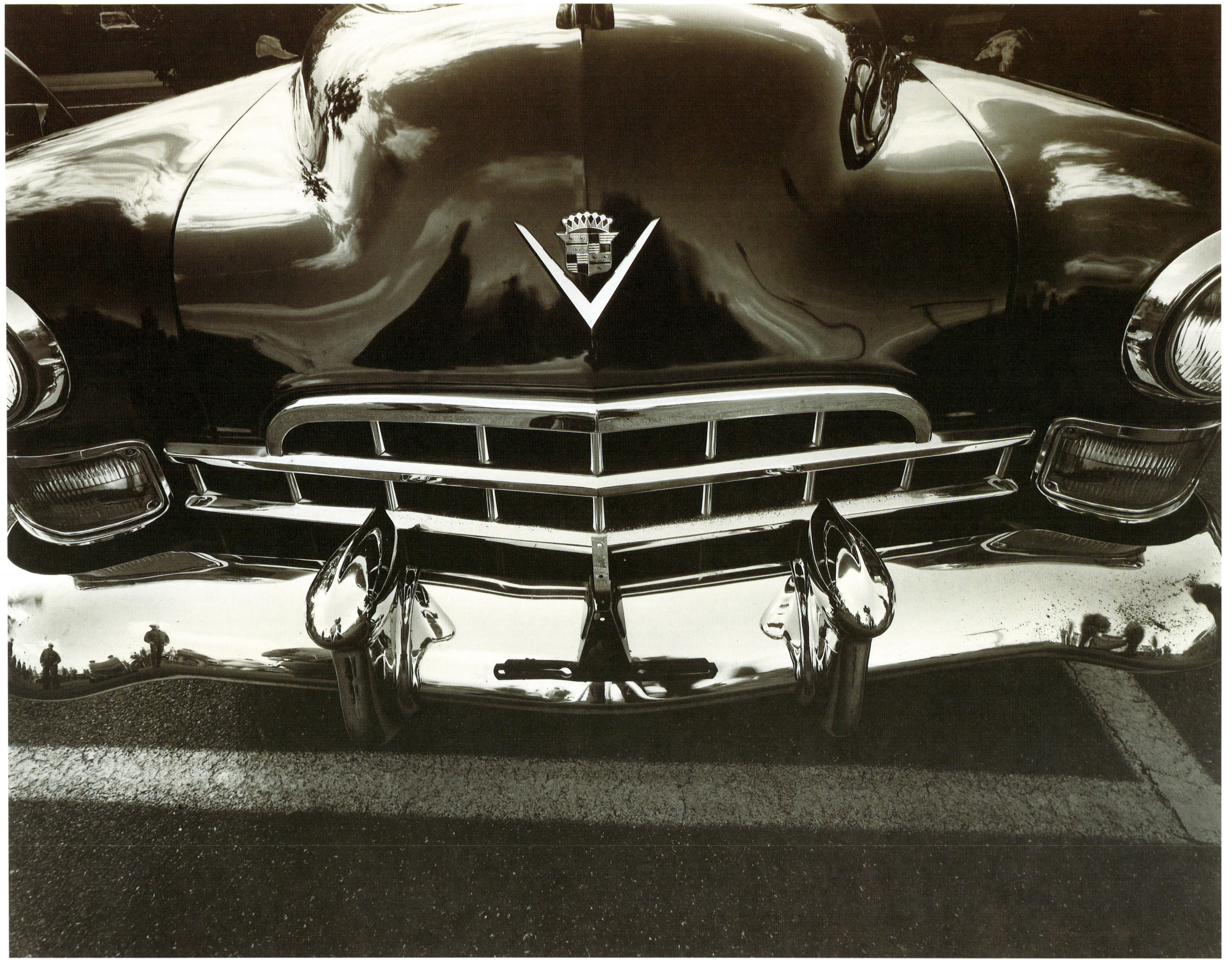

1948 Coupe de Ville; Bethlehem, Pennsylvania

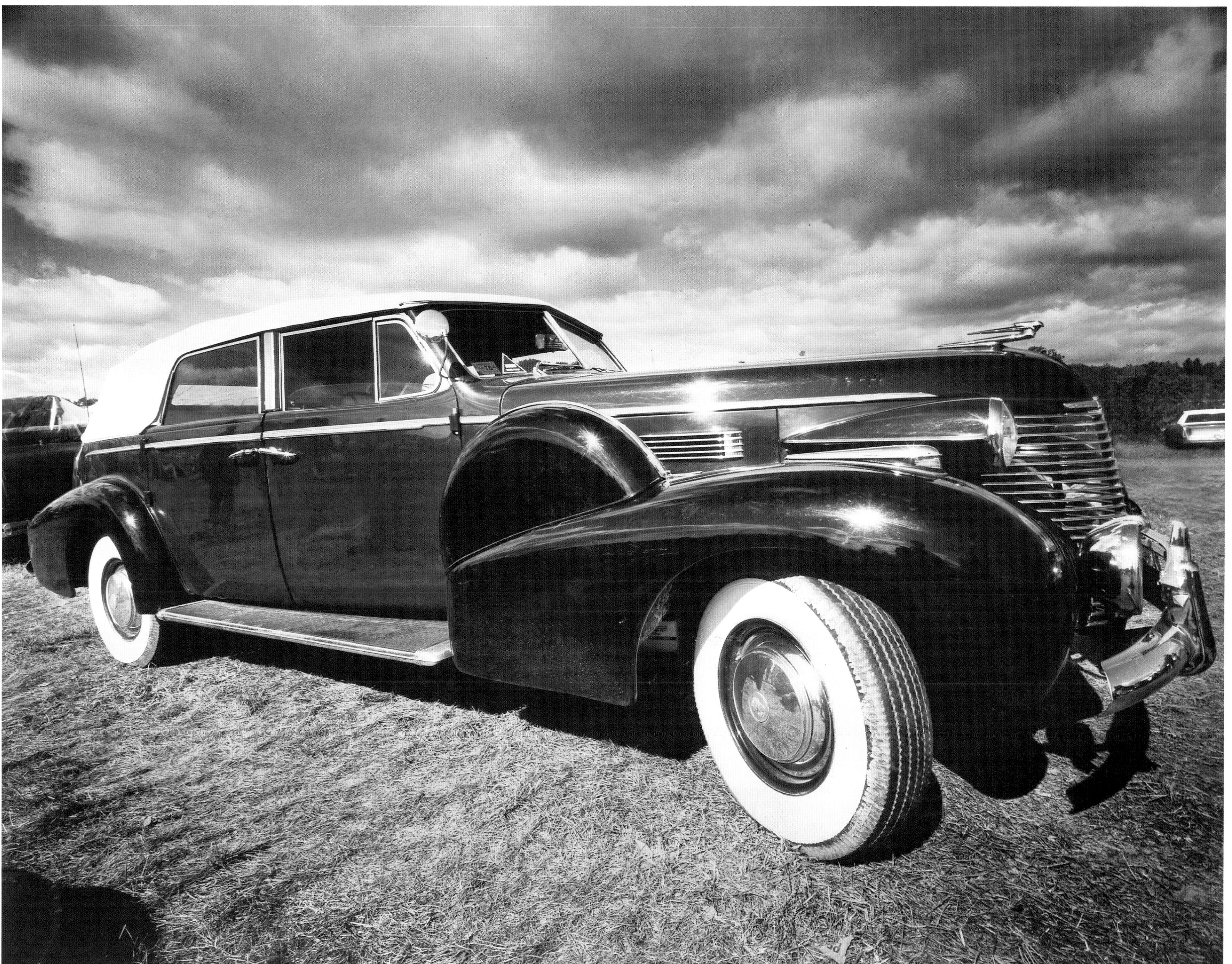

1940 Fleetwood Convertible; Hershey, Pennsylvania

The idea of directly relating a car to the high romance of a fighter plane was madly inspired. In 1948, the Cadillac sprouted discreet but unmistakable tail fins—nothing more, really, than a little swoop that housed the rear lights, but the beginning of the car's evolution toward the great swashbuckling style that made the word *Cadillac* synonymous with the joyful arrogance of success.

Through the fifties, a period that Stephen Bayley (author of *Harley Earl and the Dream Machine*) calls America's Elizabethan Age, the Cadillac departed from the image of international elegance that had dominated Detroit high-end planning since the twenties, and arrived as the apotheosis of the American car, the American frame of mind, and newly rich America itself.

Like the New York Yankees, or Cecil B. De Mille movies, or television, the Cadillac became something

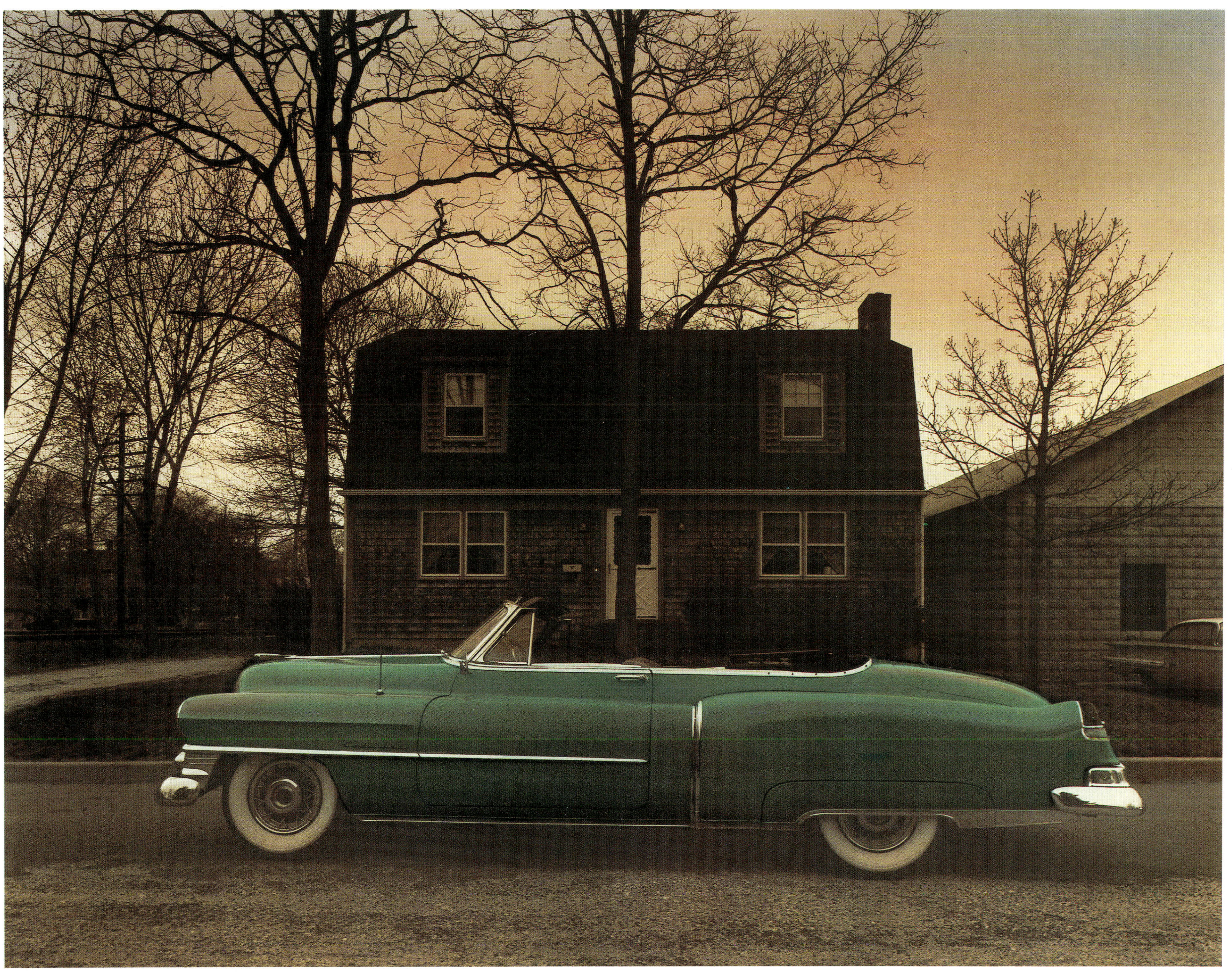

1951 Convertible; Manasquan, New Jersey

you took sides about. You loved Cadillacs or you hated them, but you did not remain indifferent. More than any other product, the cars stood for a way of life. Driving a Cadillac, or, as in my father's case, *not* driving one, made a statement that was nothing short of political. With his car, the Cadillac owner said: "I believe."

Buying a Cadillac in the fifties was subscribing to the fifties, and all the decade represented. Thus, the commitment to the make was often total, and most American families have at least one member, a prosperous uncle or a cousin perpetually on the verge of bankruptcy, who "wouldn't ever have anything but a Cadillac." Maids drove up to the middle-class houses where they washed the windows in brand-new, bright-plumed Cadillacs. People who lived in trailers passed up the chance to put a real foundation under their feet in

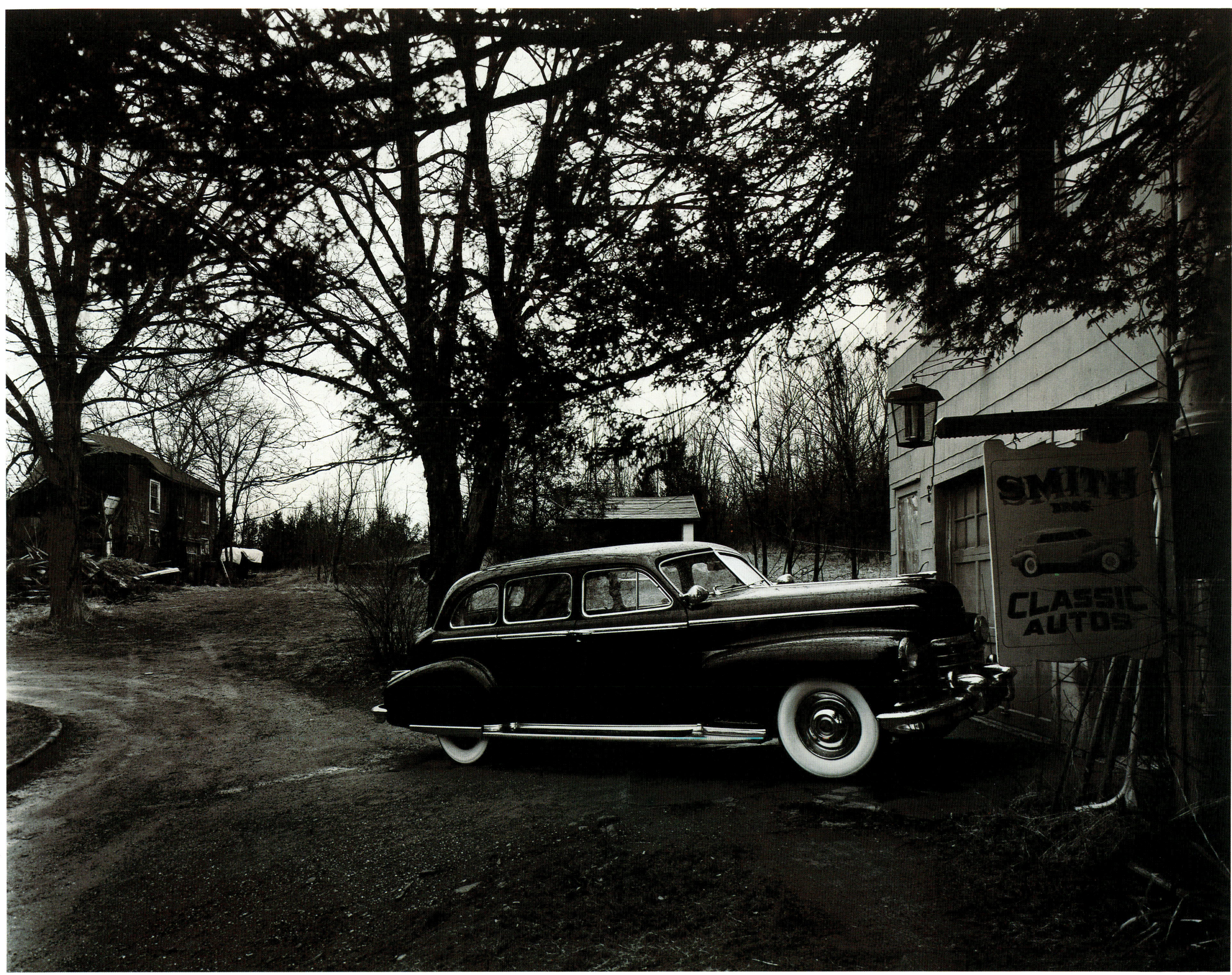

1946 Fleetwood; Fishkill, New York

order to buy yet another late-model Caddy. Bankers accepted the Cadillac as a necessary as well as desirable tool of their trade. Rich or poor, the Cadillac owner said to all who saw him (and to himself): The world that made this car, and the world that made me, are one and the same admirable place.

Increasingly, as Earl's vision of the car grew more and more ebullient, and its sheer expanse of metal began to fill the road from shoulder to centerline, Cadillacs polarized the lovers and the haters. Never mind that a prominent English technical writer would eventually write (in 1962) that the Cadillac was the car "particularly recommended for the driver who wishes to cruise quietly at 100 miles per hour," and that European magazines lavished praise on the make; for those to whom Cadillac stood for everything wasteful and nonfunctional, only the dark side could be seen. Someone who drove,

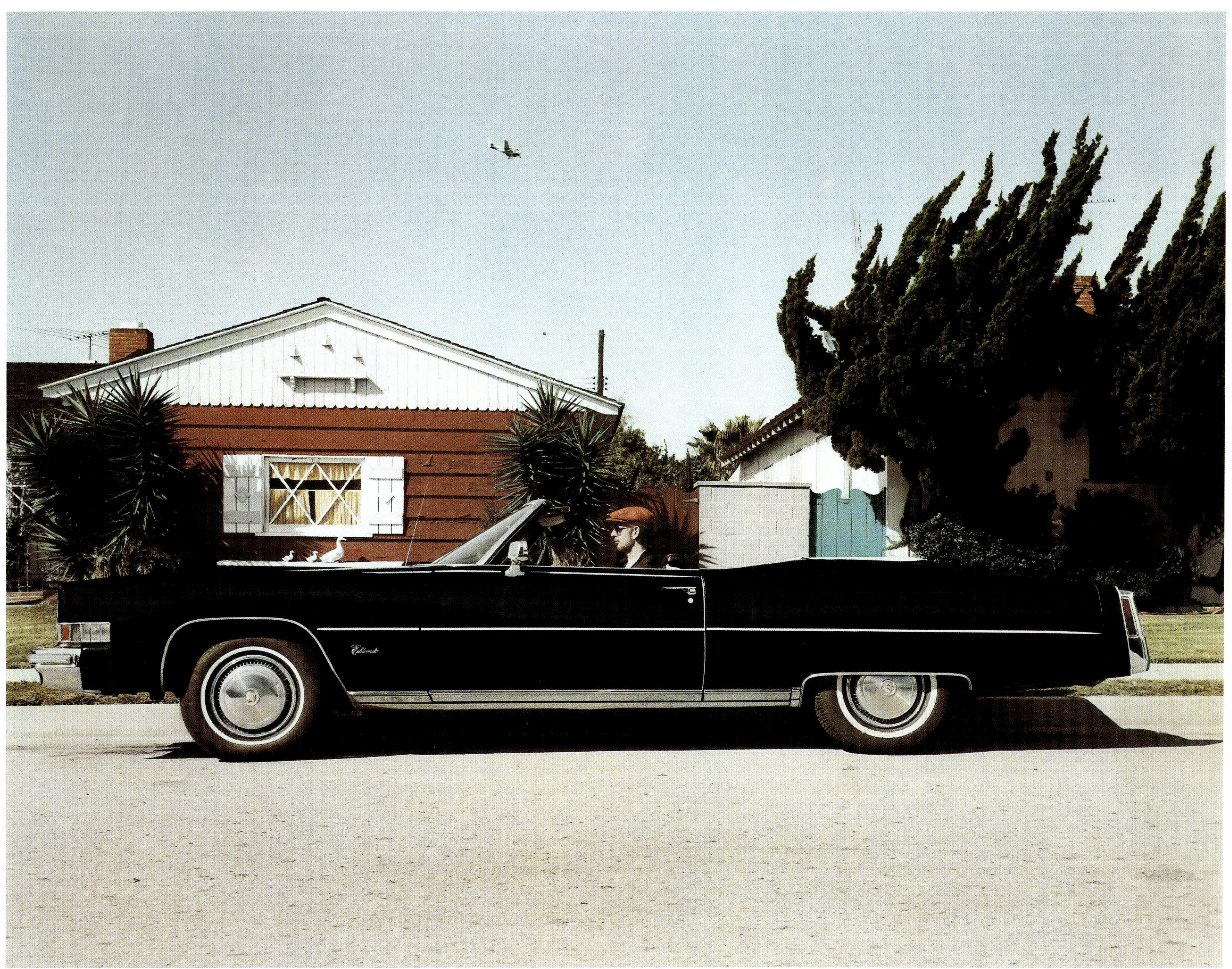

1974 Fleetwood Eldorado Convertible; Venice, California

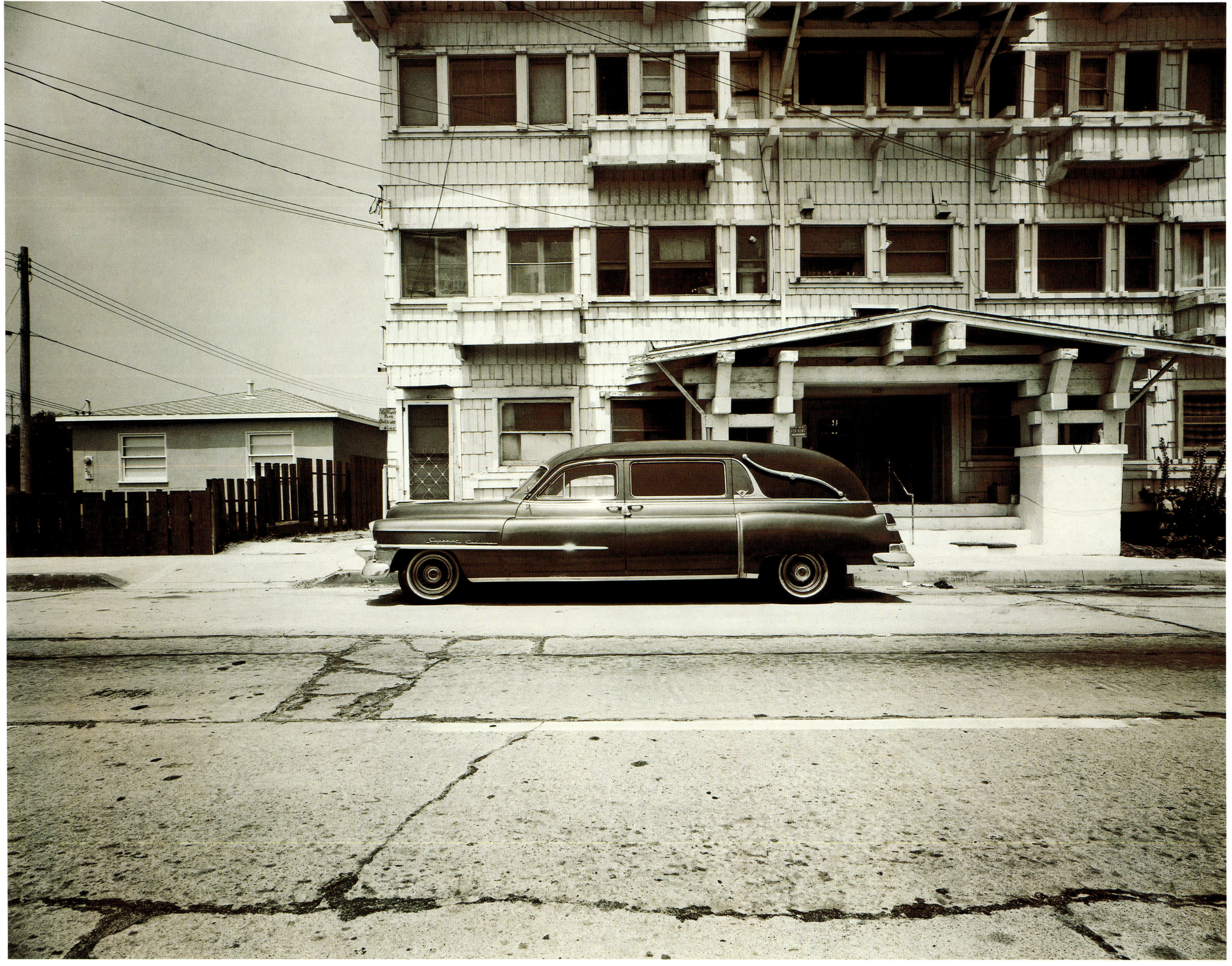

1953 Superior Landaulet; Venice, California

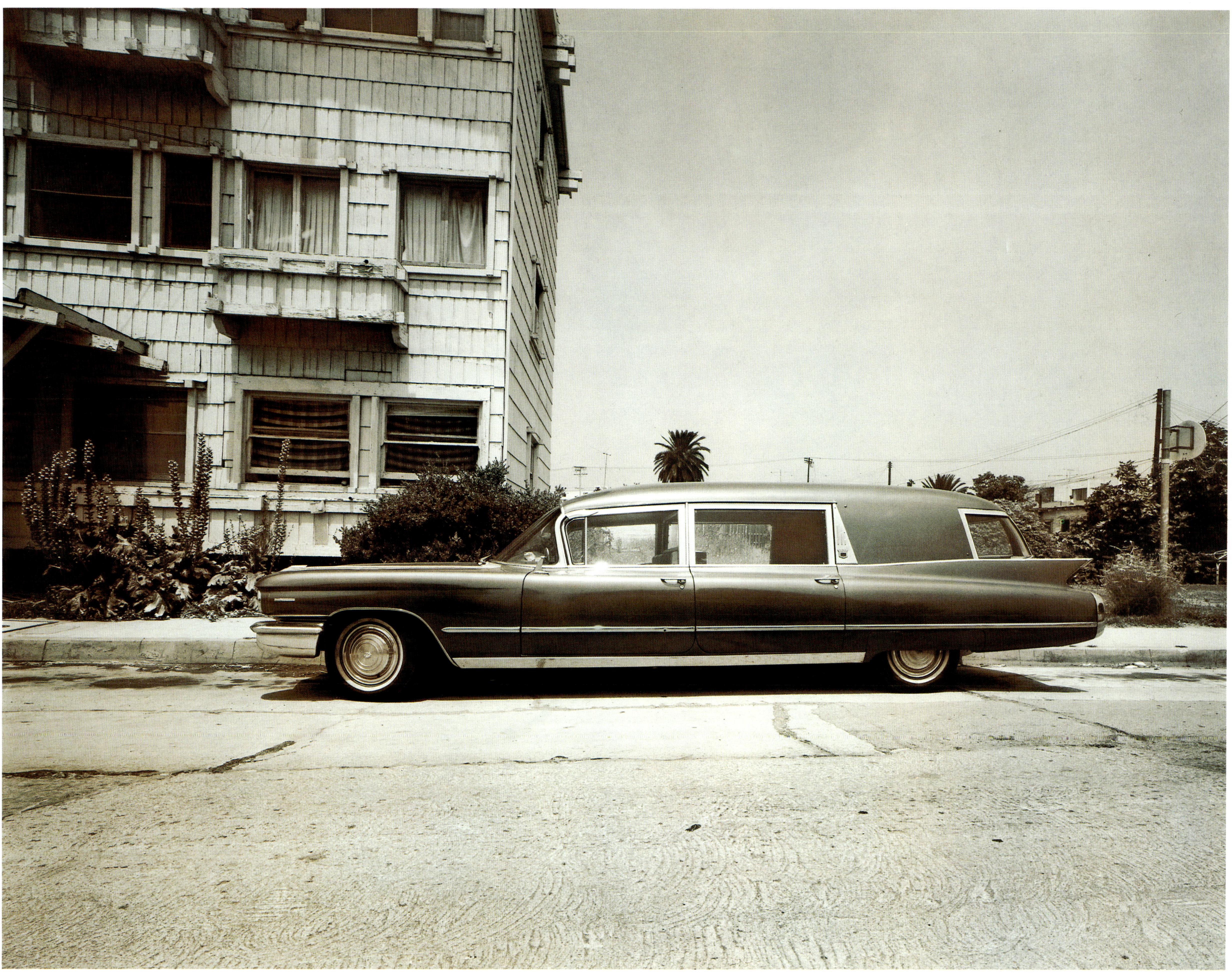

1960 Landau, Venice, California

say, a Morgan, an MG TC, or a Volkswagen beetle was bound to view the biggest and gaudiest of what writer John Keats called "the insolent chariots" as the work of the devil.

Some of this aversion was aesthetic, some was quasi-religious (the Cadillac was the established church; smaller, more efficient cars were the Protestant Reformation) but much was simple snobbism. And there is nothing quite so twittable as a snob. Having been one of those arch-sports-car-acolytes, I remember hearing an interview with Juan Fangio, the legendary racing ace for the Ferrari factory team, and leaning forward expectantly when he was asked what car, given the choice of any in the world, he would select to drive across America. Without hesitation, Fangio said, "An air-conditioned Cadillac, of course." Consternation!

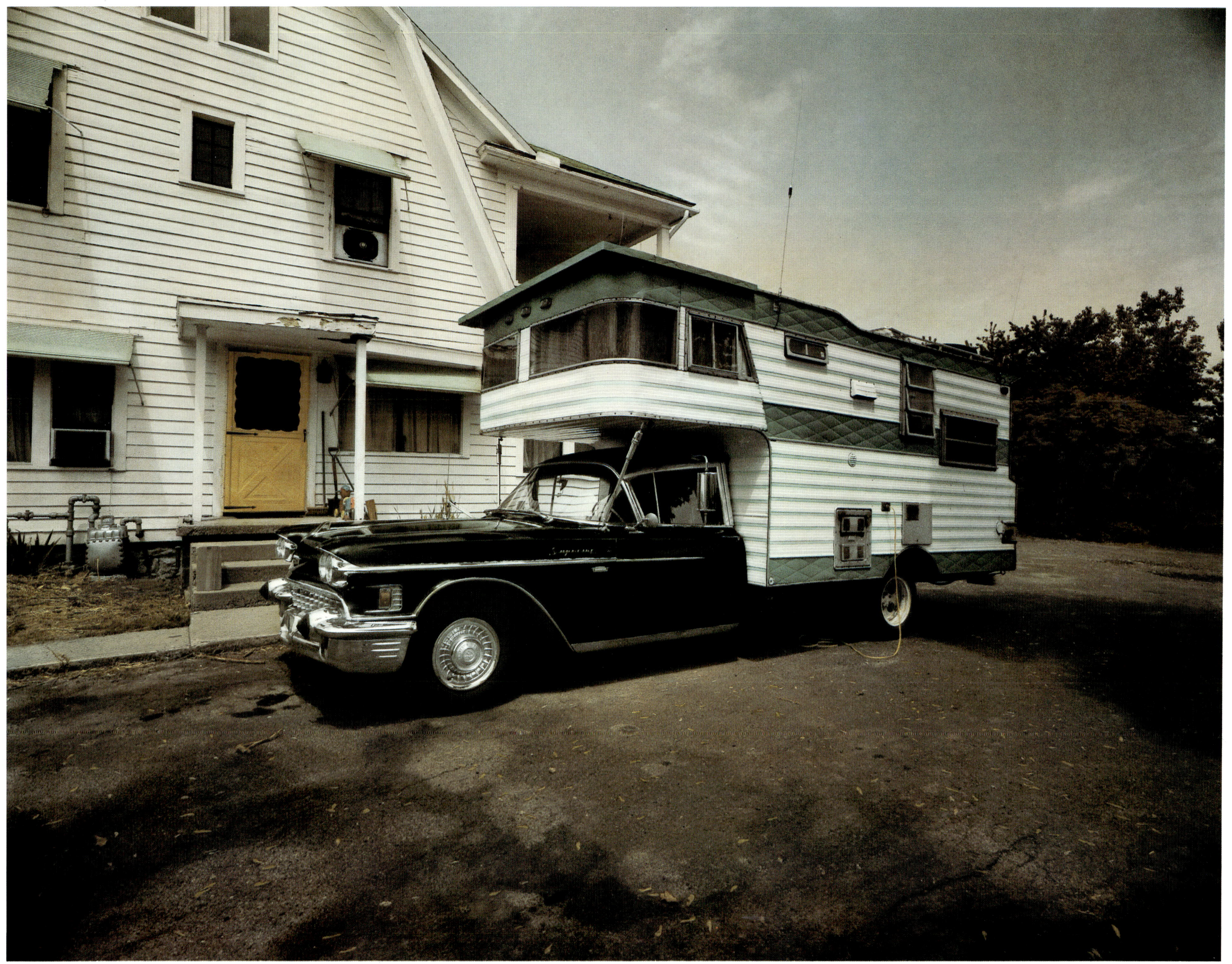

1958 Caddy Camper; Woodstock, New York

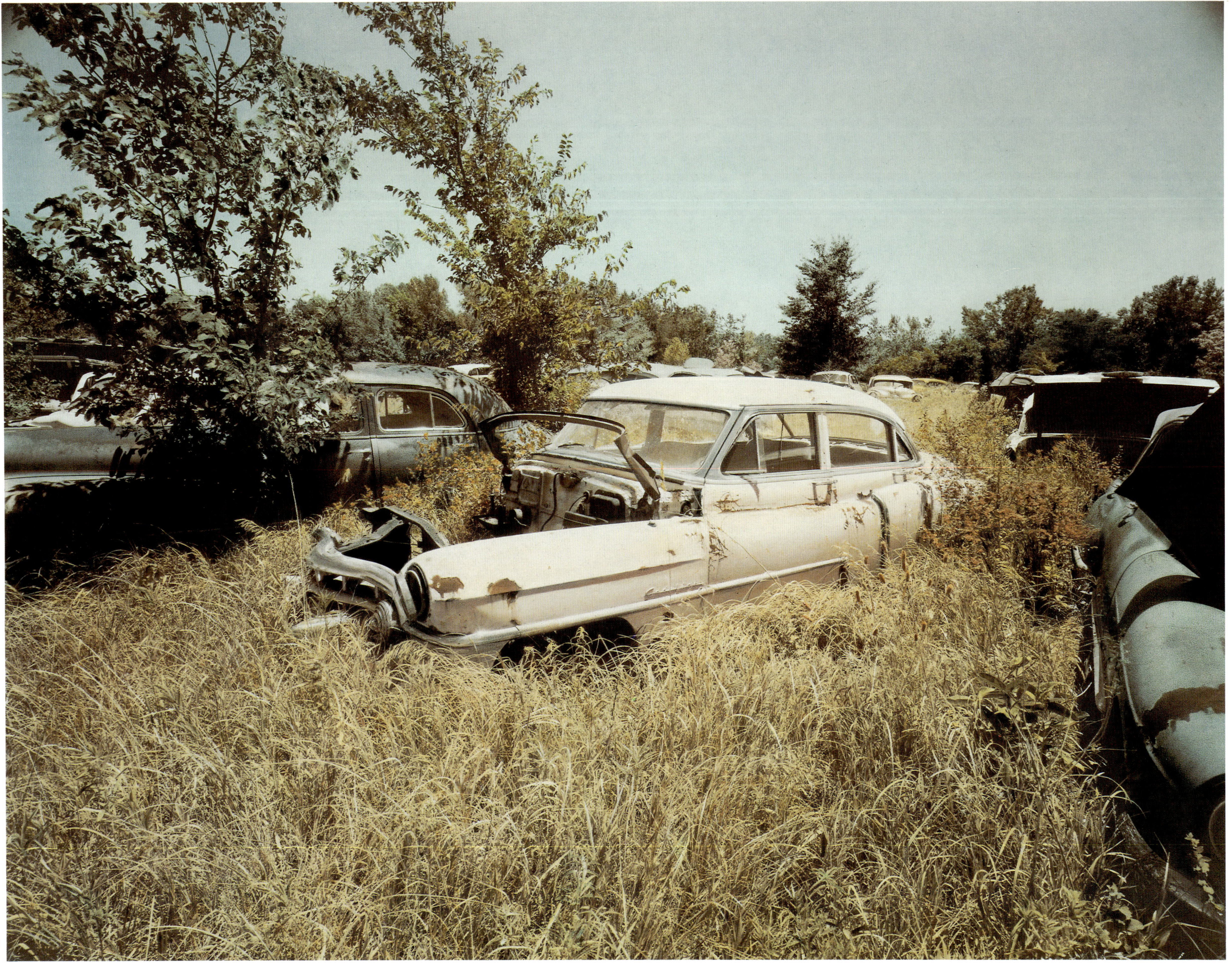

1952 Fleetwood Special; Woodstock, New York

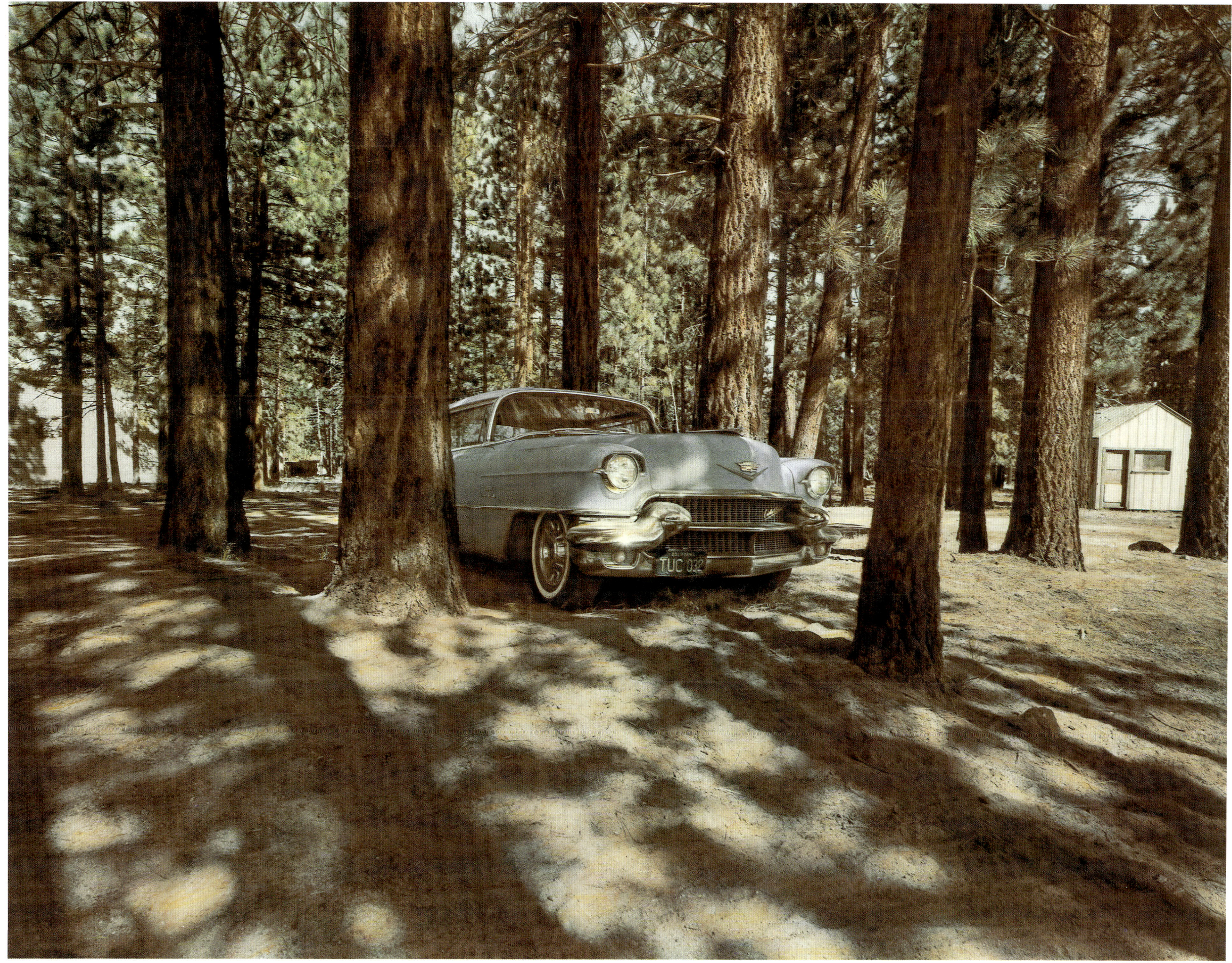

1956 Coupe de Ville; Lake Tahoe, Nevada

Horror! Treachery! The scholarly option of a man who had earned the right to value comfort in a car above all, but pure blasphemy to Caddy-baiters.

In the Le Mans race of 1950, American Briggs Cunningham entered a stock Coupe de Ville and a special-bodied open racer on a standard chassis and engine (called "Le Manstre" by the French press). We snobs greeted his irreverence with sneers, and neither car did much, but Cunningham's faith in the high compression Cadillac V-8 engines paid off in a highly successful sports car he produced by combining Cadillac power with an English-built body and chassis.

The disdain of the snobs was, however, meager stuff compared to the adoration of the legions of Cadillac zealots. Gradually, from year to year, the car came to symbolize the new American dream, a dream not of being wealthy but of *getting* wealthy (the dream was not new, of course, but simply dreamed more widely than ever before).

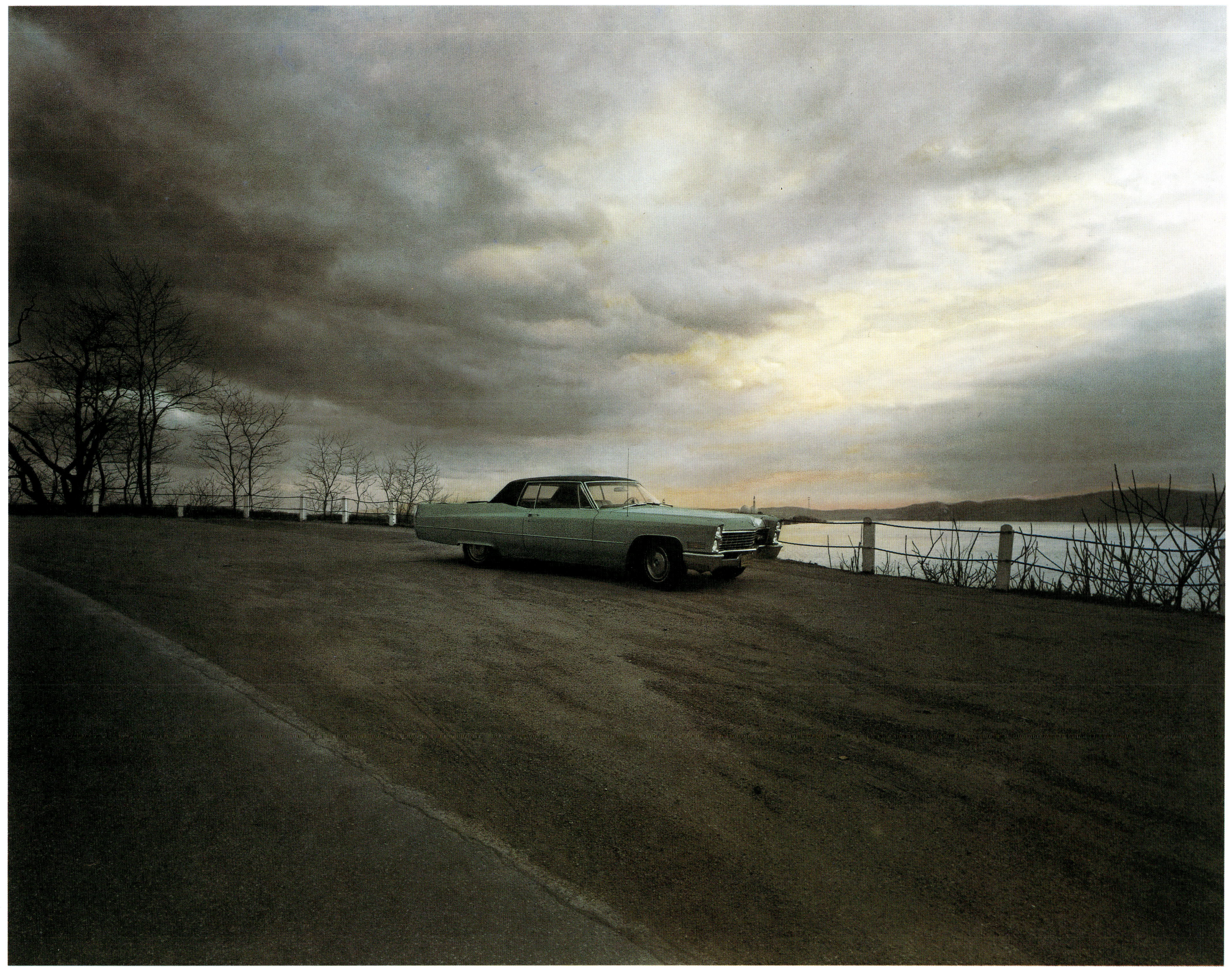

1967 Coupe de Ville; Peekskill, New York

In a spiraling mating ritual, the Cadillac grew more elaborate, more phenomenal, in order to further excite its adoring public, and the public responded with a heightened ardor that triggered yet more extraordinary changes. Through such a process, evolution has produced curious creatures like the flamingo, the mandrill, and the star-nosed mole. GM and Harley Earl, at the dizzying height of the spiral, produced the 1959 Eldorado.

The '59 was, in every conceivable way, the ultimate. Its tail fins flared up to an astonishing height, each bisected by a pair of streamlined tail lights. The car's dual headlights (a trend-setting style introduced on the Eldorado Brougham in 1955), vast grille, and wide bumpers with protruding rubber-tipped points gave a feeling that the car could devour blacktop, entire lanes at a time. It was as if, with the 1959 model, Harley Earl

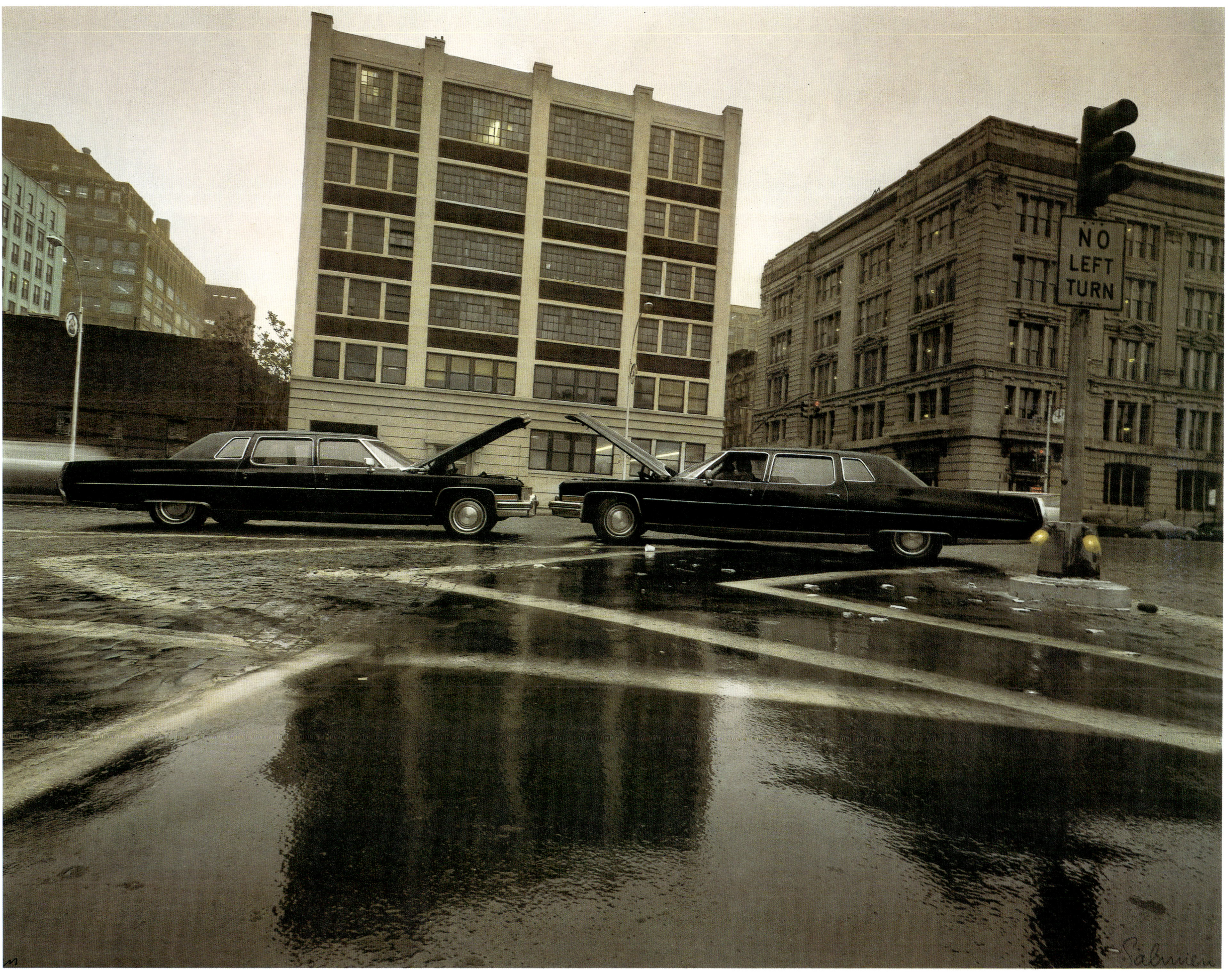

1973 Fleetwoods; New York City

and his merry band of stylists had decided to weed out those habitual Cadillac buyers who were insufficiently devoted to the breed, and build something that demanded deep convictions and courage no less profound. Perhaps, too, with the long shadow of Sputnik cast over the land, Earl sensed that a new, more cautious age was coming, and that he'd better shout his last hurrah.

Never has a car lived up to its name more fully than the brash, daring, and eccentric Eldorado. Here, surely, was the dazzling destination at the end of Detroit's yellow brick road. If the Cadillac was the holy grail, this was the holiest of the holy. To truly understand such a formidable and antic automobile, no mere casual devotion would suffice.

In Michael Cimino's movie *The Deer Hunter*, the central character, a steel worker and hunter played by Robert DeNiro, lives in a hillside trailer and drives a

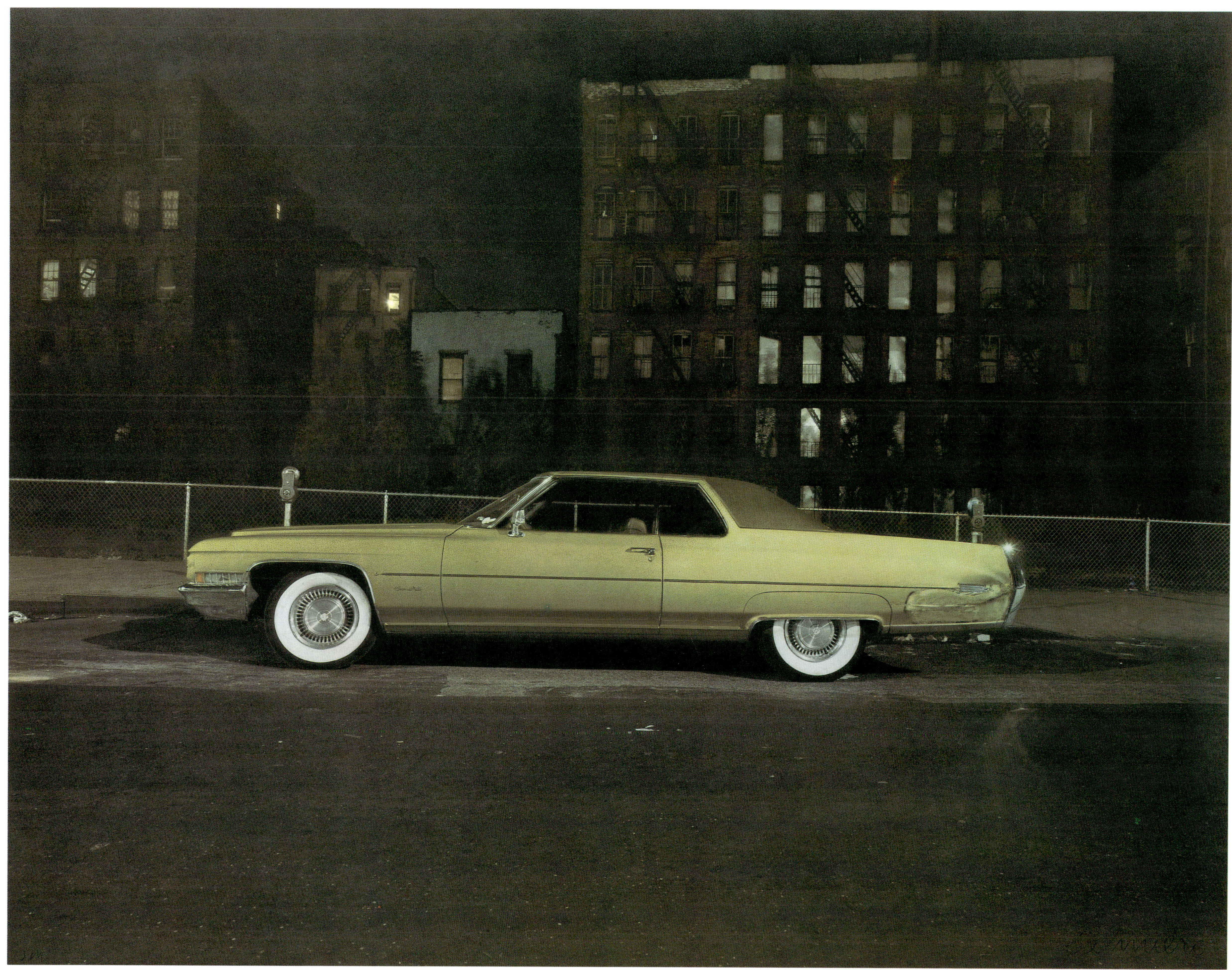

1971 Coupe de Ville; New York City

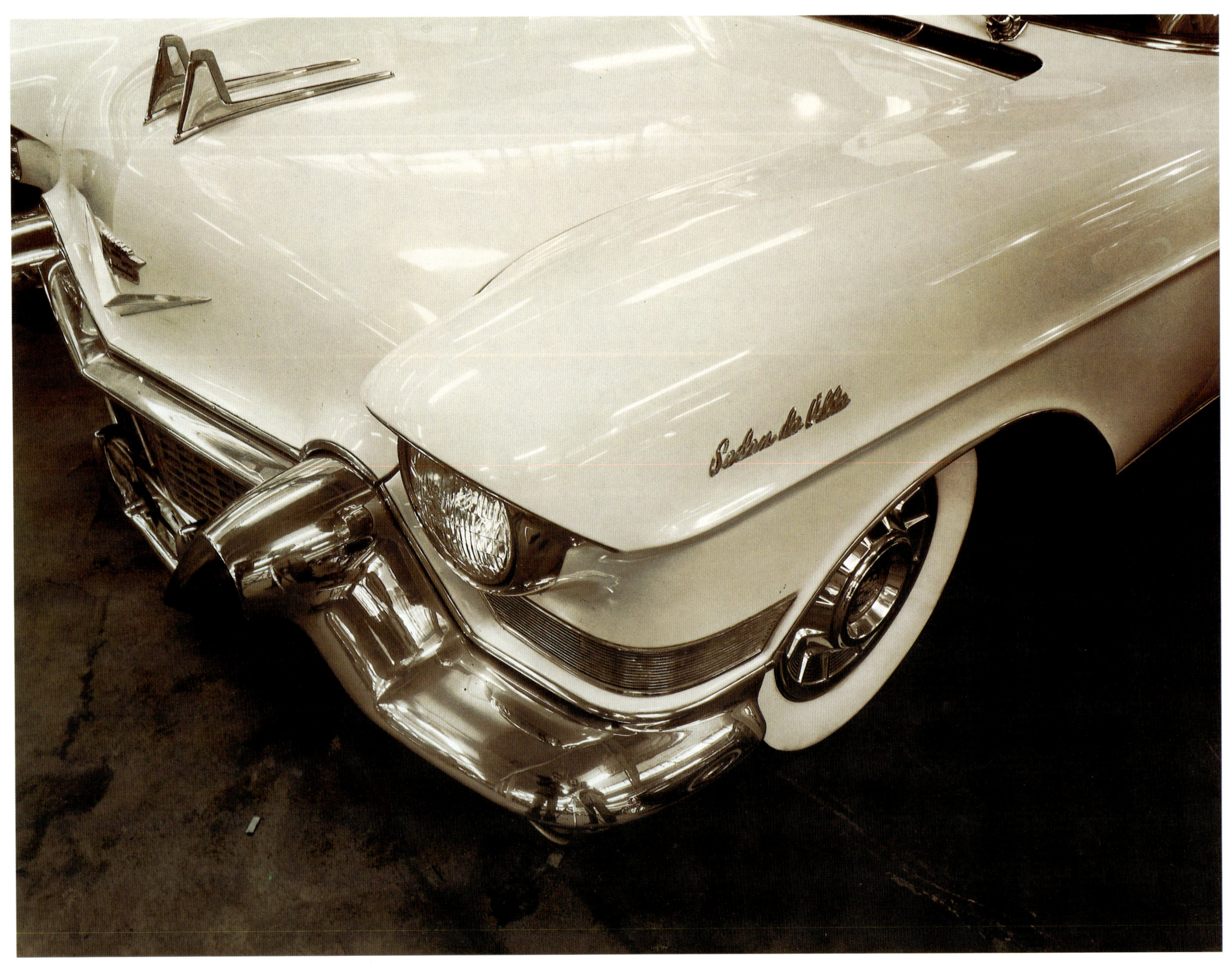

1957 Sedan de Ville; Philadelphia, Pennsylvania

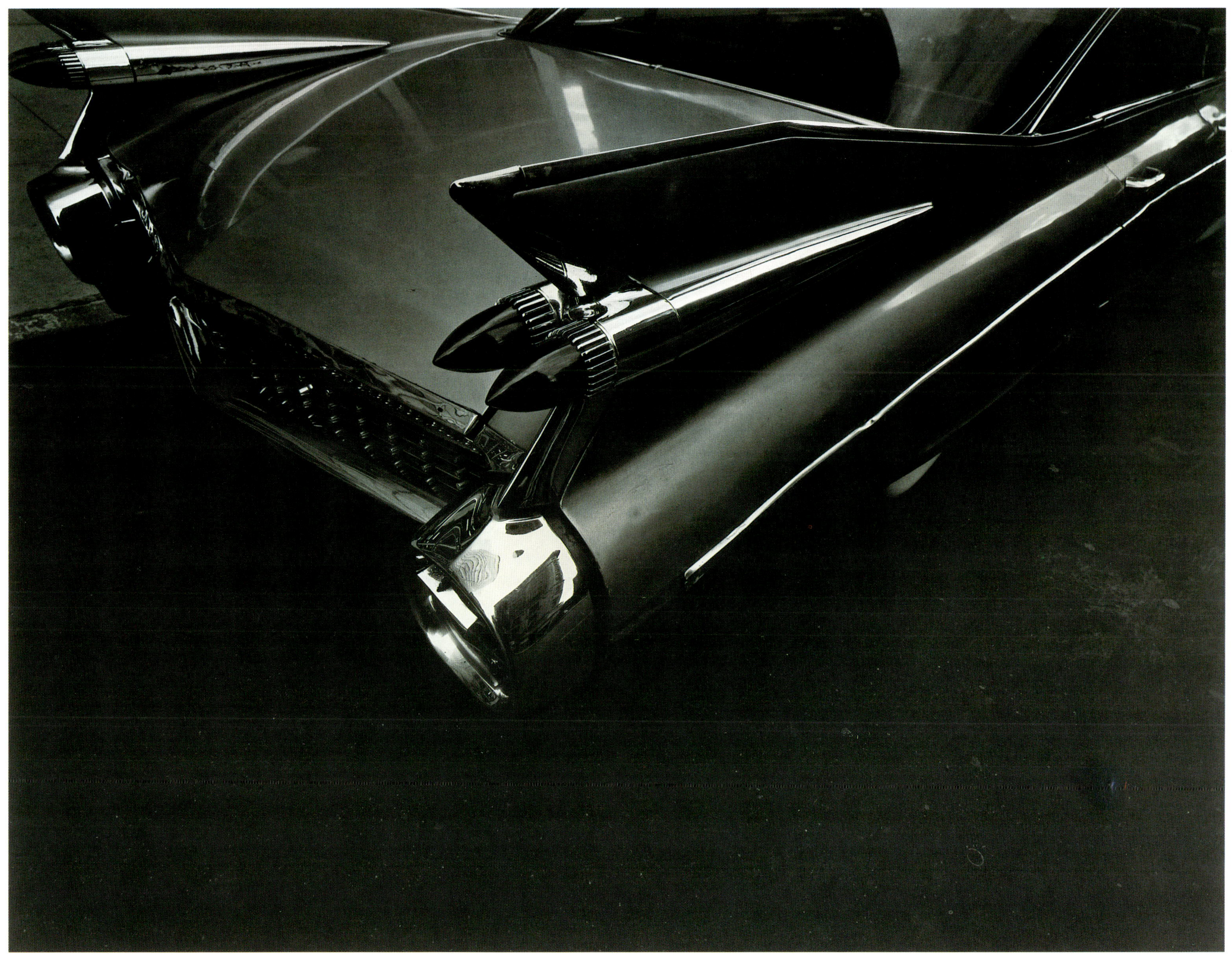

1959 Sedan de Ville, New York City

white 1959 Coupe de Ville. A few days before he reports to the army for duty in Vietnam, as he and his friends pile into the car to drive into the mountains, one of the group says, "I like Michael's car. It makes me feel safe." He is not talking about safety on the road, I suspect, but a larger safety. Within the padded cave of the Cadillac interior, we experienced the incomparable luxury of being safe within the fastness of America. The car was big, as the country was big, and its blithe, heedless use of precious materials said that in here, in this car and this country, we would always be safe.

The metaphor held for all of us, friends of the car and phobes alike. And as our birthright of luck ran out, as we began to realize there was no safety and that the days of our all-encompassing contentment were coming to an end, the Cadillac of vaulting and innocent lust grew in our hearts as it inexorably diminished before our eyes.

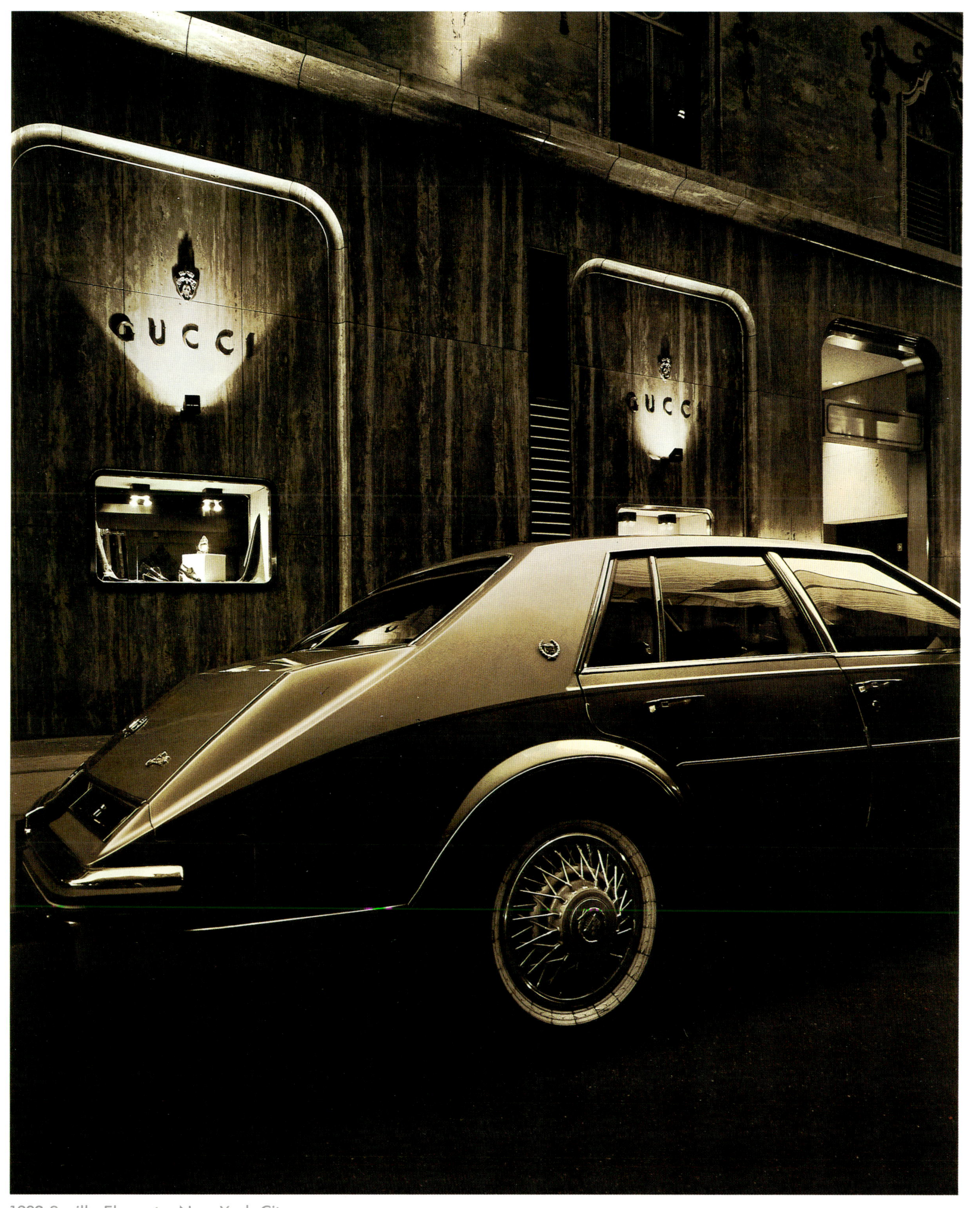

1982 Seville Elegante; New York City

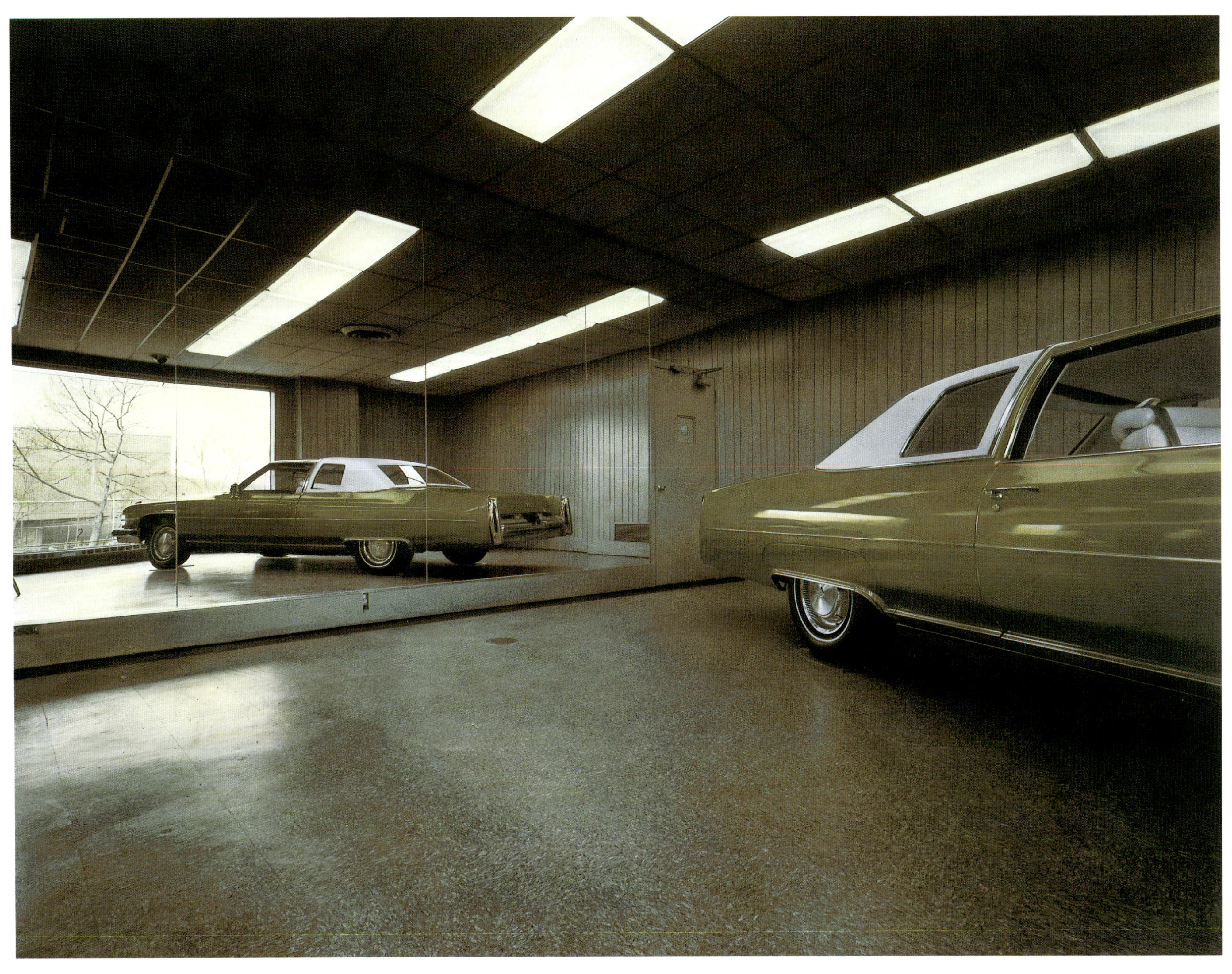

1974 Coupe de Ville; New York City

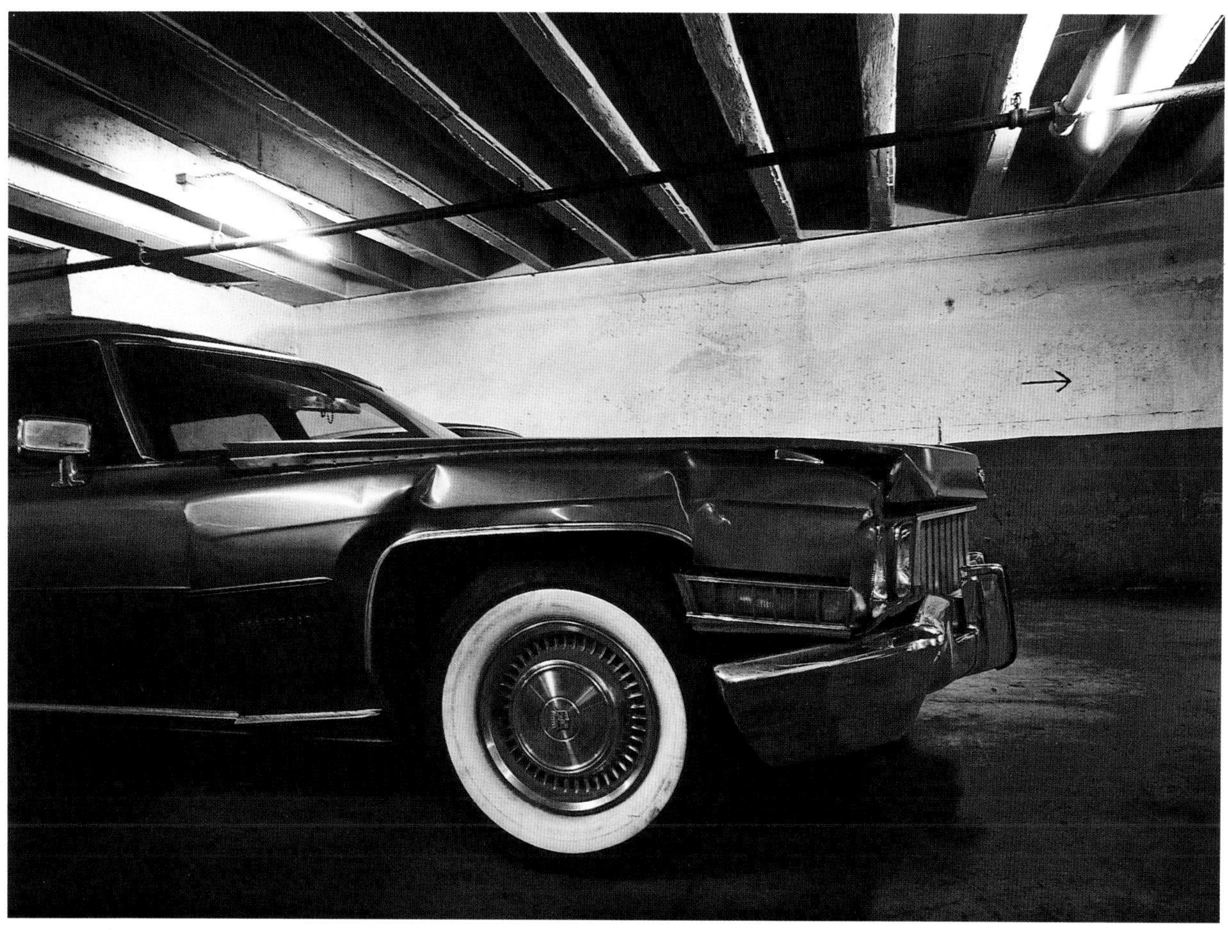

1971 Sedan; New York City

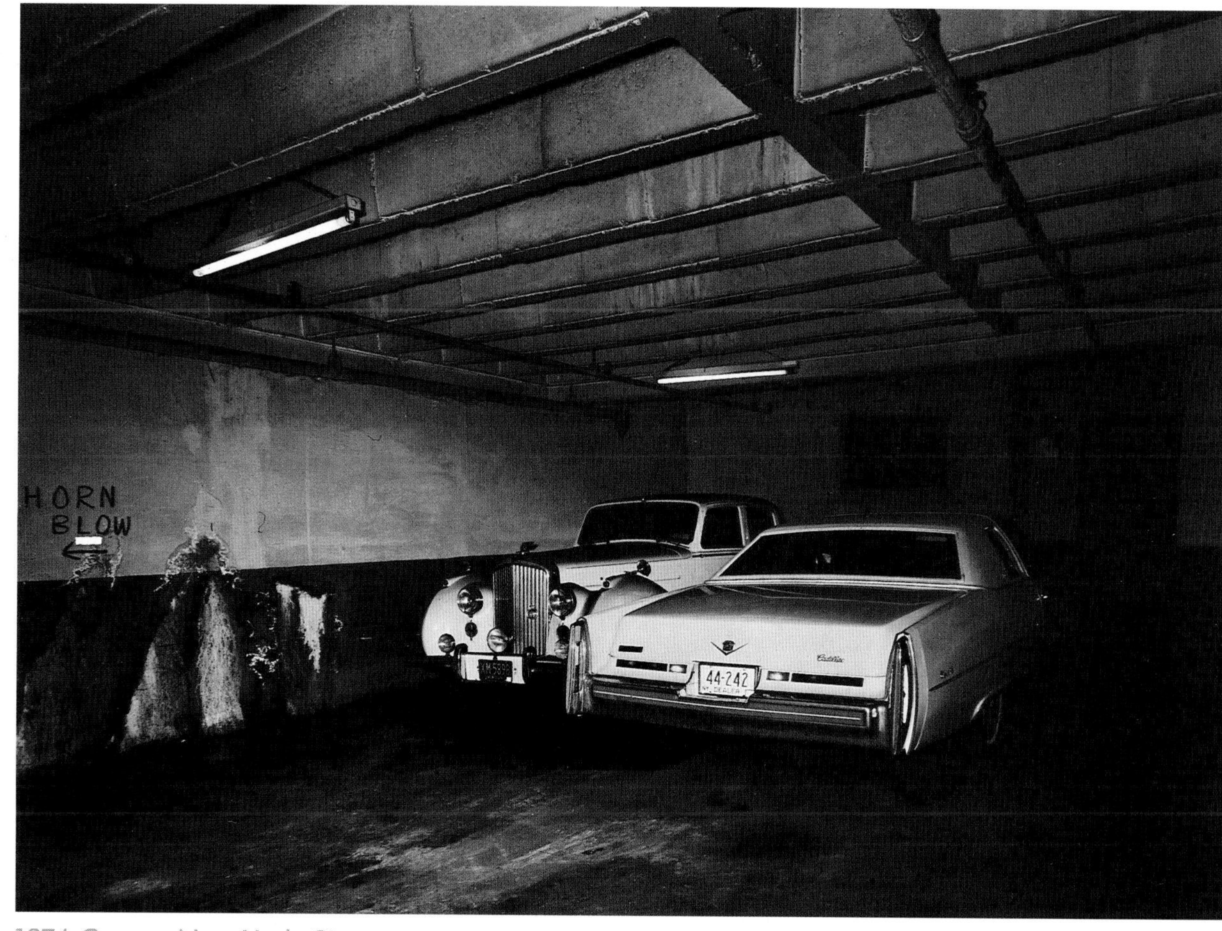

1974 Coupe; New York City

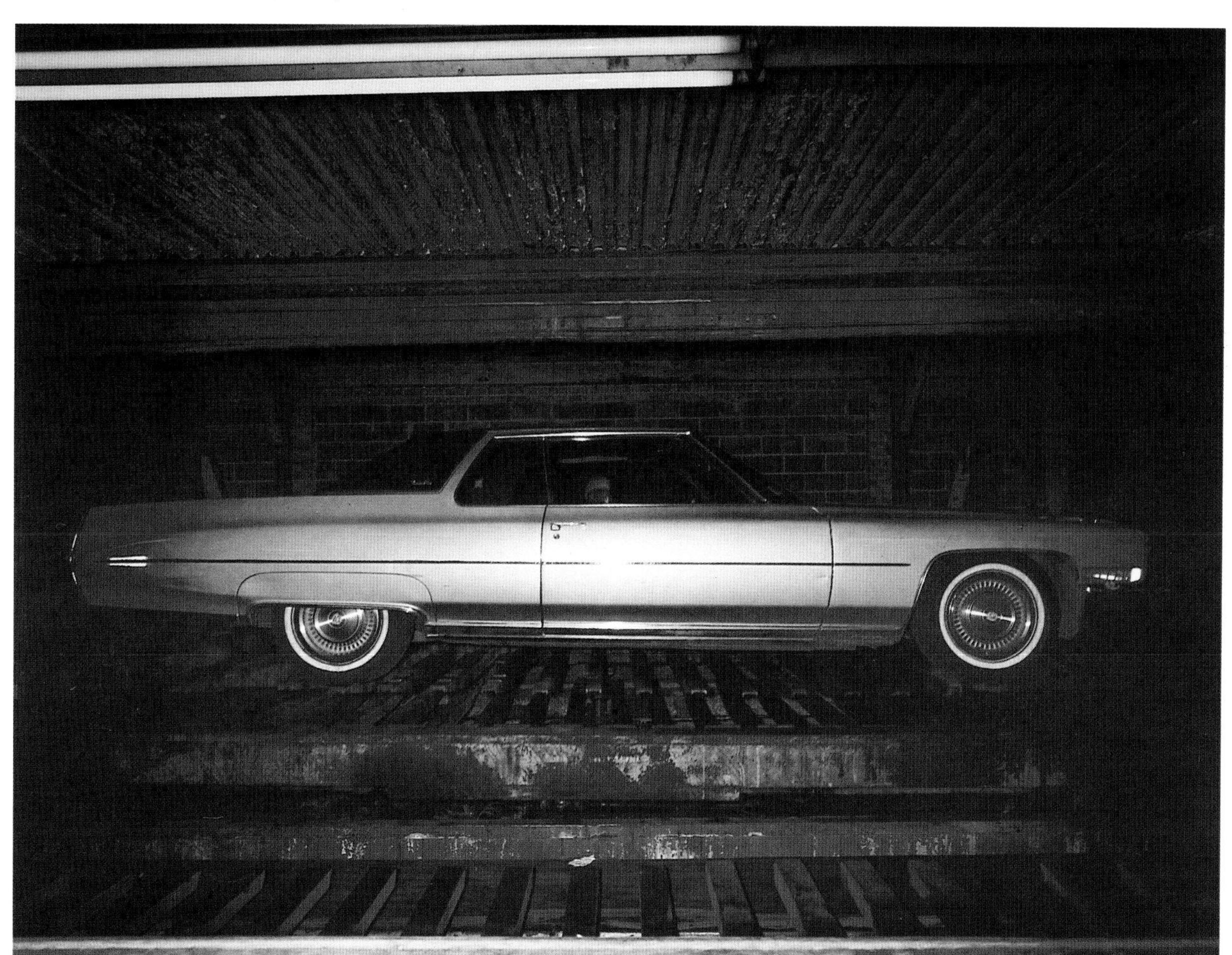

1972 Coupe; New York City

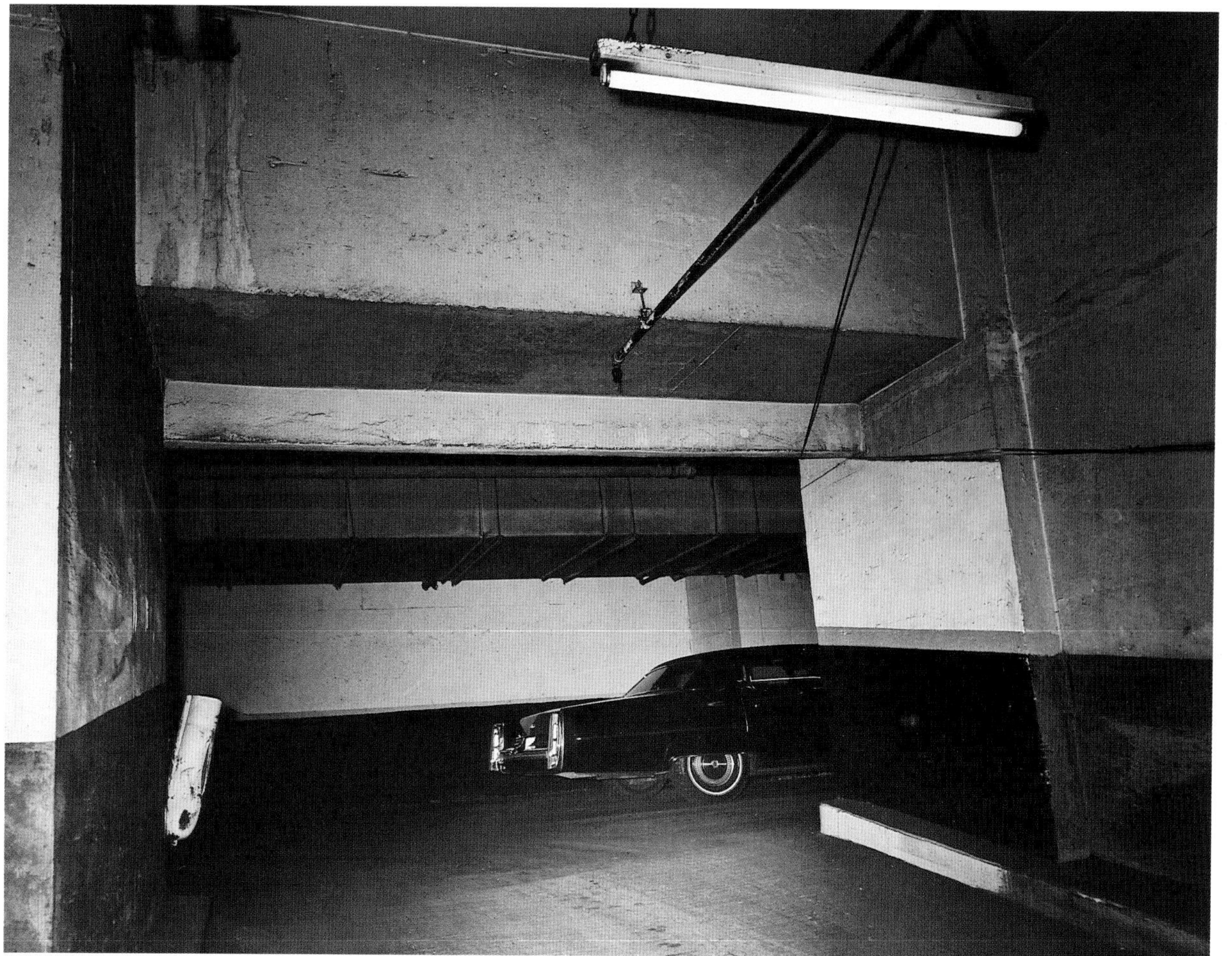

1973 Sedan; New York City

In 1973, Stephen Salmieri, a New York City portrait photographer, went to look for America. This search, in itself, is hardly without precedent. In fact, it is as much a heritage of our frontier-lured past as the Marlboro man and Saturday-night specials. Artists and Okies, writers and drifters, eventual winners and perpetual losers have all done the same when luck, inspiration, or patience dried up. Salmieri's idea, however, was not to go in search of a place, but to piece together the kind of visual tapestry with which photographers attempt to make sense of things.

Unlike writers—or drifters—who can make up whatever stories please them and their audiences as they go along, photographers are indentured to the way things appear to be, and even more narrowly to the *surfaces* of things. Mark Twain could send Huck Finn off down the river and recreate the world however

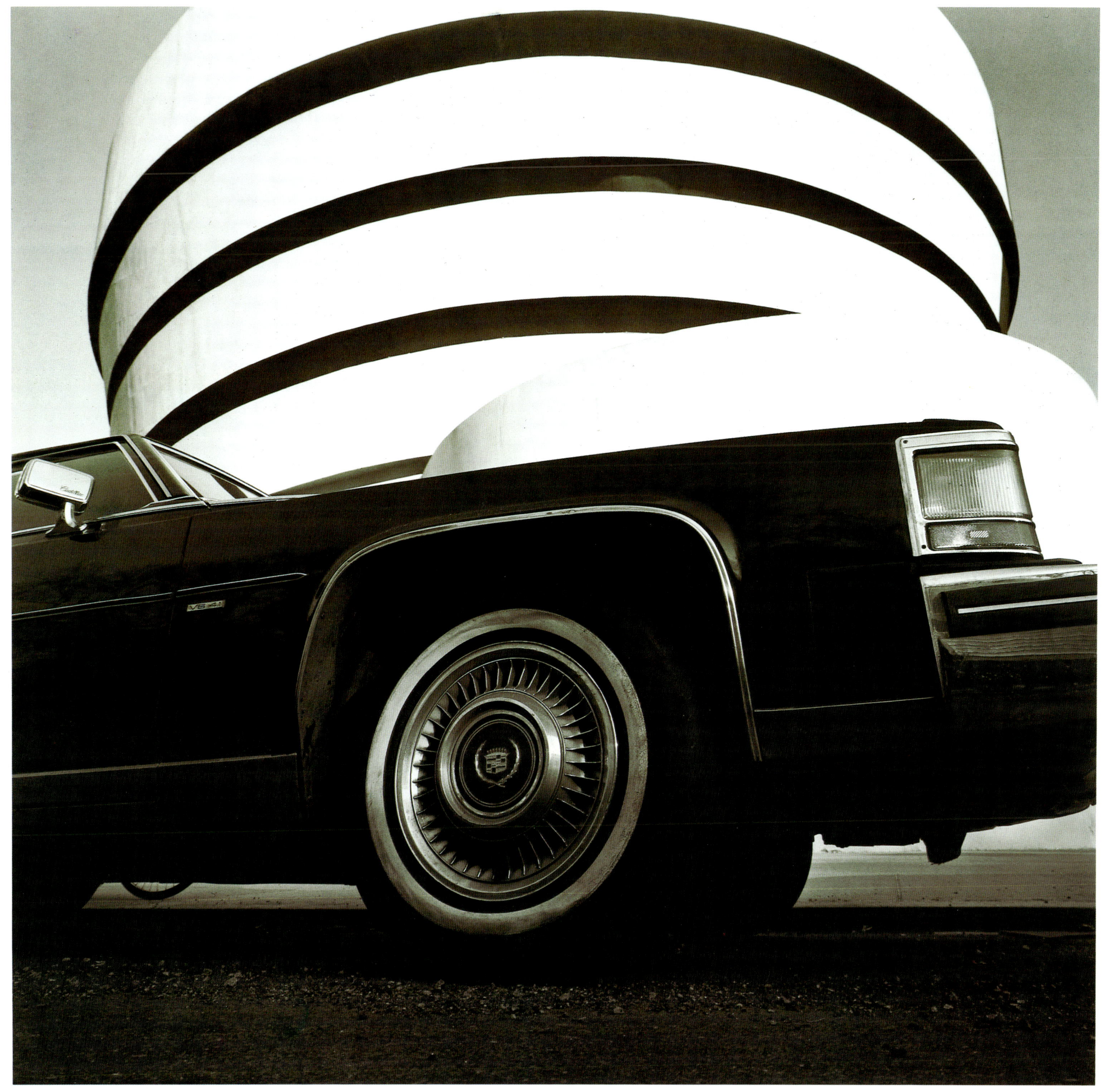

1980 Sedan de Ville; New York City

he wished, but a photographer must present the world more or less as it is, reduced to two dimensions and shaped only by an ability to filter reality through a glass darkly or brightly in such a way that it emerges artistically his own.

Given the limitations of their medium, ironically combined with its overwhelming mechanical profligacy, photographers may be forgiven their often desperate grasping at metaphors. Without some specific goal, what newspaper editors dourly call a hook, a photographer can be devoured by the insatiable appetite of his own machinery. The camera without a controlling idea is nothing more or less than a visual vacuum cleaner.

When Salmieri had first begun to think about going to find America, his notion for a metaphor to hold the tapestry together was an appropriate one: cars.

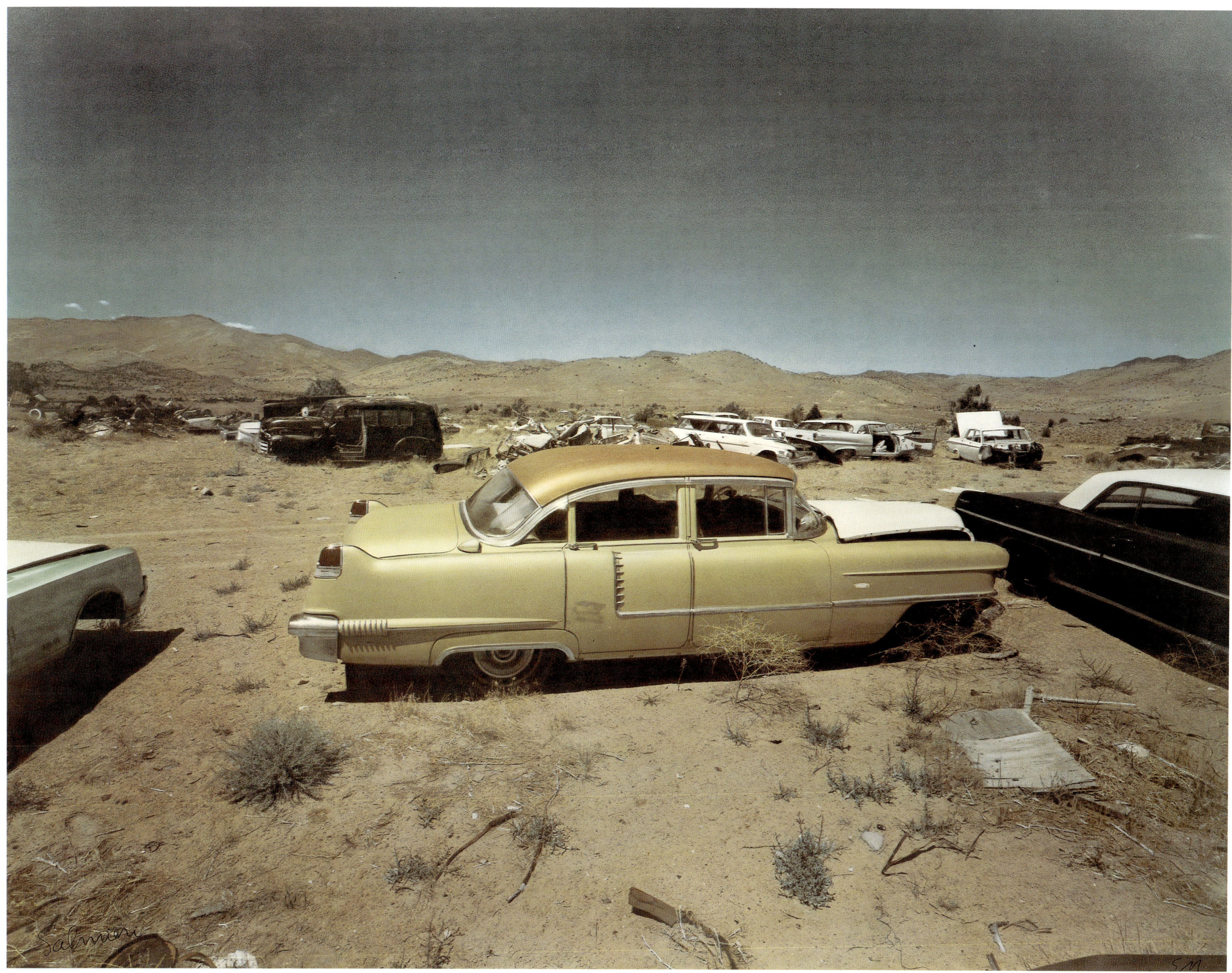

1956 Sedan; Utah

If wagon trains, and then railroads, created the broad patterns of travel in America—created, in fact, the dream of endless betterment through bugging out and moving on—then it was the car that filled in all the vast spaces between the trails and rails.

Salmieri's car metaphor was good but vague. He wanted a metaphor within the metaphor, an automobile of automobiles, the ur car. That the Cadillac percolated up through the vast mass of American motoring metal was proof of its symbolic capacity to prevail against all odds.

The Salmieri family of Brooklyn, New York, like the New Jersey Edwardses, never had a Cadillac. But in an Italian neighborhood, no less image-conscious than the New Jersey suburbs and far more un-self-deprecating, there was nothing ambiguous about the car. Not having a Cadillac made only one statement: You did not have

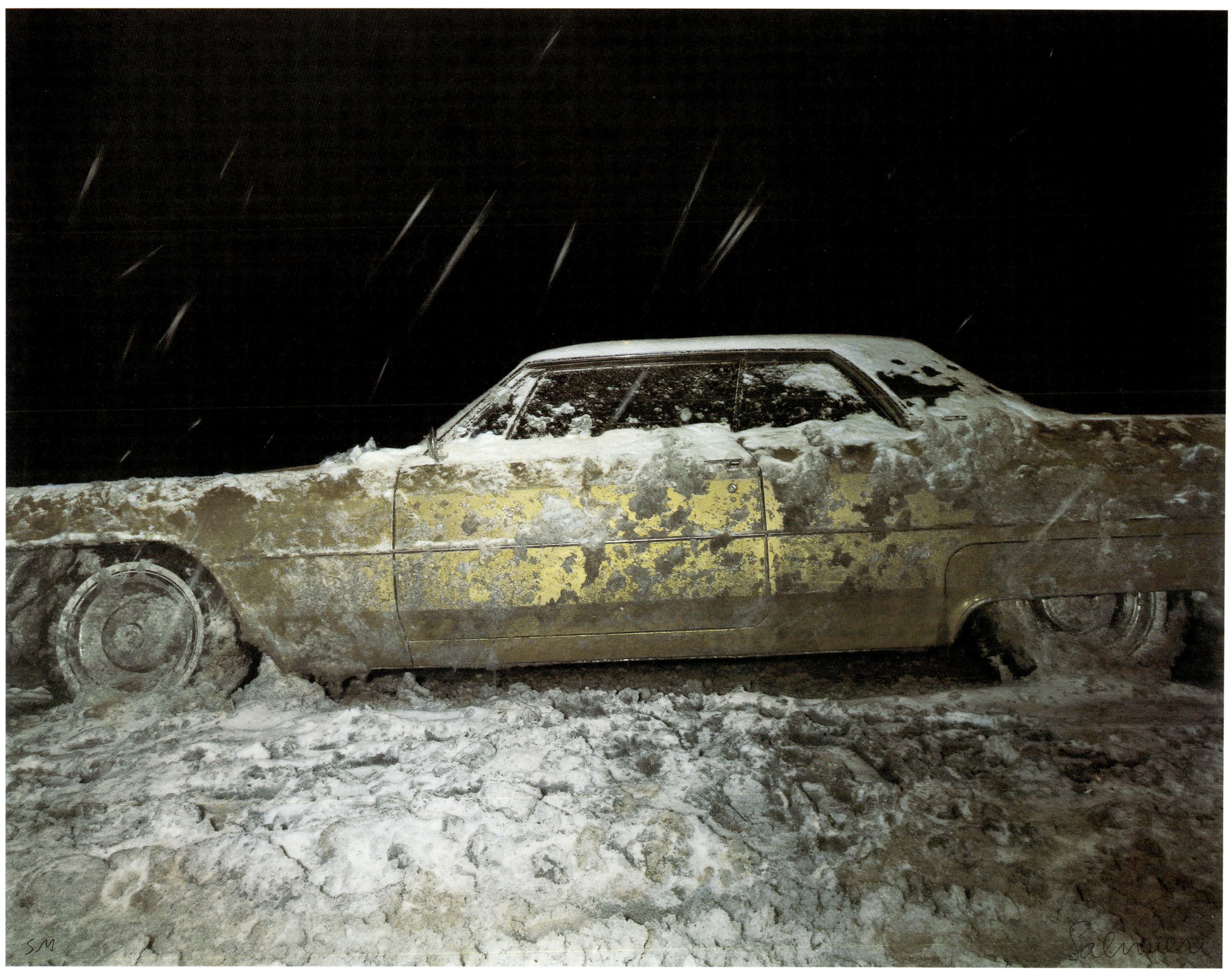

1965 Coupe de Ville; Route 9, New York

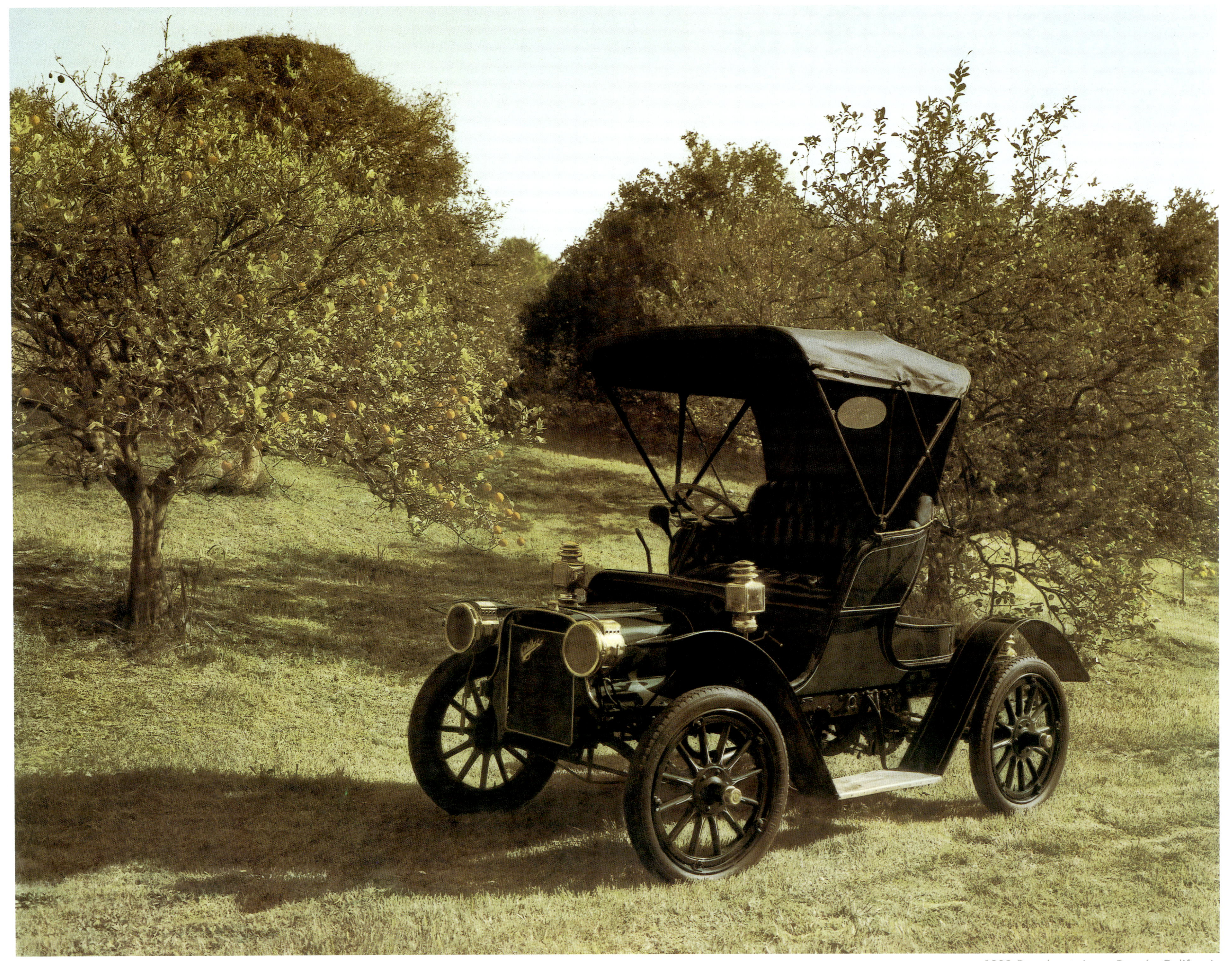

1908 Runabout: Long Beach, California

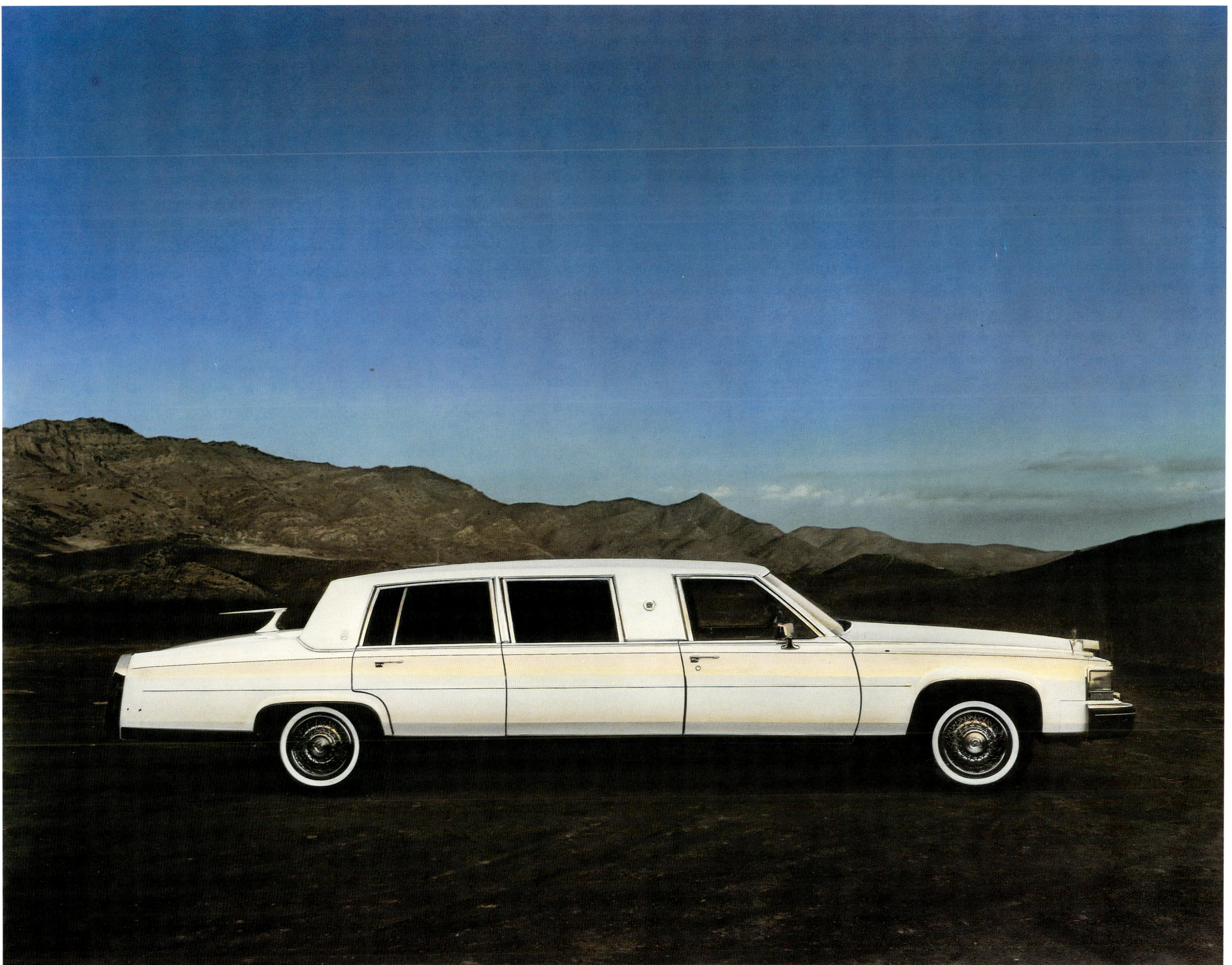

1985 Fleetwood; San Fernando Valley, California

a Cadillac. In sum, you had not yet arrived, however close you might be, to that ultimate point where you would be accorded automatic *respetto*. In Brooklyn, the Cadillac was understood, deeply, just as General Motors meant it to be understood: as the chariot of the gods.

Salmieri could not ignore his family's Cadillac-lack. There was no stubborn pride in the fact that his father drove a Ford, no chance to take refuge in the subtle suburban superiority of understatement. And on weekends, he washed cars to make money, which as often as not meant sponging down the broad backs of the Caddys owned by the fathers of his friends. He remembers the introduction of each year's new Cadillac models as the main issue of the day in neighborhood conversations that he could enter only as an onlooker, a pre-novitiate.

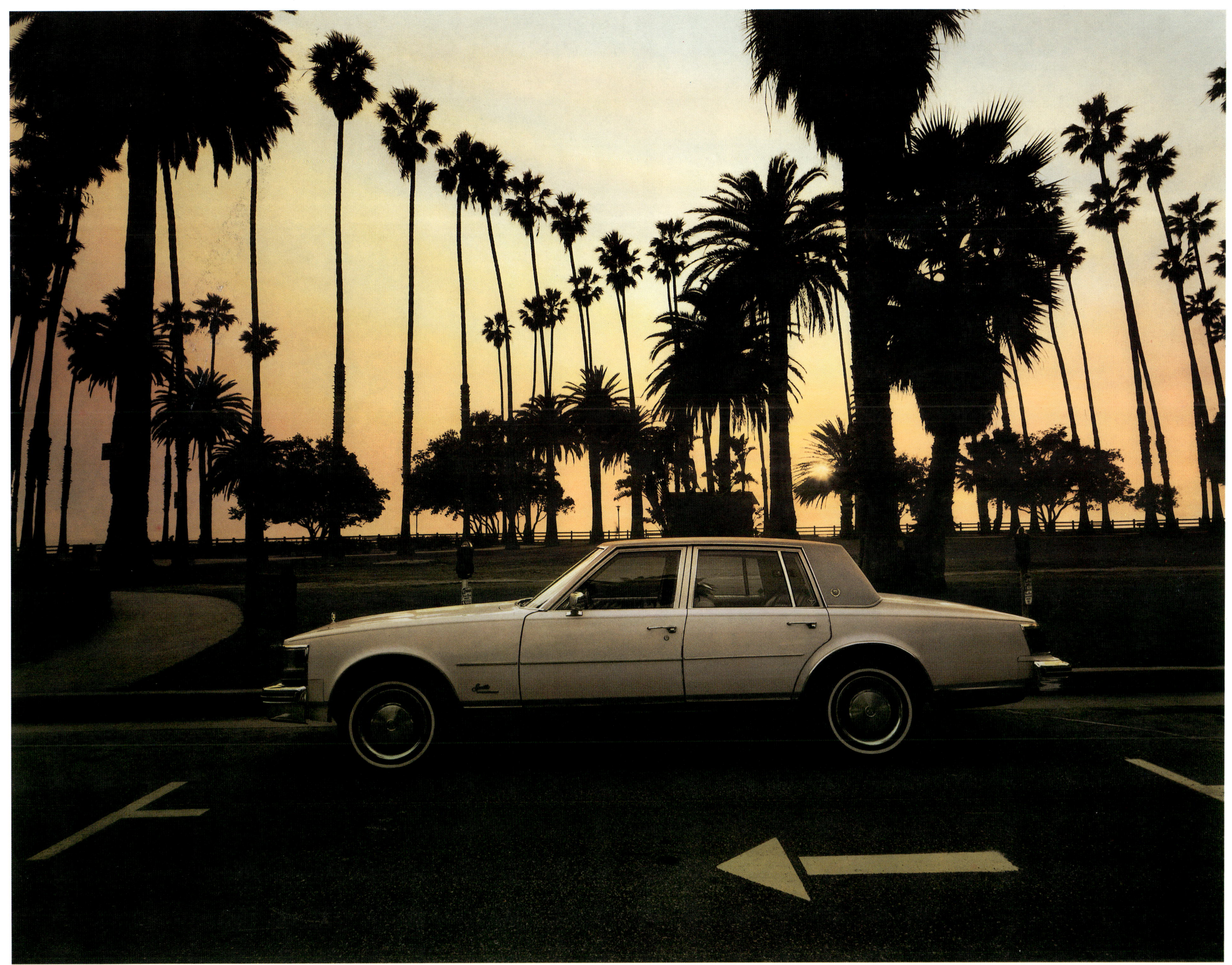

1976 Seville; Santa Monica, California

When it came to the twin spires of community faith—Catholicism and car worship—young Stephen must have been a problem. He was to end up as an artist, after all, which in Brooklyn is still not really considered a career. Making a living with a camera, however good that living might turn out to be, was at least slightly suspect, and so it may be concluded that from the beginning his values were skewed. Serving as a material reminder that the family's status was not quite what it could be, the Cadillac was no friend. And when Salmieri learned to drive, and came to judge cars for their usefulness and the intelligence of their design, he concluded that the Cadillac was not for him. When Salmieri left Brooklyn for the far-away shores of Manhattan, he emphatically left the Cadillac behind.

And yet it was the scorned Caddy that became his photographic hook, grail, passion and, finally,

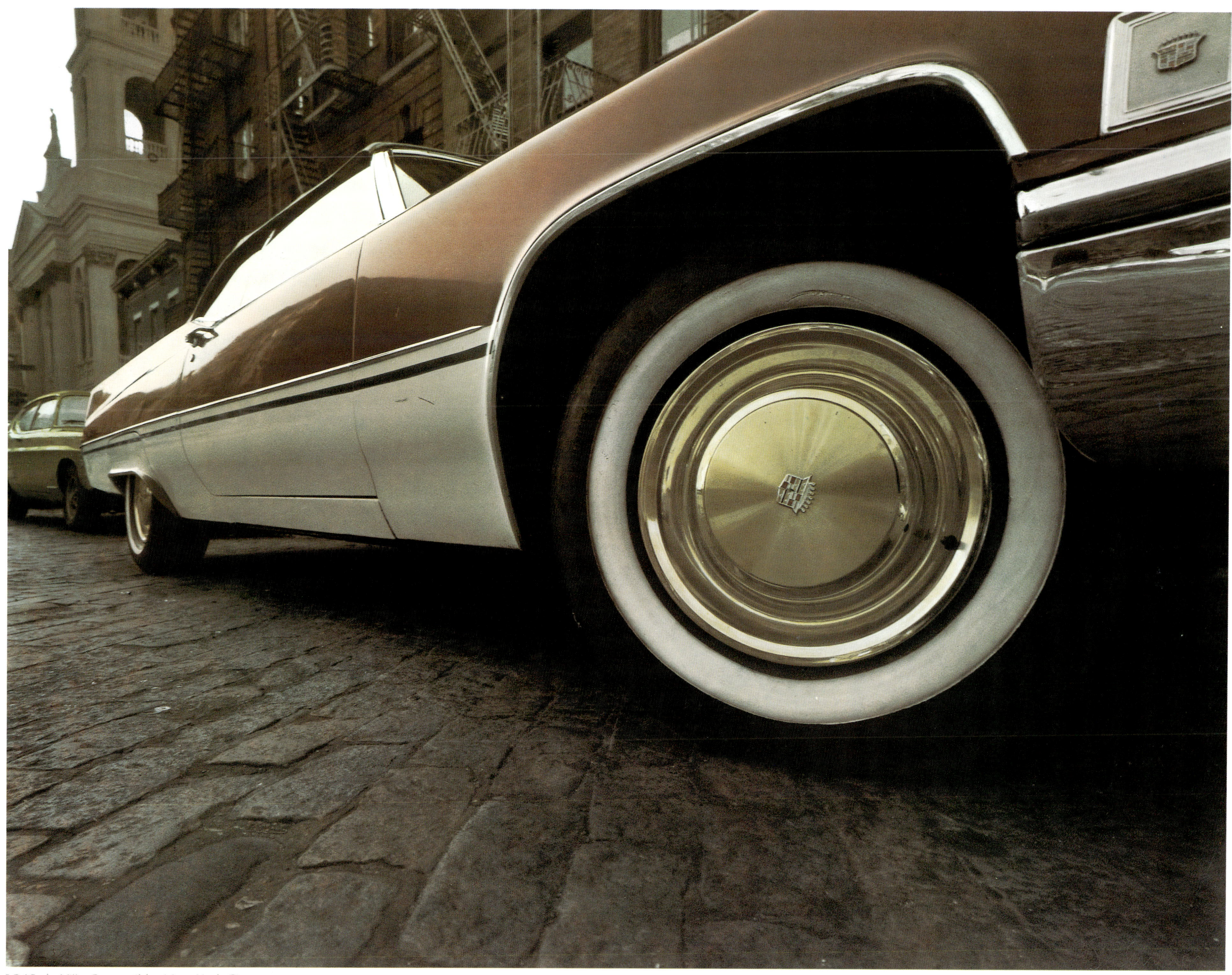

1969 de Ville Convertible; New York City

obsession. The abandoned icon would become his unavoidable artistic vehicle, in which and through which he would travel for years.

True obsessions have a manic magic about them. Like oracles, they may speak obscurely, but their omens are often dramatically evident. In the earliest days of Salmieri's Cadillac fixation, when the idea of doing something with the car was vague and unformed, he met a painter named Sydnie Michele, and the two rather precipitously decided to join their lives. On the day Salmieri had decamped from his apartment and moved his belongings to Sydnie's loft, he was driving a rented van back to its roost when he saw a matched brace of 1975 Cadillac limousines, parked grille to grille in a classic exchange of battery energy.

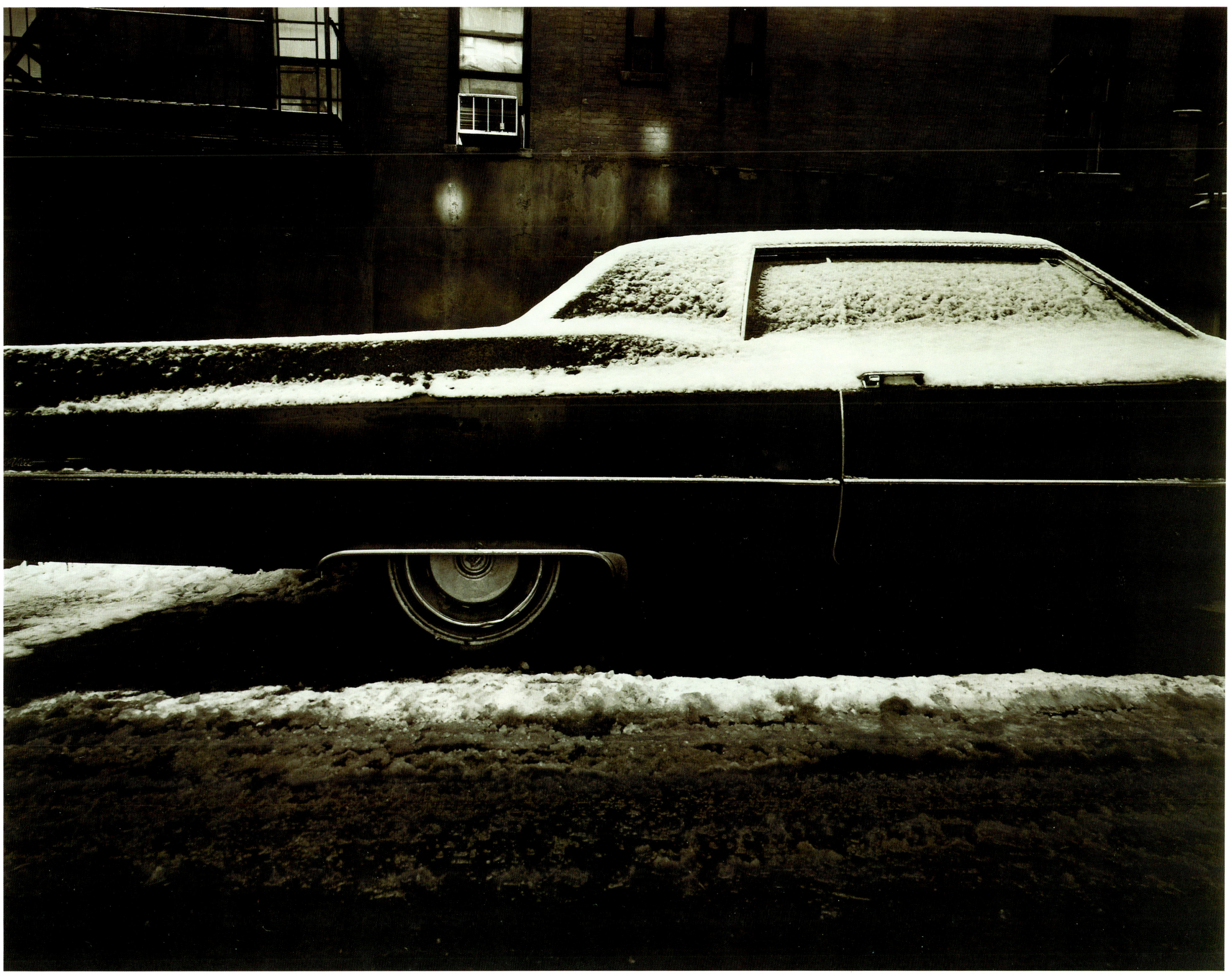

1967 Coupe de Ville; New York City

The great creatures languished there voluptuously, symbolically (this being the day of meaningful mating), seeming to wait expressly to give Salmieri his first picture, like a gift from some opportunistic demiurge. Except that, just this once, the ever-ready photographer didn't have his camera with him. Racing the van along a rats' maze of one way streets back to the loft, Salmieri unpacked his camera, then raced back, sure he would be late. There the cars sat, still agape, the exchange completed, the drivers conversationally engaged.

"I can't believe you're still here," shouted the excited hunter. "You've changed my life!"

History doesn't record whether the drivers understood what Salmieri's particular problem was, or if they cared. The city is full of crazies, after all. But the Cadillac project was launched. The message was clear, at least to someone waiting to hear a message and

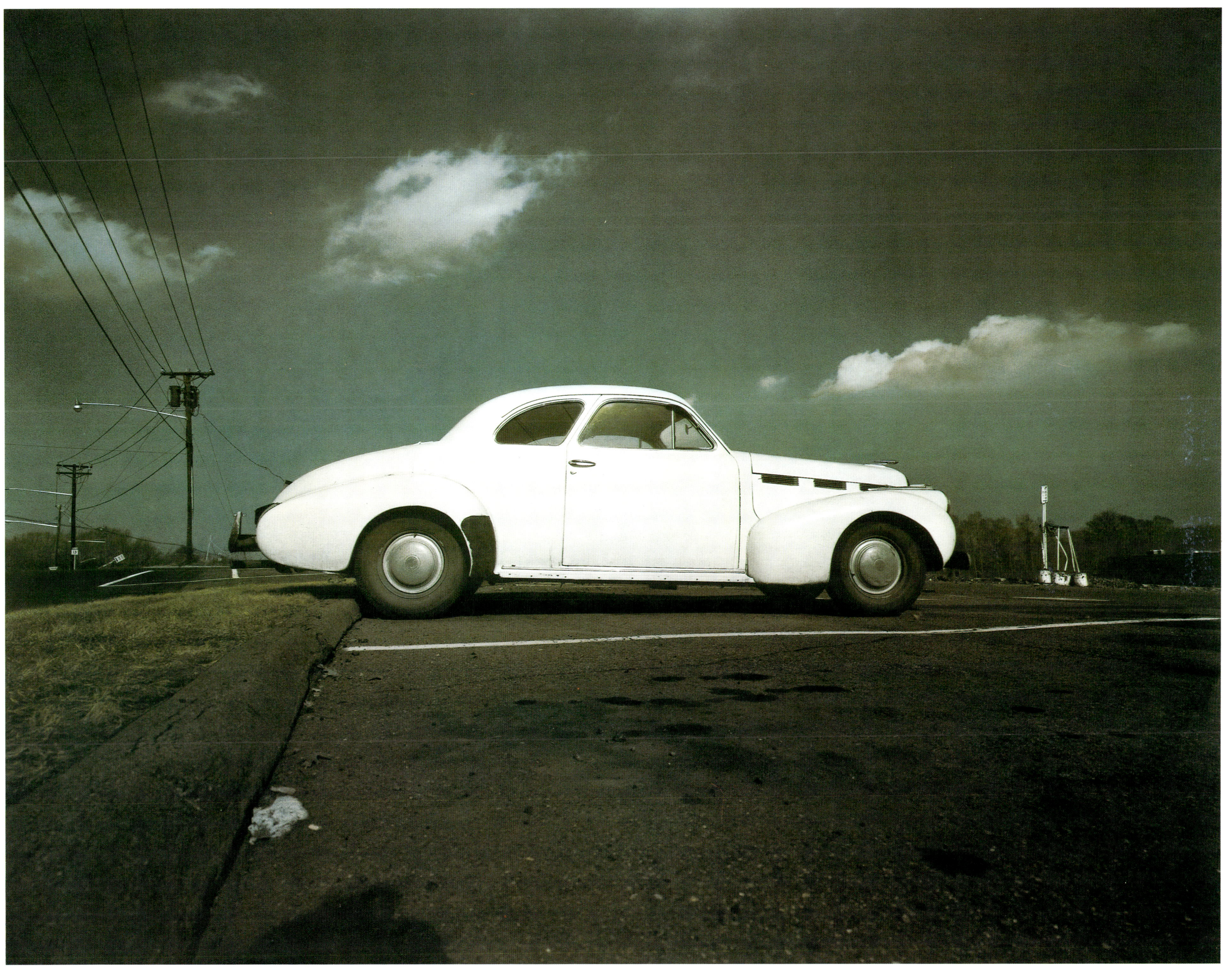

1940 La Salle; Englewood, New Jersey

hypersensitive to symbolism oddly combining pairs and cars. And the idea for a Cadillac project naturally gelled. After all, the mating cars might have been Buicks, but (since the gods obviously *wouldn't* rather have a Buick) they were not. Within a few days, Salmieri and Sydnie had jettisoned their past, packed up their car (a dutiful Dodge Dart) and started west.

For five months the two zigzagged across the country. Like a wildlife photographer roaming the bush in search of a vanishing species, Salmieri looked for Cadillacs in all their natural habitats, and in all states of being. In driveways and junkyards, as limousines waiting with showy importance and as derelicts rusting into oblivion, as powerful symbols of both hope and despair, Salmieri came upon Cadillacs in all sorts of places and all manner of forms.

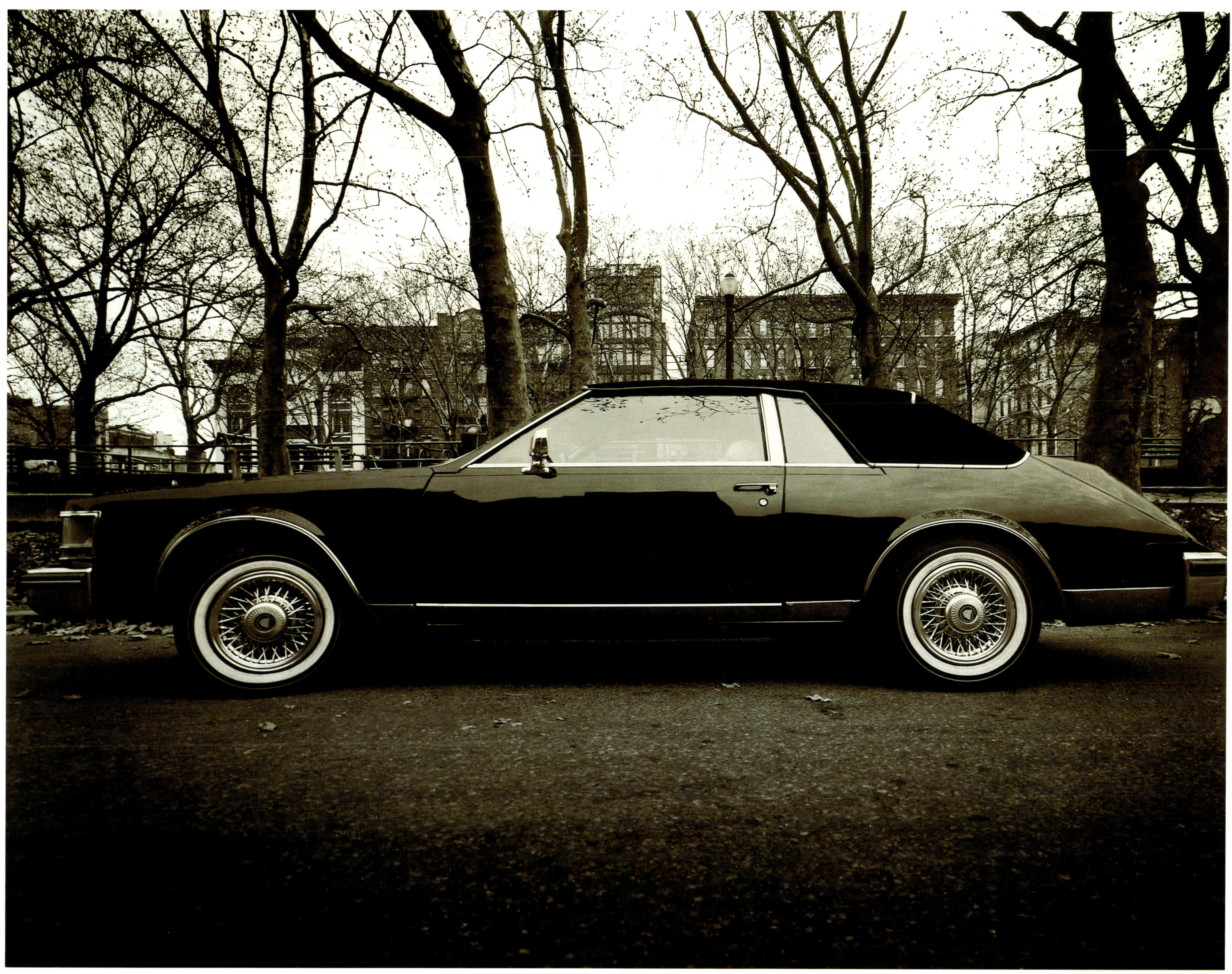

1982 Seville; New York City

The obsessions of artists, like those of shoe salesmen, can be tamed simply by overfeeding. They are useful for simplifying life (anything unrelated to the X obsession need not be considered important), but often lack stamina. If you paint skulls or peek up dresses, a steady enough diet may exorcise the demons. If not, art and life may suffer, since obsession alone makes a misleading muse.

But five months of tracking the Cadillac turned what might have been a short-lived obsession into an abiding passion. Whatever Salmieri may have felt about the Cadillac when he started out on the first stage of the project that would eventually become this book, by the time he had reached California he had come to feel that he had found a vein of ore more valuable than he had at first imagined. As a car, the Cadillac still aroused in Salmieri only disdain (true to his earlier principles, today

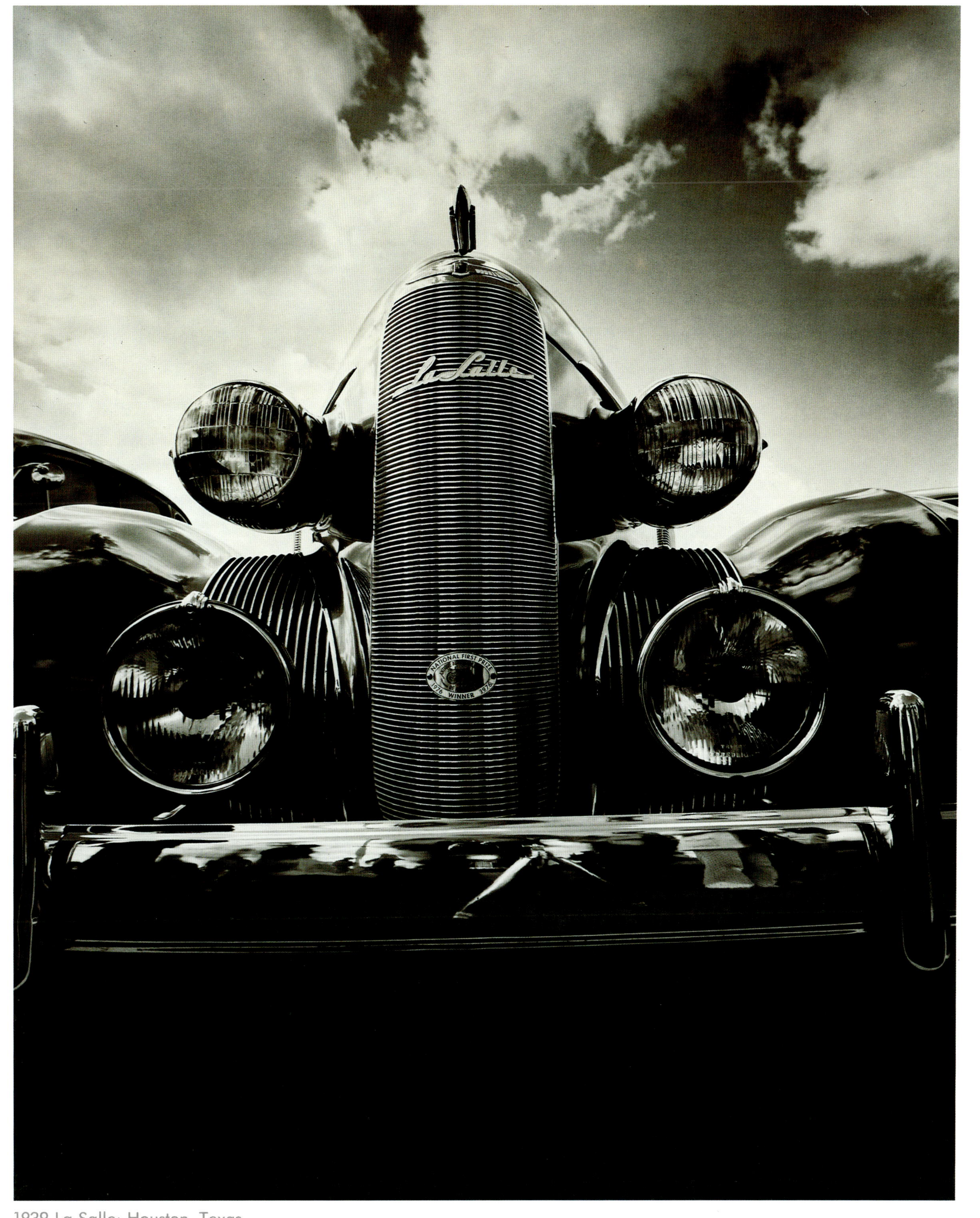

1939 La Salle; Houston, Texas

he drives a Jaguar), but as a metaphor it can't be improved upon. The late Eugene Ormandy's Philadelphia Orchestra has been described as "the solid gold Cadillac of orchestras." The term is instantly understandable. No American could ever respond as feelingly to the image of, say, a solid-gold Lincoln.

Los Angeles, a town shaped by and for the automobile, filled with giddy charioteers indebted to their mobility and often in debt to their car dealers, was for Salmieri the kind of annealing experience that traditionally strengthens the resolve of grail seekers. Southern Californians celebrate cars with a fine fervor unknown to New Yorkers, and even with the pyrotechnic displays of Rolls-Royces, Ferraris, and exotically rigged Mercedeses, the Cadillac retains a paternal presence there. Salmieri's five-month journey to L.A., with its random sightings and increasing excitement, had turned

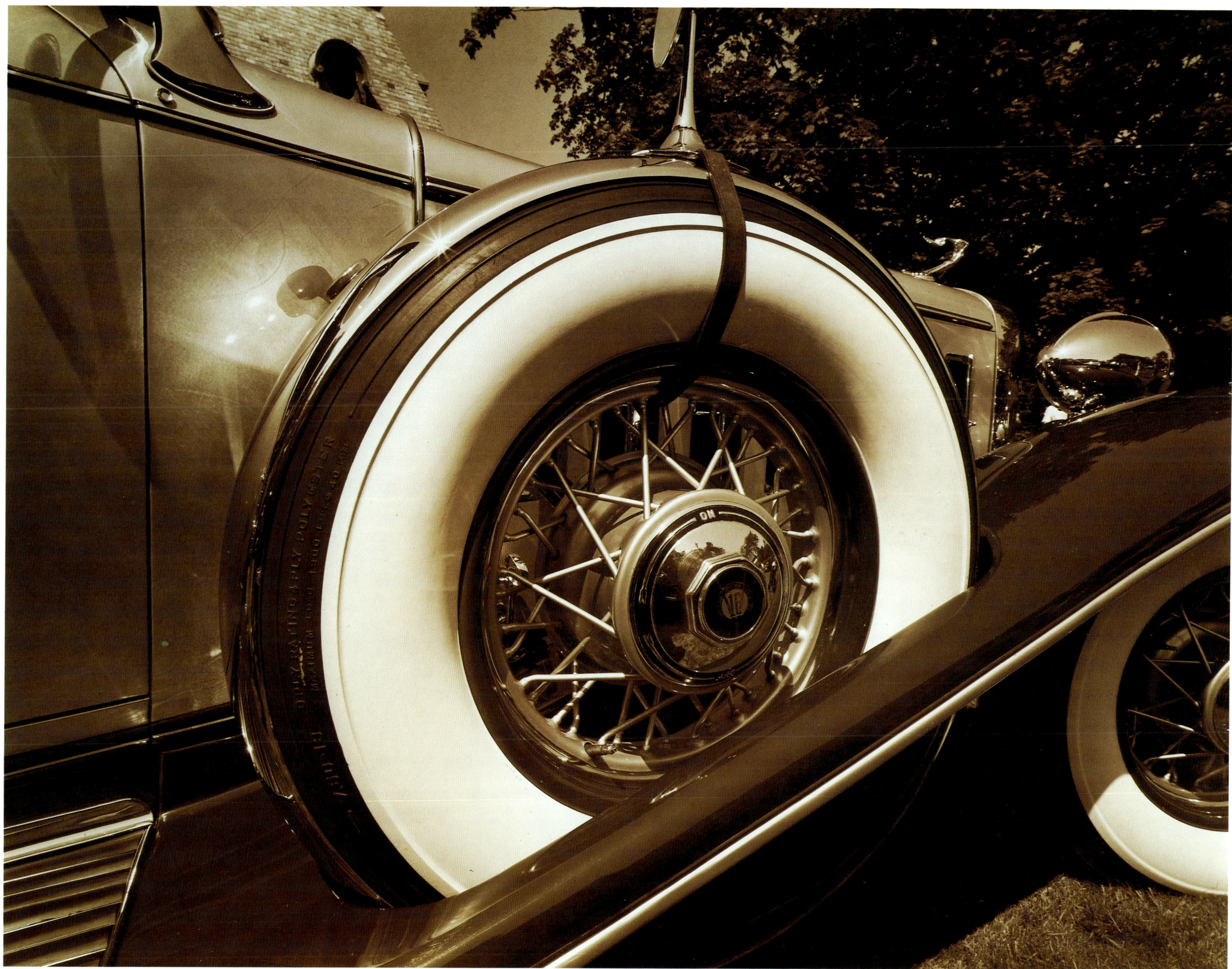

1932 V.16 Fleetwood; Newport, Rhode Island

a dilettante into an enthusiast; the panorama of Caddys, vintage and fresh-minted, straight and strangely customized, grazing splendidly along the trails of this auto Serengeti, completed the process and produced a connoisseur. And since chance favors the eye sharpened by lust, Cadillacs appeared as if by psychokinesis. Did the hint of desire to see that *rara avis* , the flamingo-pink late-fifties Eldorado, drift into his mind? Within half an hour the very thing would obediently appear, mystically abandoned at the side of the freeway. Did he briefly long to encounter something classic and black, say a late forties model, looming up on the drive of an equally classic California bungalow? His wish was the *Zeitgeist's* command, and soon enough there it would be. And so on for weeks on the happy hunting grounds.

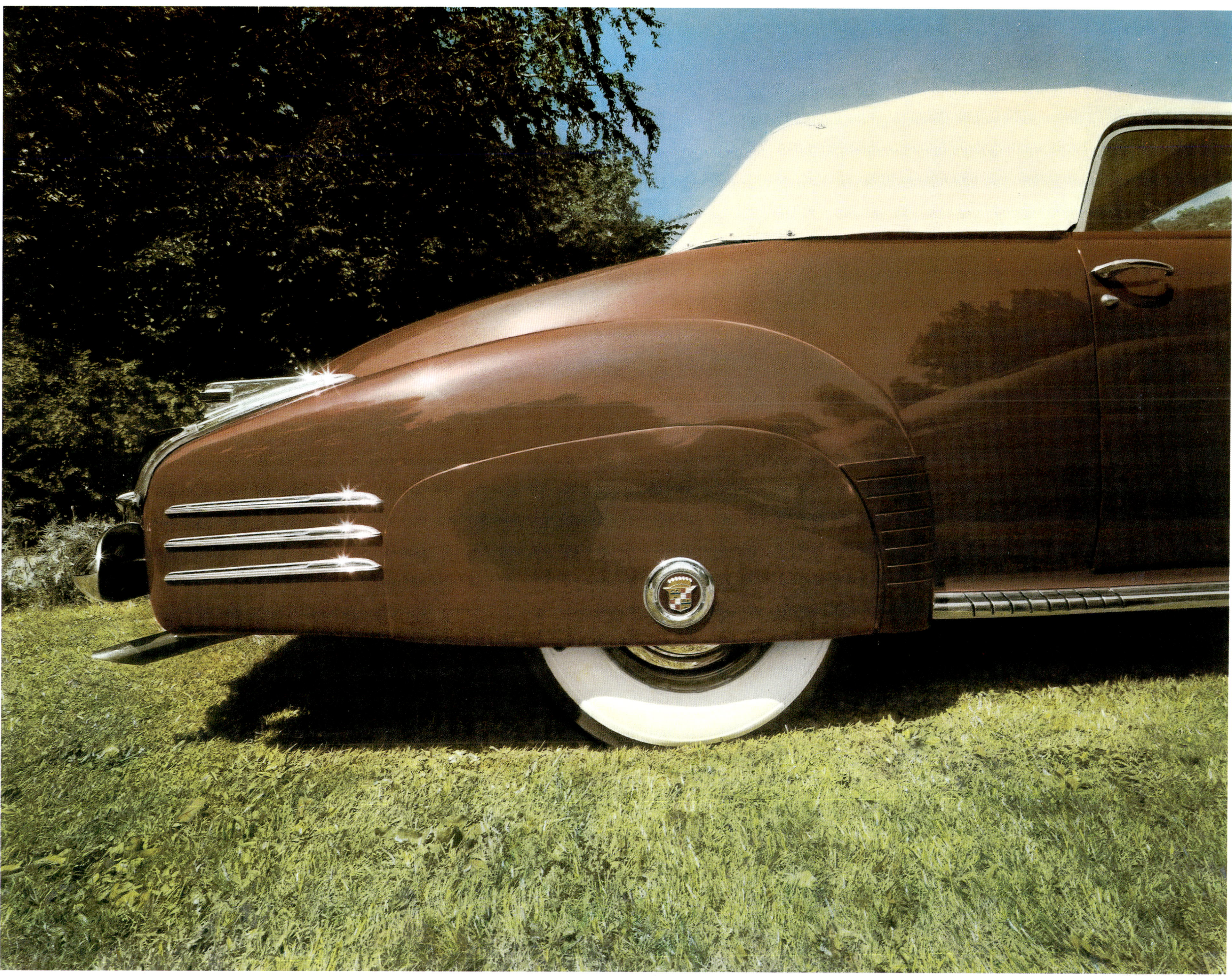

1941 Convertible; Danbury, Connecticut

By the time the Dodge Dart headed east on Route 1, Salmieri's pact with destiny, Detroit-style, was (as they say on the coast) almost inked. Approaching the Arizona border, in a town whose name he didn't quite catch, Salmieri spotted a white '61 serenely parked in front of a sedate, solidly middle-class house—dead center and serenely afloat between two white markers painted on the macadam. Jumping out of his car, setting his camera up on a tripod as the daylight faded, tripping the shutter, Salmieri sealed the deal.

"This says it all," he shouted, "this car in front of this house." It became the quintessential image.

After California the project "took on a life of its own," according to Salmieri, and became a photographic quest not just for Cadillacs, but for *all* Cadillacs, or at least models from as many years as he could find, encompassing the first model to the present. What had

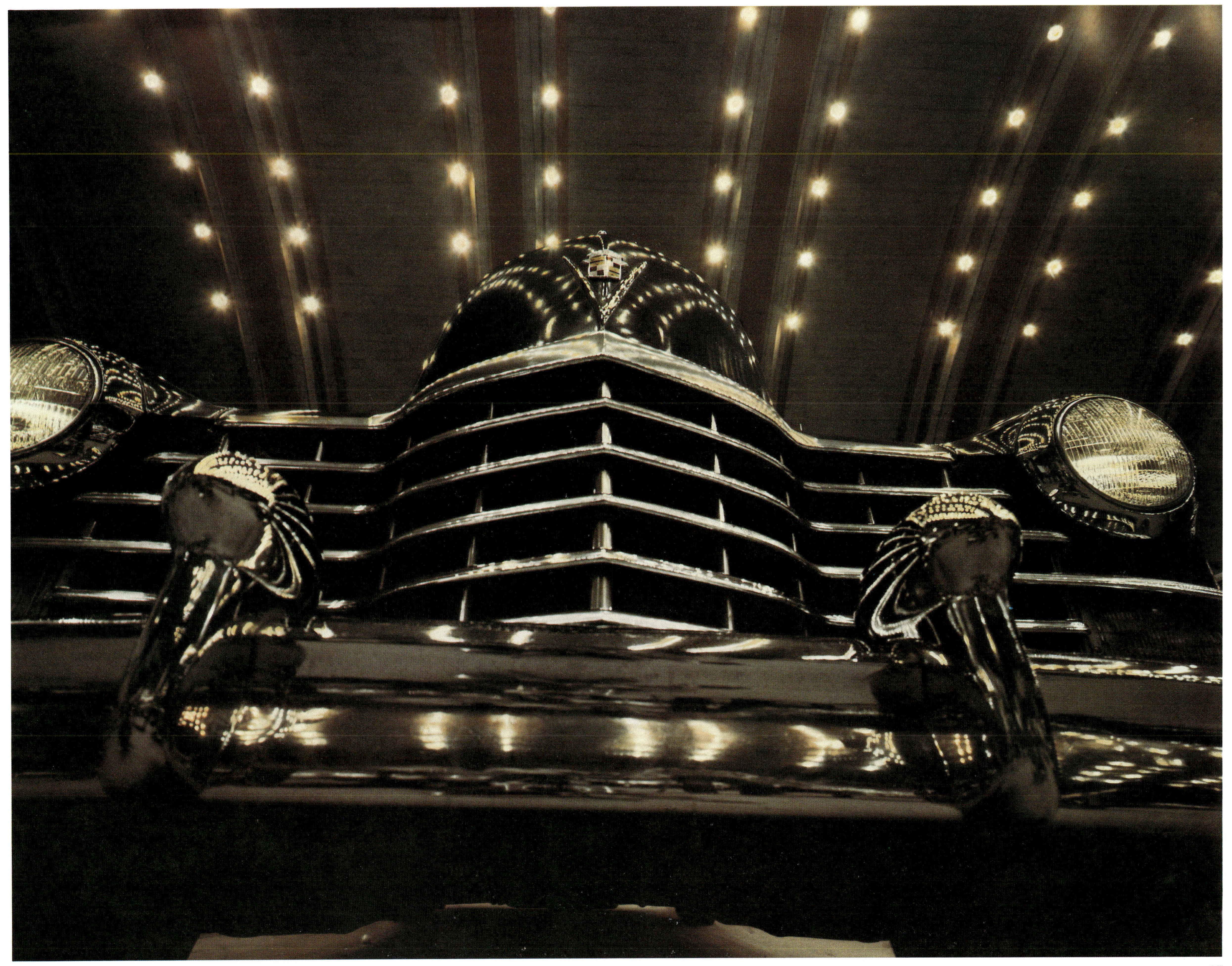

1946 Fleetwood; Atlantic City, New Jersey

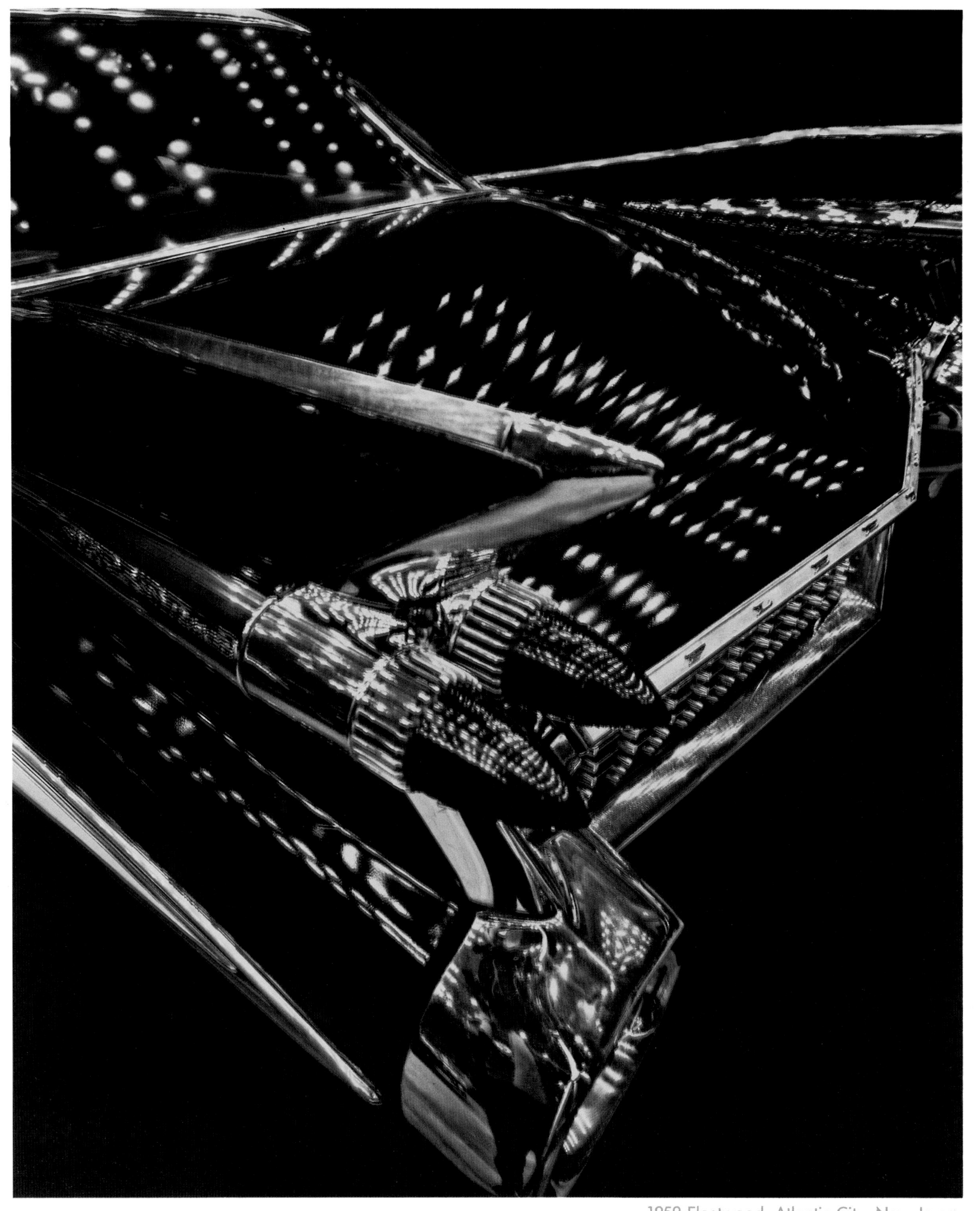

1959 Fleetwood; Atlantic City, New Jersey

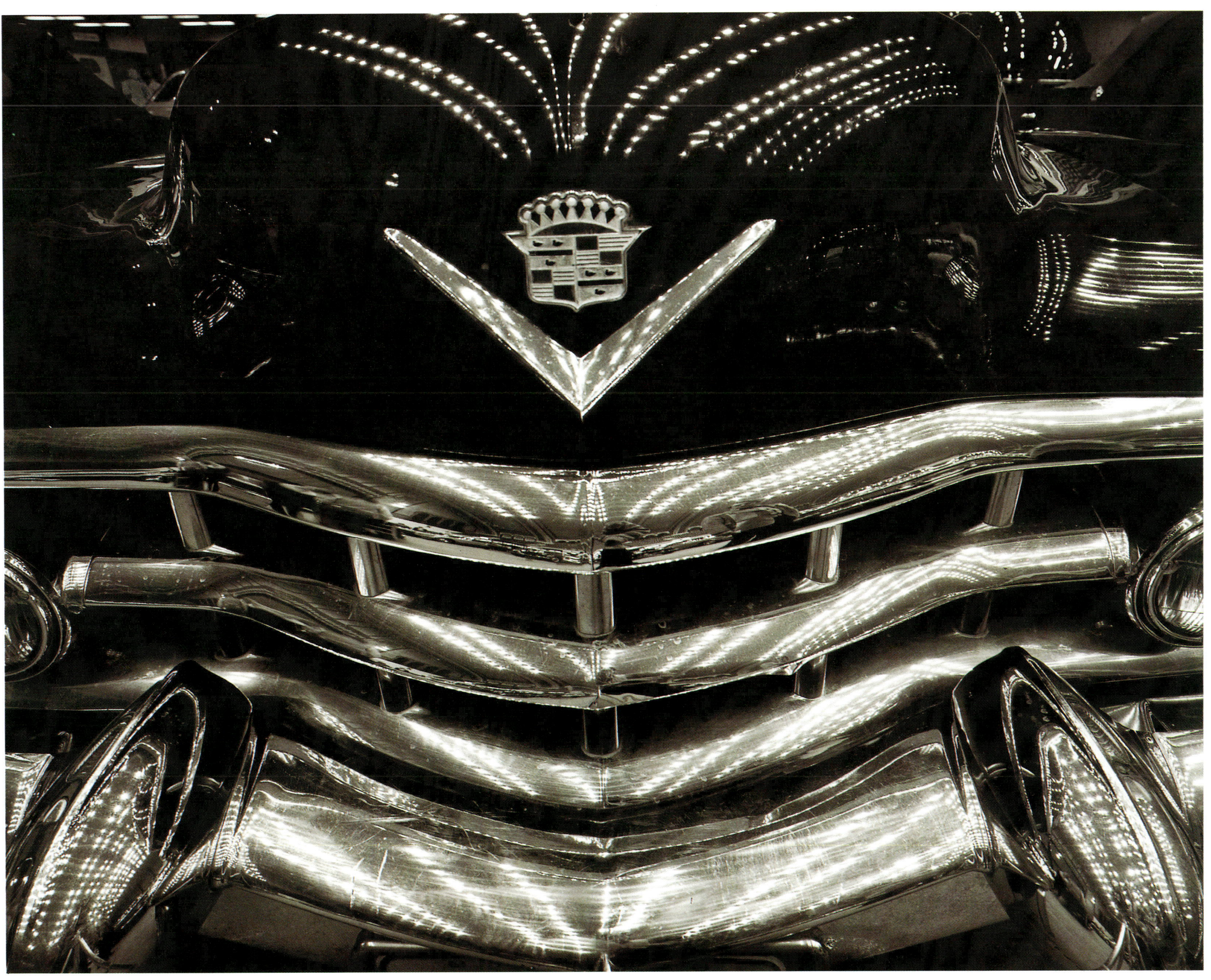

1955 Coupe de Ville; Atlantic City, New Jersey

evolved from obsession to passion became, over the course of the next several years, a sort of social scientific census, involving him with car clubs, historians, and automotive designers, as well as car freaks, unregenerate zealots of the breed, and astonishing acolytes like the man in Bayshore, Long Island who maintains a stable of twenty-four models—the complete set—from the watershed year of 1959.

To be the self-assigned Audubon of the Cadillac meant being ready to go where the machines were, as well as being ready to catch them when they appeared unexpectedly. It meant keeping the Cadillac always in mind, despite a hundred other ideas and projects that intervened in the years between 1973 and now. It meant retaining passion, and a utilitarian kind of egomania that let Salmieri believe that the project, like the car itself, was singled out by fate to endure.

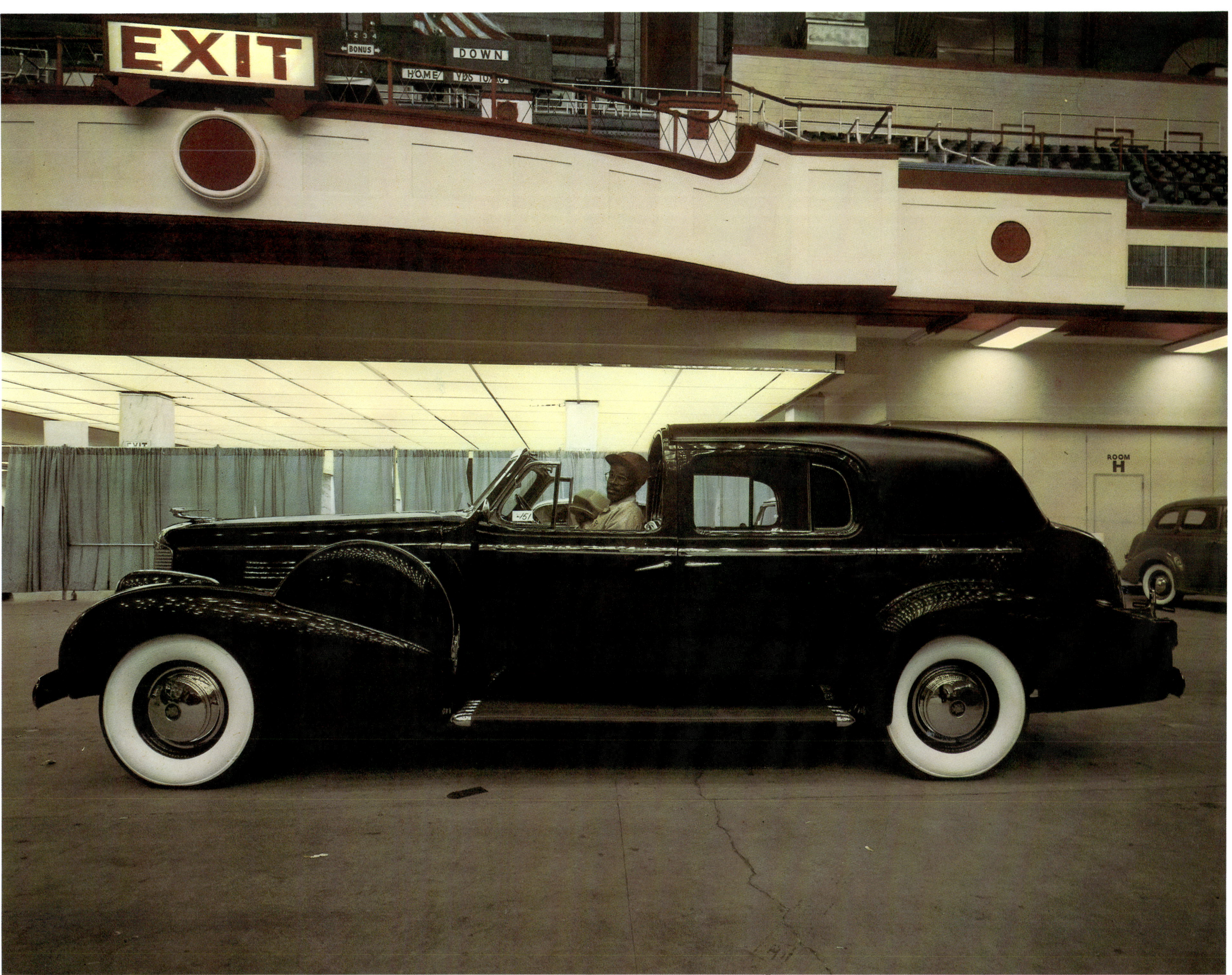

1938 Fleetwood Town Car; Atlantic City, New Jersey

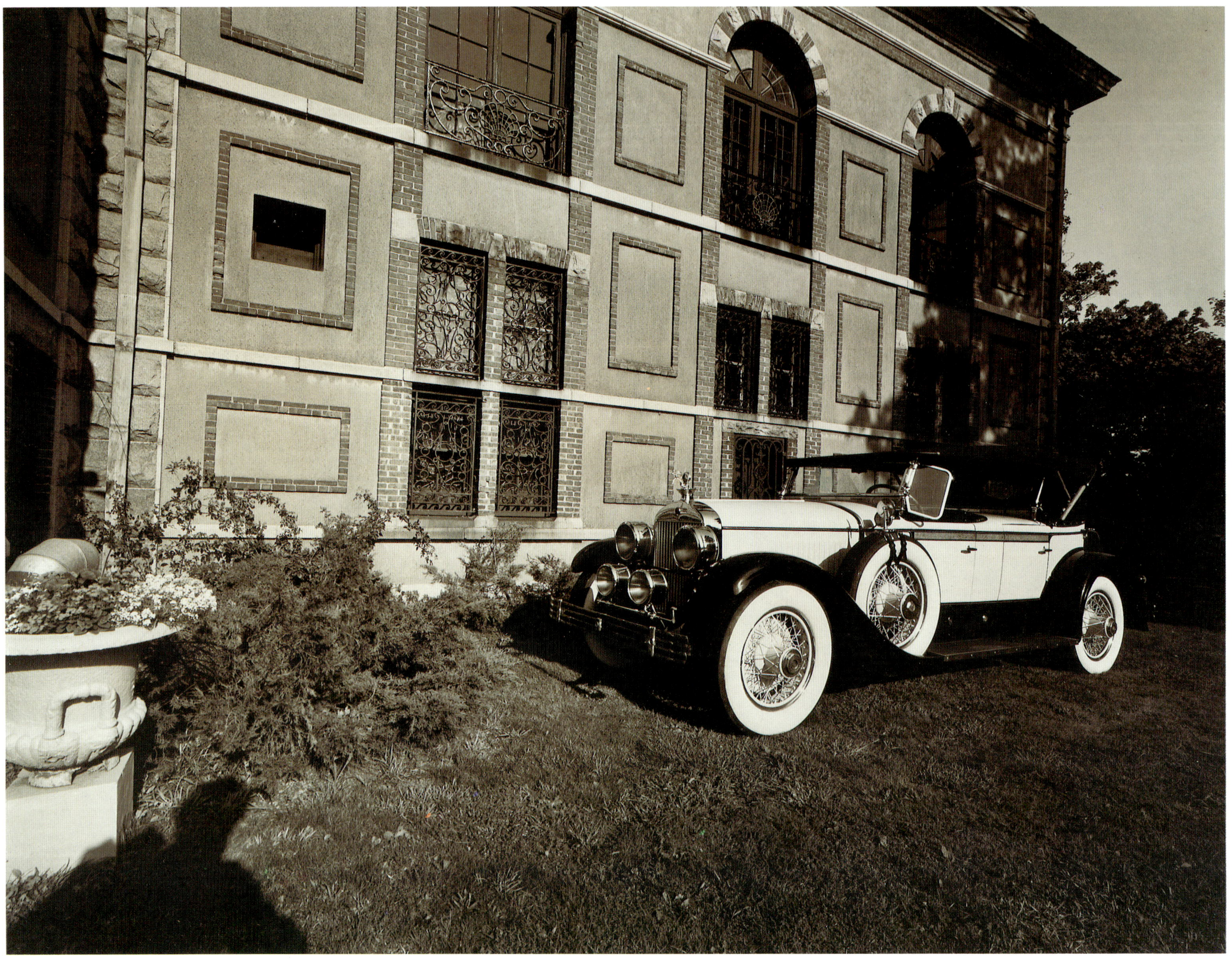

1927 Roadster; Newport, Rhode Island

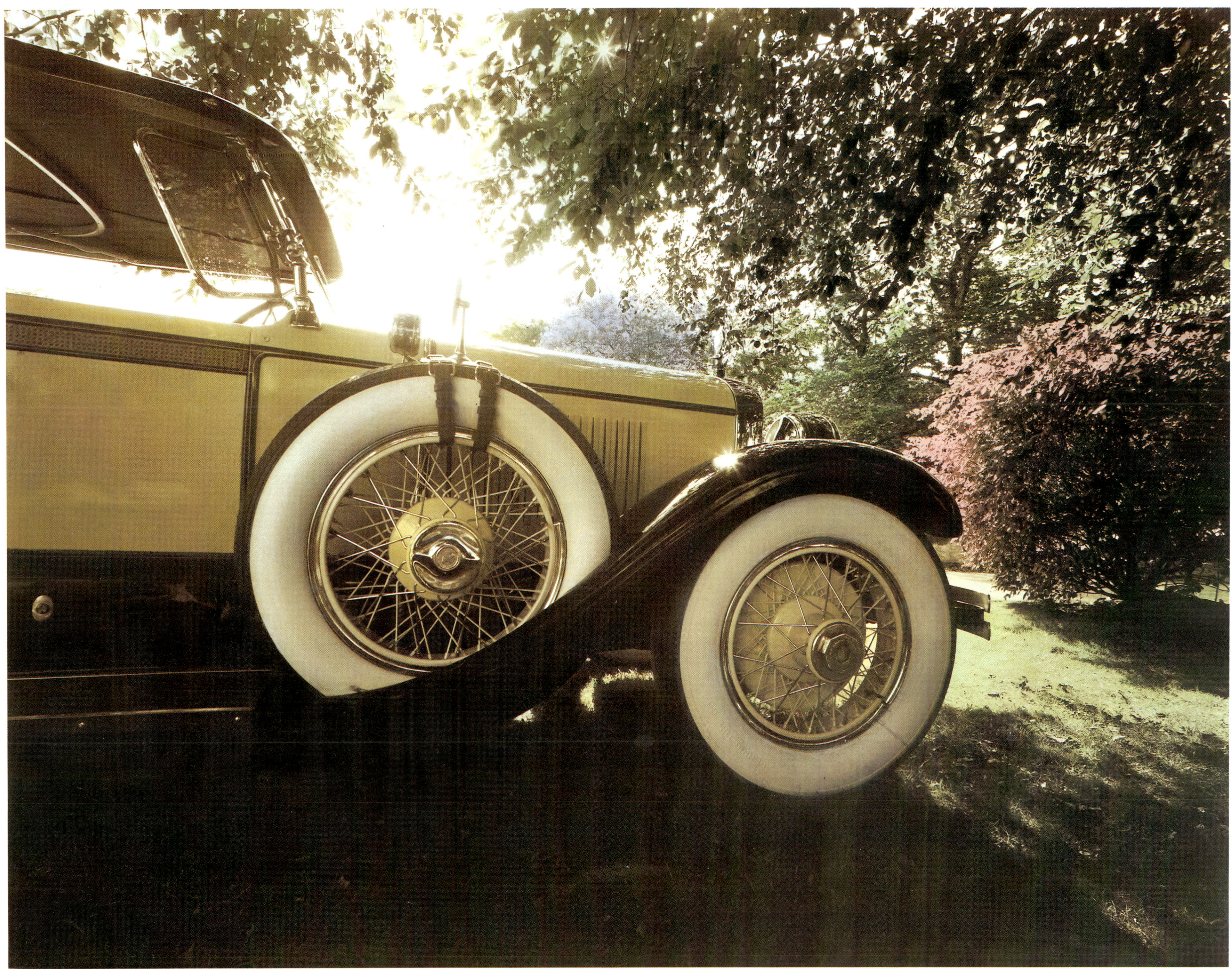

1927 Roadster; Newport, Rhode Island

Salmieri's hovering demiurge continued to help. In the winter of 1982 the Bleecker Street building that housed the Salmieris' sixth-floor loft and studio/darkroom caught fire and burned for three days. In it were hundreds of four-by-five black-and-white negatives from the great Cadillac roundup, and as many prints: the entire harvest of nine years' work, shimmering up into the frigid air as indiscriminate toxic fumes. When time and the fire department had reduced the blaze to a smolder, Salmieri and Sydnie picked their way up the icy stairs of the ruined building, pushed open the blackened door of their loft, and discovered that the fire had inexplicably passed the place by. Though Salmieri claims he would have done the work all over again had everything been lost, the pictures that make up this particular, peculiar book would not have been retrievable. Photographers know too well that once

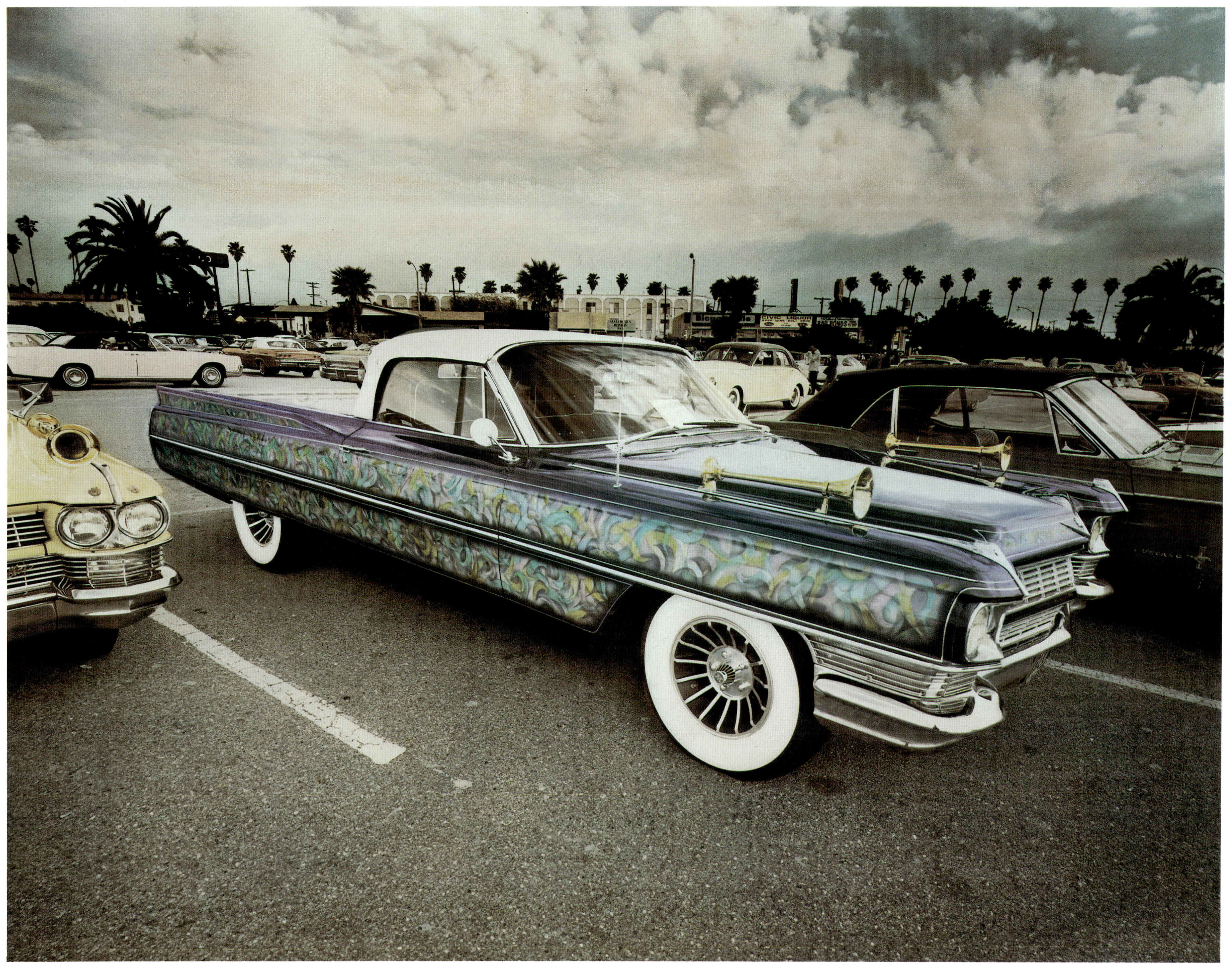

1964 Ranch Wagon; Santa Monica, California

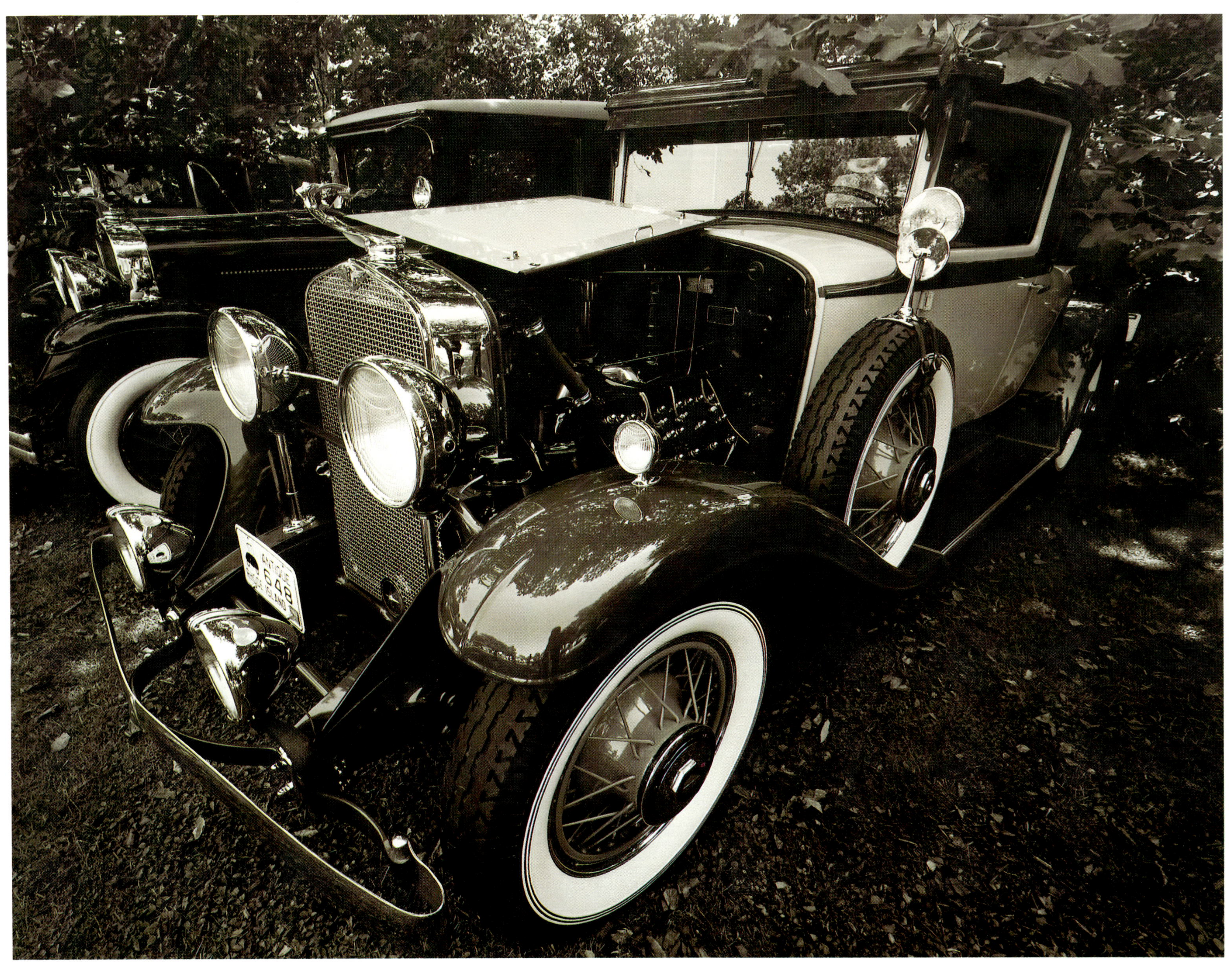

1931 La Salle; Virginia Beach, Virginia

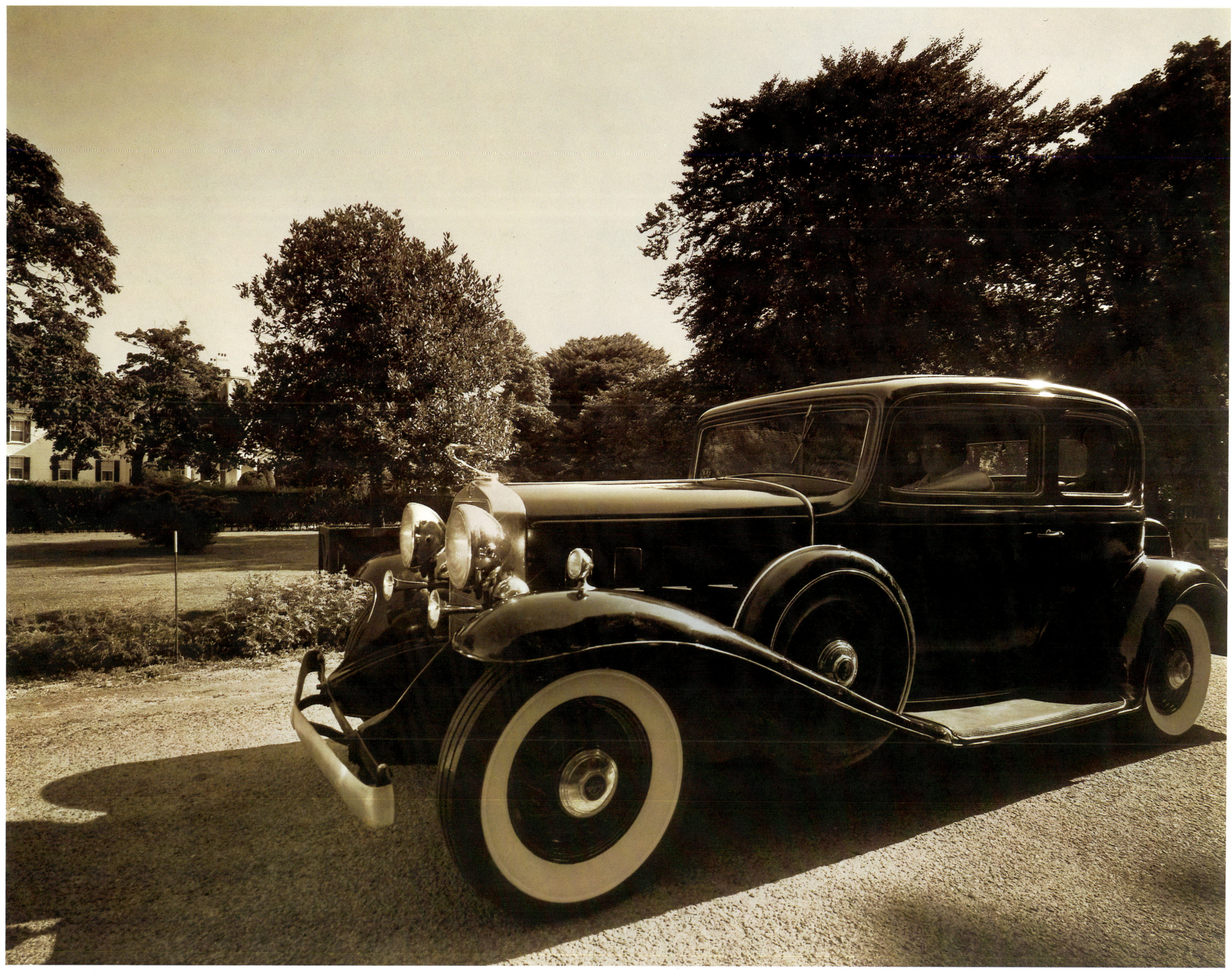

1932 La Salle; Newport, Rhode Island

gone, or missed, a picture can never be exactly recaptured. Given the unlikelihood of the salvation of the Cadillac pictures, one might wonder just what Harley Earl's ectoplasm was up to that winter.

If ever a dream has been persistently in Technicolor, it is the Cadillac dream. Yet Salmieri had photographed in black and white in order to control the mood of his pictures and not surrender that control to the often blunt chemistry of color film. Nevertheless, the project had become a romance with the breed that seemed to suggest the kind of mildly hallucinatory hues common to early autochrome photography. As an experiment, Sydnie began to brush color onto the black-and-white prints, inventing a spectrum that pleased her. The happy result is that many of the photographs have the added evocative dimension of an entirely unreal and irresistible chromatic fantasy.

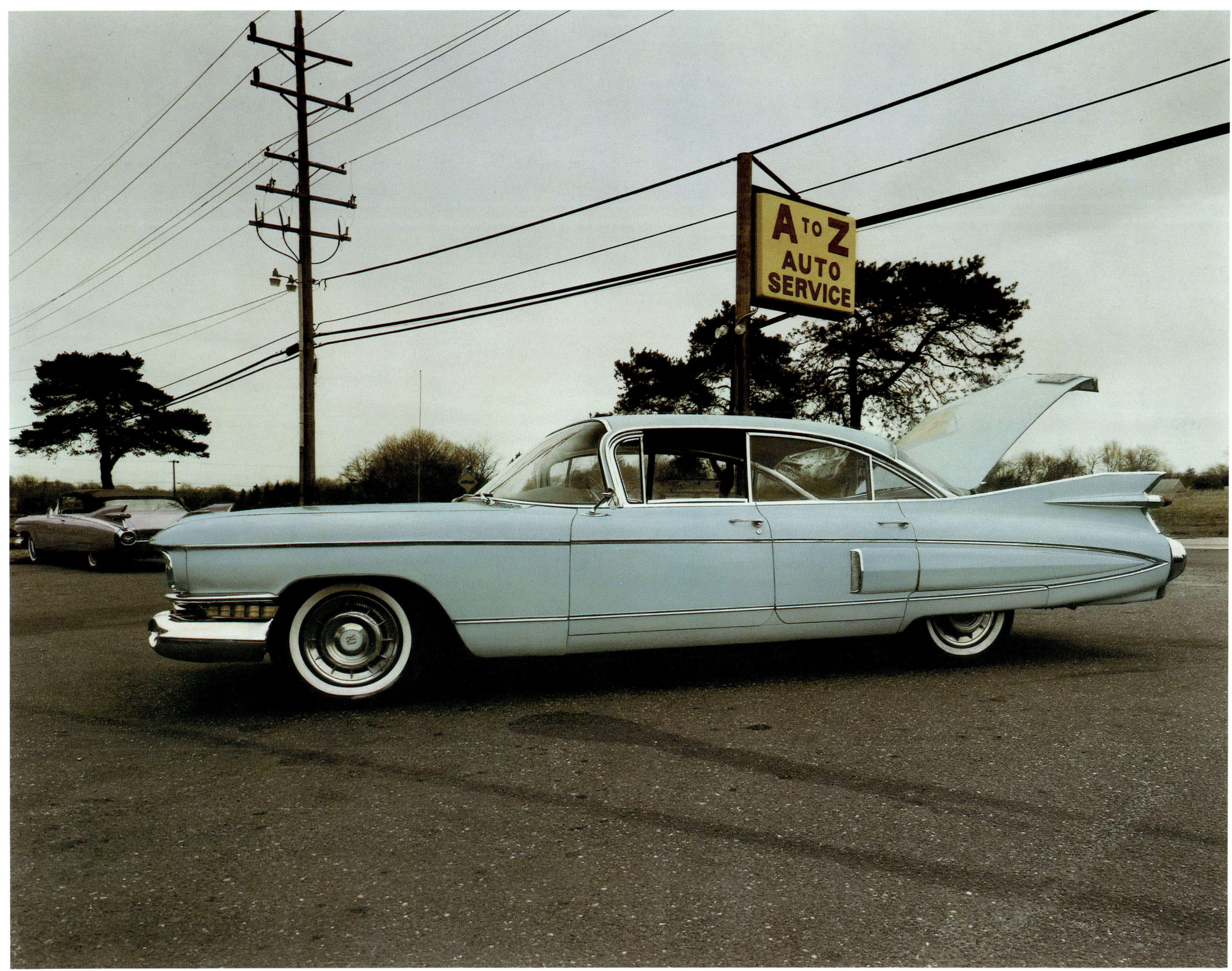

1959 Fleetwood; Manasquan, New Jersey

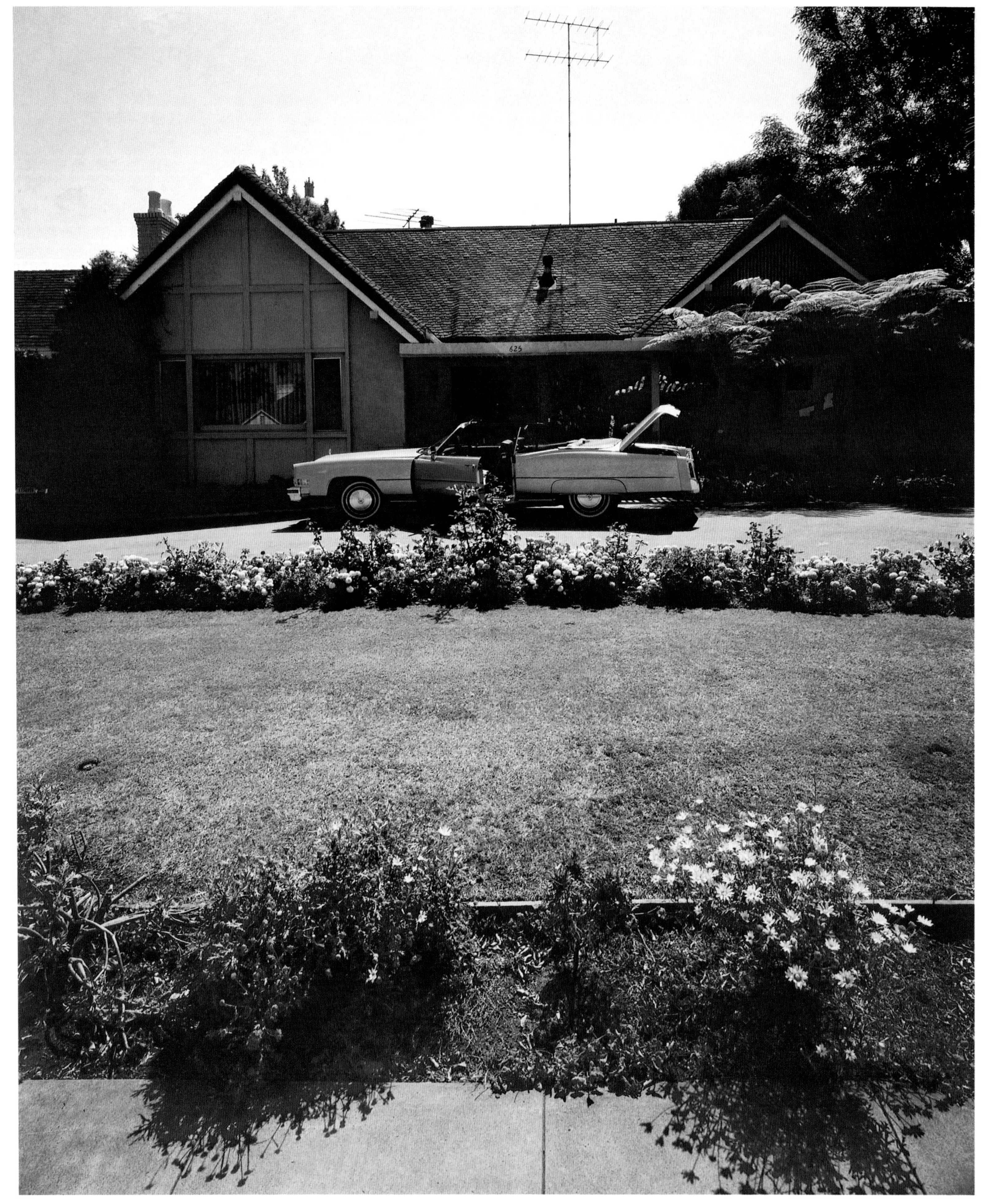

1974 Eldorado; Scarsdale, New York

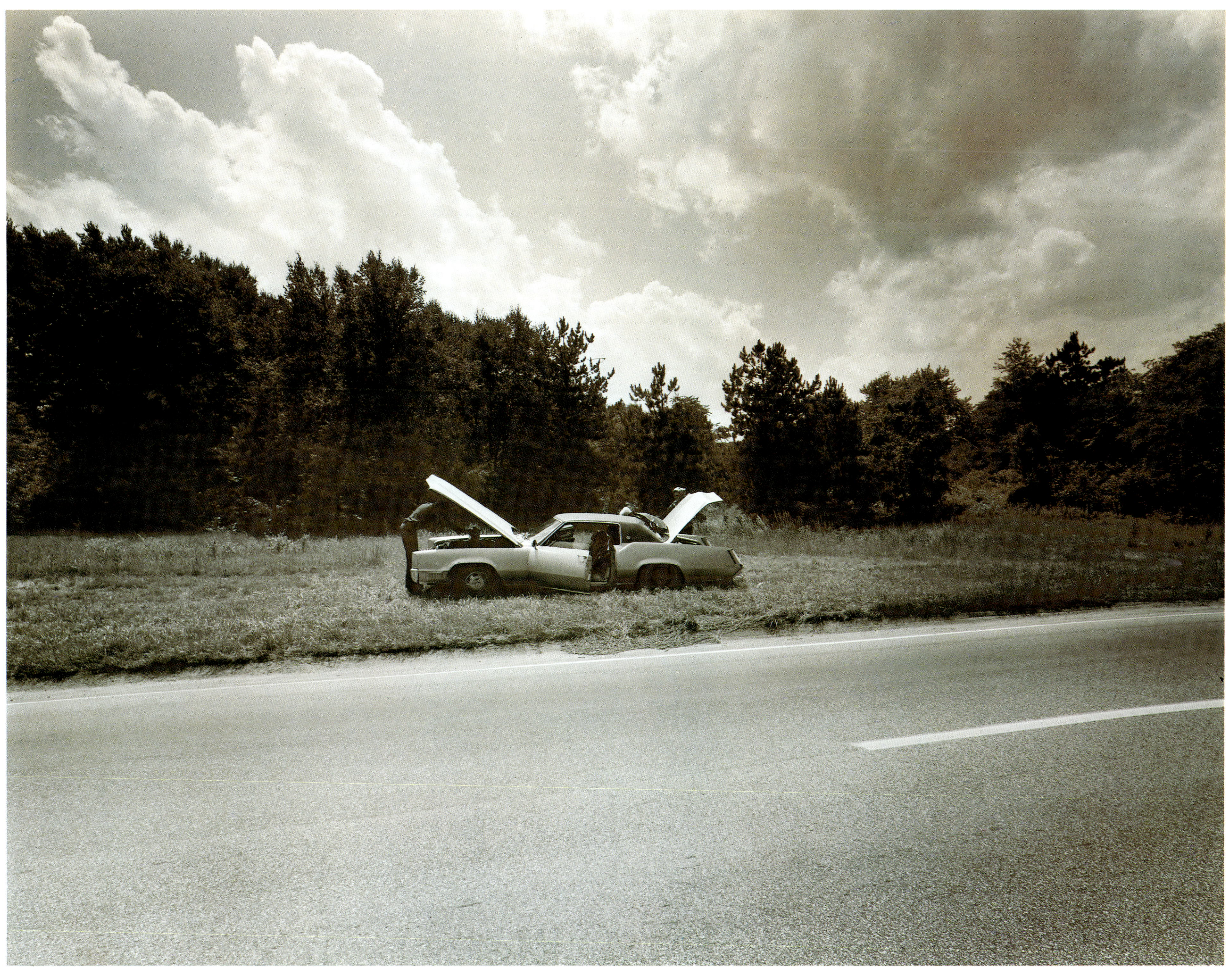

1967 Fleetwood Eldorado; Route 9, New York

During the years of Salmieri's pilgrimage, despite a rapt interest in a specific piece of numinous hardware, he never ceased being fundamentally a portrait photographer. In his effort to portray the spirit of the Cadillac in America, he found himself making portraits not just of the cars themselves, but of what he calls "the invisible character in each photograph, the owner." Even when he found a car abandoned at the side of a road, its owner gone for help or simply gone for good, Salmieri felt that the owners of these mass-produced machines breathed life and energy into them and made each one as singular as a human face.

Of course, Cadillac owners knew of this special animus long before the kid from Brooklyn lit out on his personal expedition. Even those rare owners who came by their cars unintentionally, for whom the

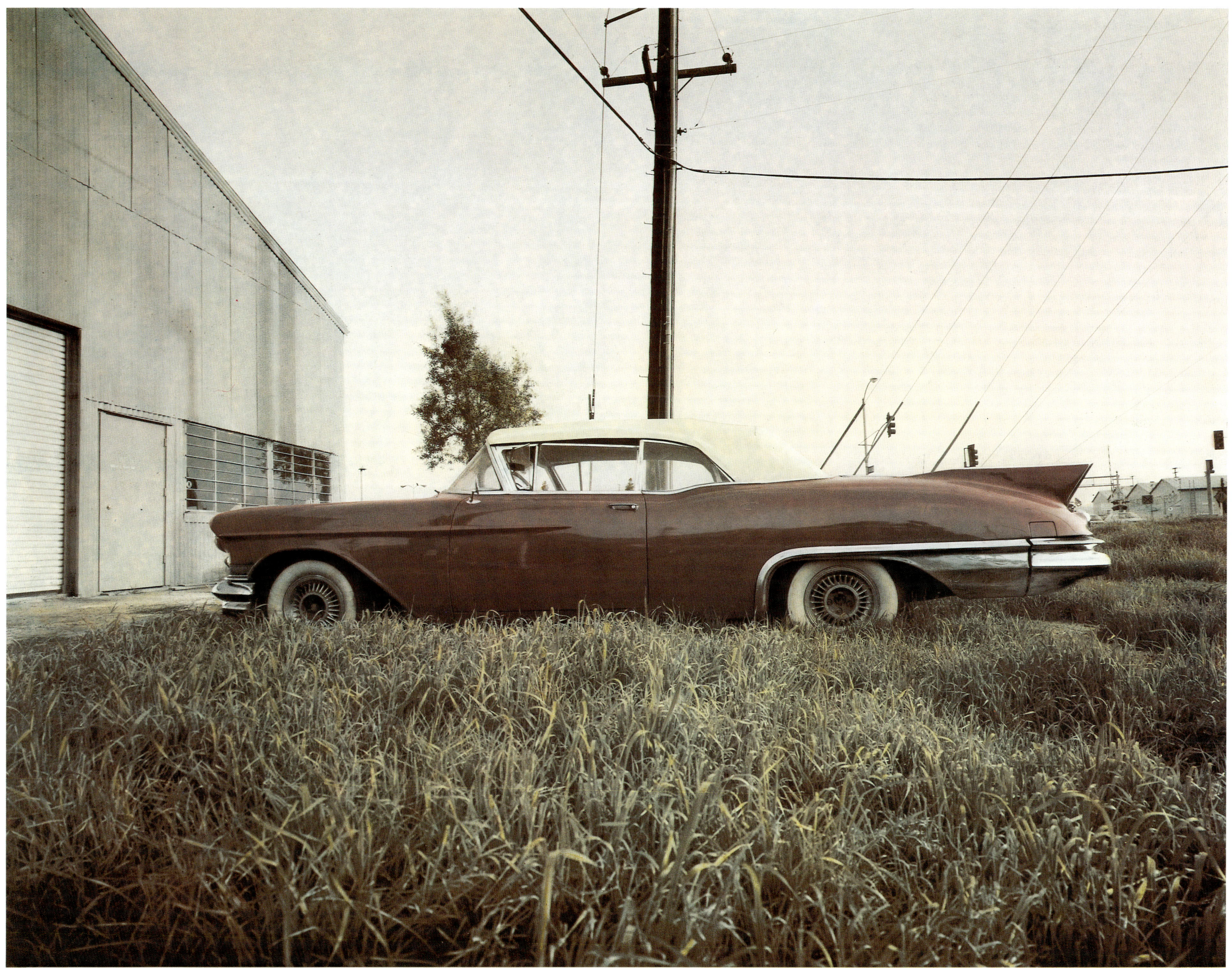

1957 Eldorado Biarritz Convertible; Santa Monica, California

Cadillac ethic was a matter of happenstance and not a philosophical decision, understood in a flash the idea that Salmieri was coming to terms with over a long stretch of time. Early in the spring of this year, in Venice, California, the photographer found himself somewhat laboriously trying to explain his project to a woman who had inherited a Sedan de Ville, fixed it up in an elaborate nautical motif, and named it "The Whale." The woman heard Salmieri out, then blessed him with one of those sun-bleached, beatific smiles never seen east of Death Valley and said; "I understand, now, that you are on a mission from God."

Not even the vice-president in charge of corporate optimism at General Motors can fail to realize that the Cadillac is not what it used to be. It is different. Arguably better, in some ways, but different. In the

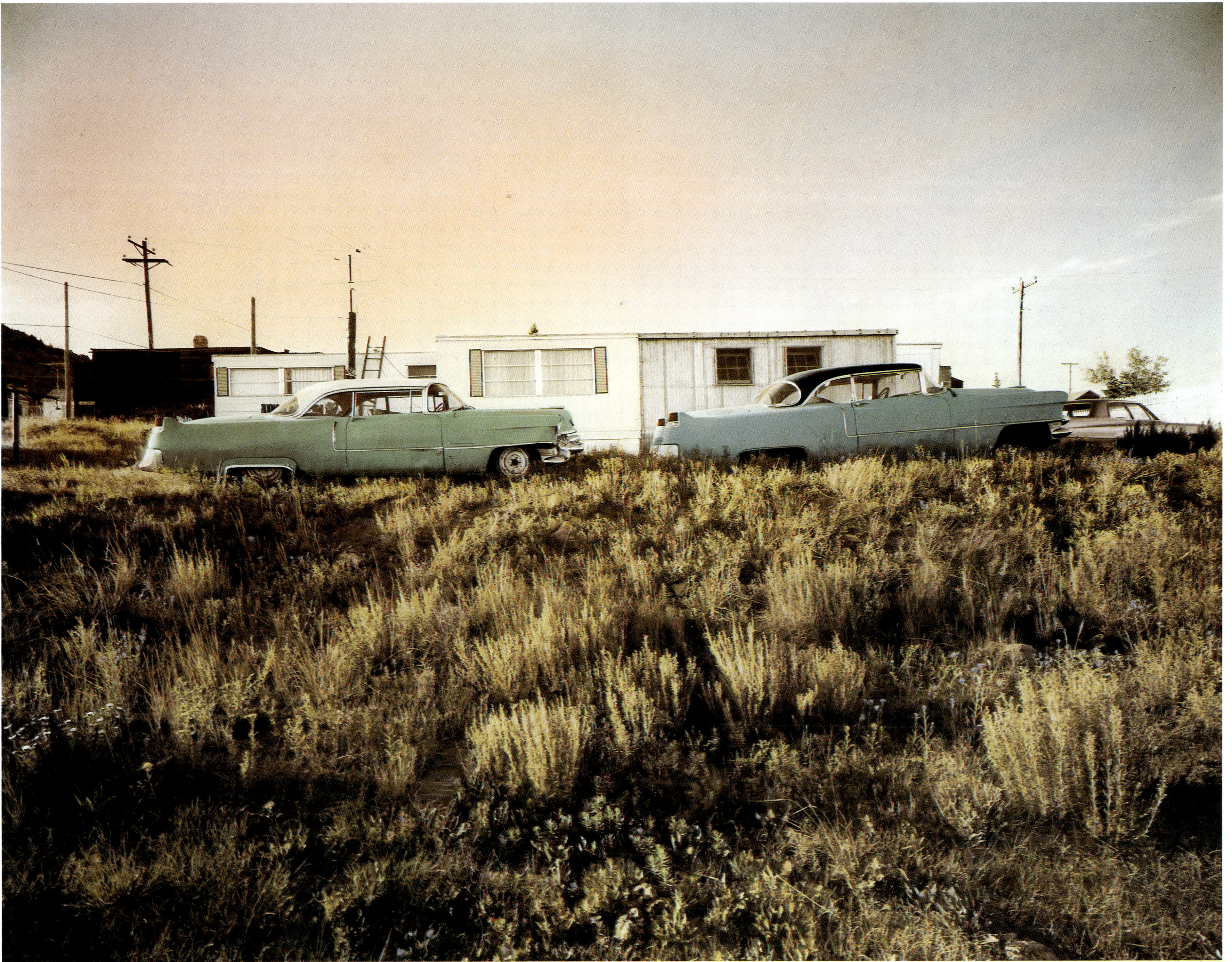

1955 Coupe de Ville; Cripple Creek, Colorado

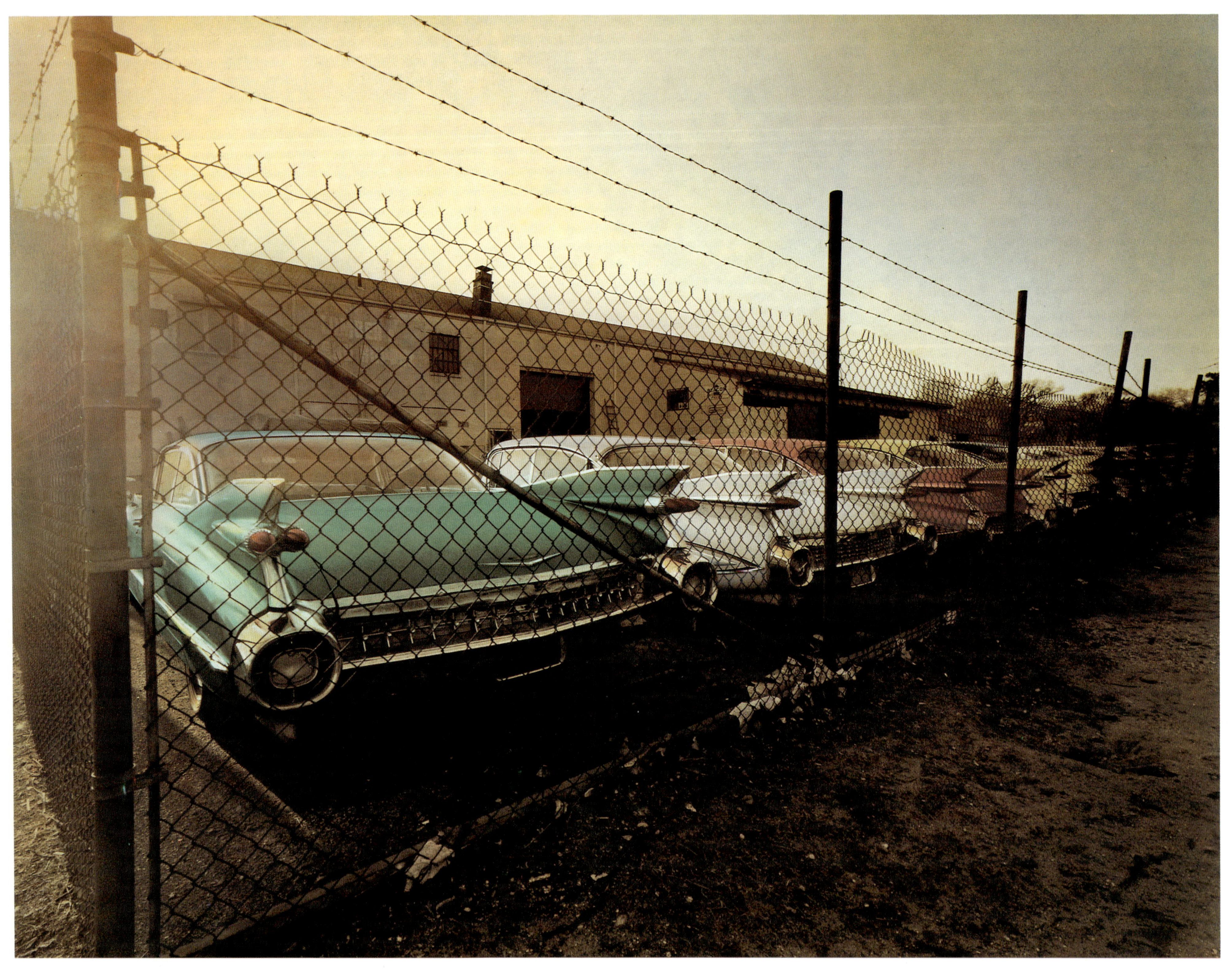

1959 Cadillacs; Long Island, New York

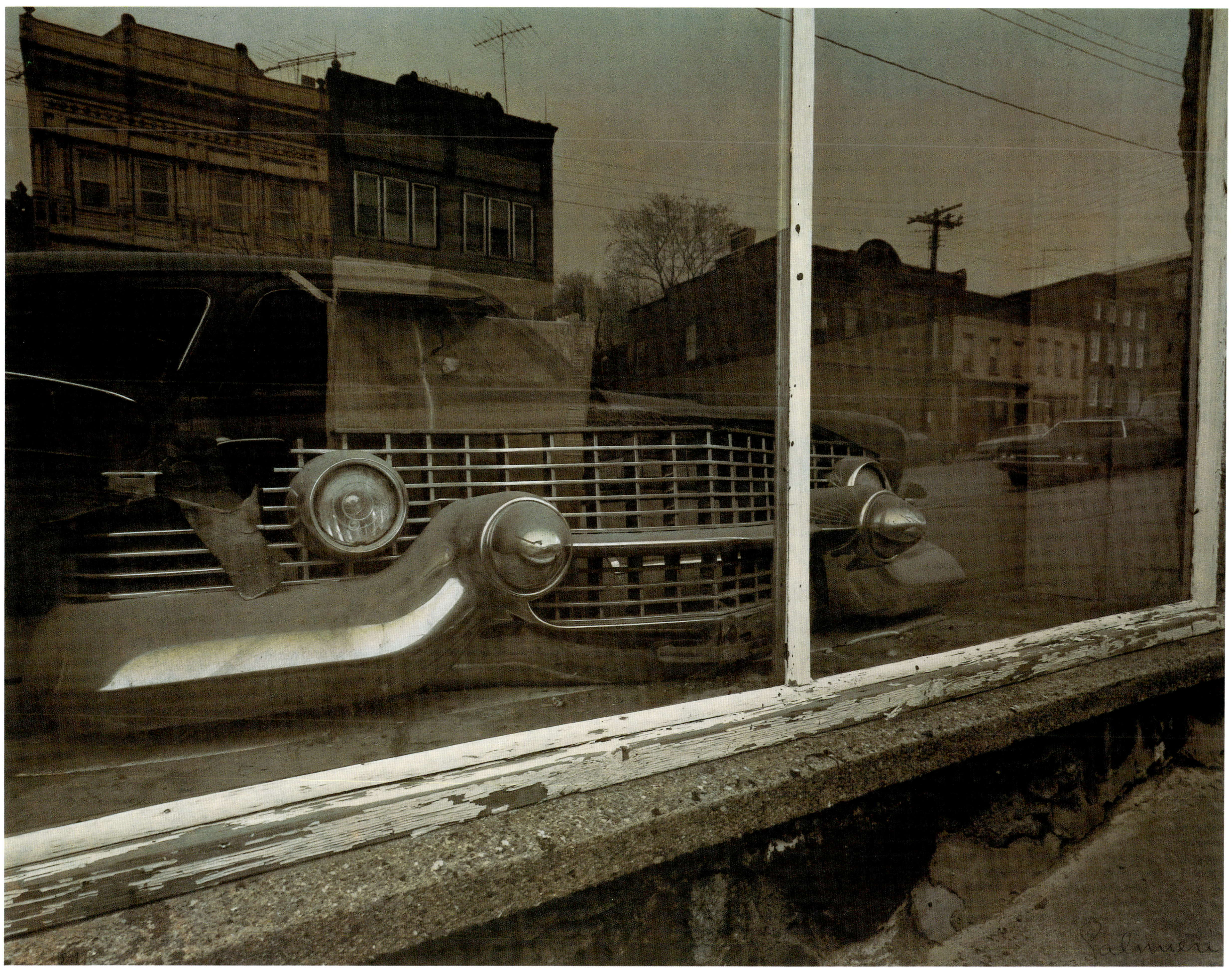

1954 (Grille); Cold Springs, New York

eighties, at last, and quite properly, Detroit has got religion, a new, Calvinistic faith in aerodynamics, fuel economy, and "scaled down" sensible engineering. Gone are the high-kicking gods of the Saturnalia, the happy bombastics like Harley Earl and Raymond Loewy (of jet-prowed Studebaker fame), and in their place have come the gloomy priests of high efficiency with their apocalyptic fervor and nerd packs.

And curiously, it is those of us who twenty years ago were railing at the profligacy of Detroit's ways—tight-mind auto-didacts like Salmieri and I—who end up missing the glittering yearly panoply of great chromium beasts. We never drove them, and never missed a chance to castigate their excesses, and yet, we now know, their lumbering presence was unexplainably comforting, in the way that the existence of whales may be comforting even to those who have never seen them and have no desire to do so. The Cadillac, the most

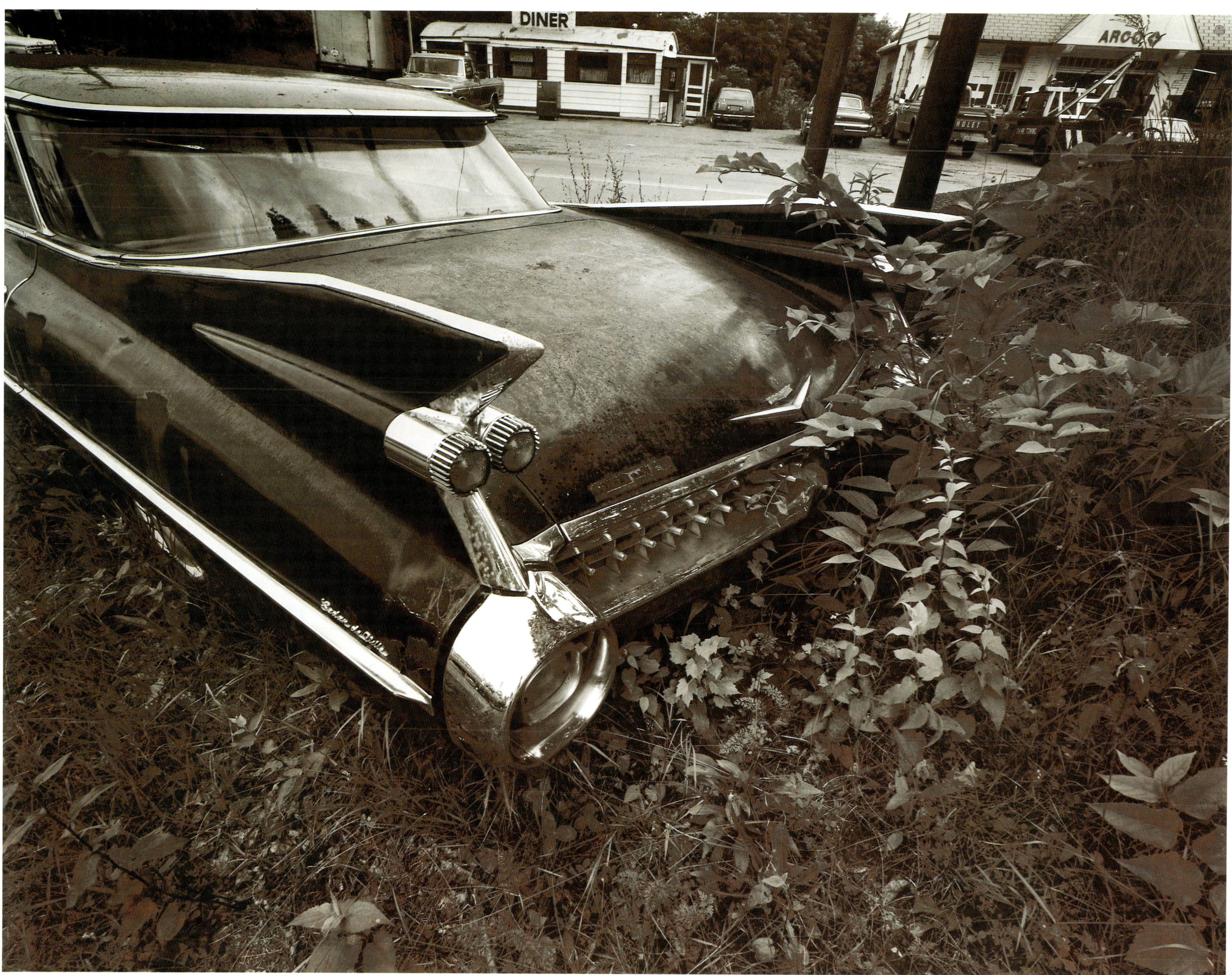

1959 Sedan de Ville; Poughkeepsie, New York

phenomenal and thus most reprehensible of Detroit's insolent chariots, is a more appropriate car now, but—diminished, diminutive, civil, and civilized almost to the point of meekness—it is simply not the chest-thumping, go-to-hell Cadillac of yore. It's harder, somehow, to envision the current generation of twelve-year-olds ever reserving a special place in their fantasies for the car, or agonizing over whether their fathers have one or not, though no doubt many still dream of Eldorado as hopeful ads claim. Yet, for many the upward aspiration that once focused on the Caddy has shifted to the terse, Teutonic Mercedes-Benz, which has also forsaken all the stylish swagger of its earlier, undaunted days. Who would have predicted, twenty-five years ago, that bankers, doctors, and even archpatriotic small town lawyers would someday look to pragmatic Germany to provide ultimate status?

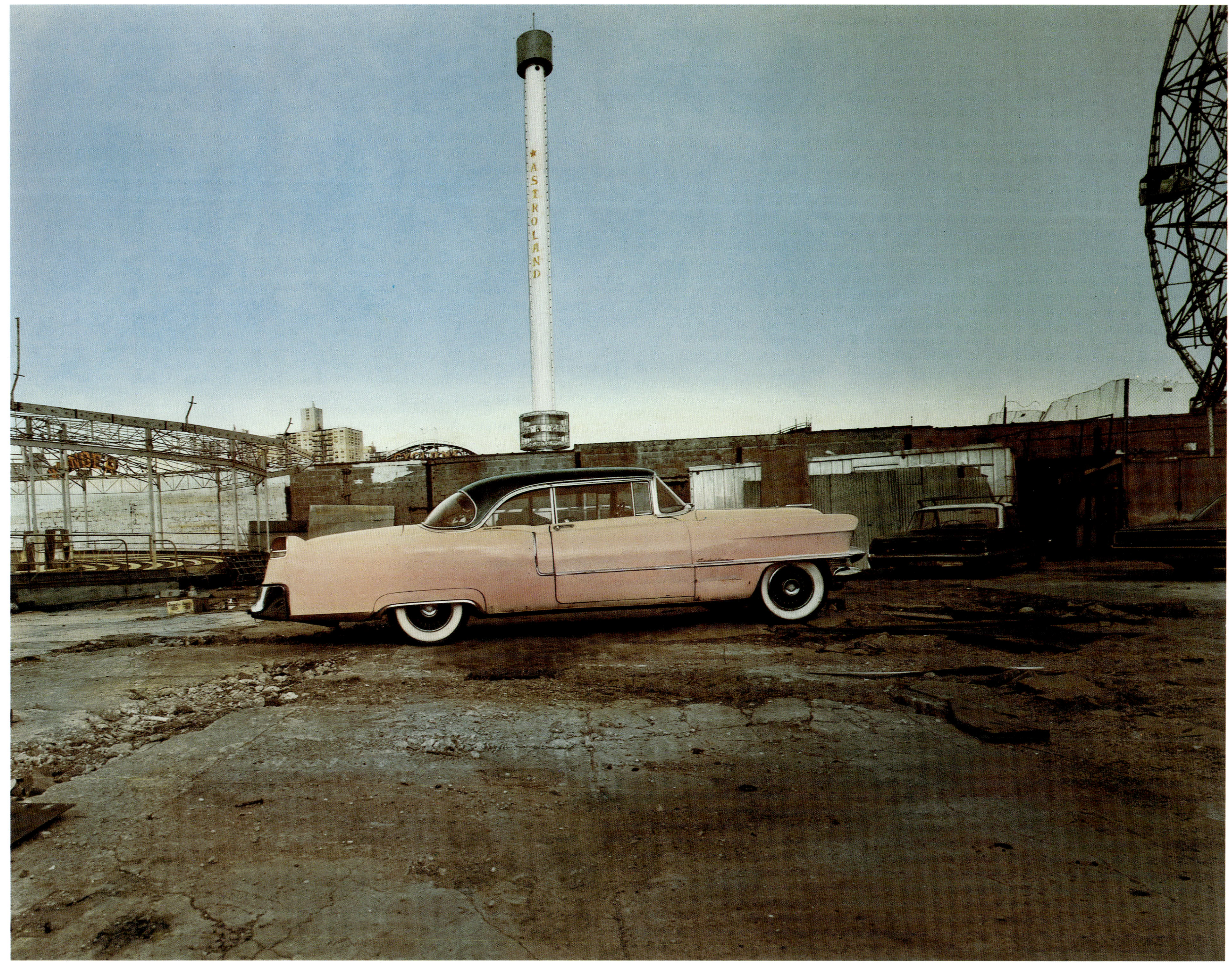

1955 Coupe de Ville; Coney Island, New York

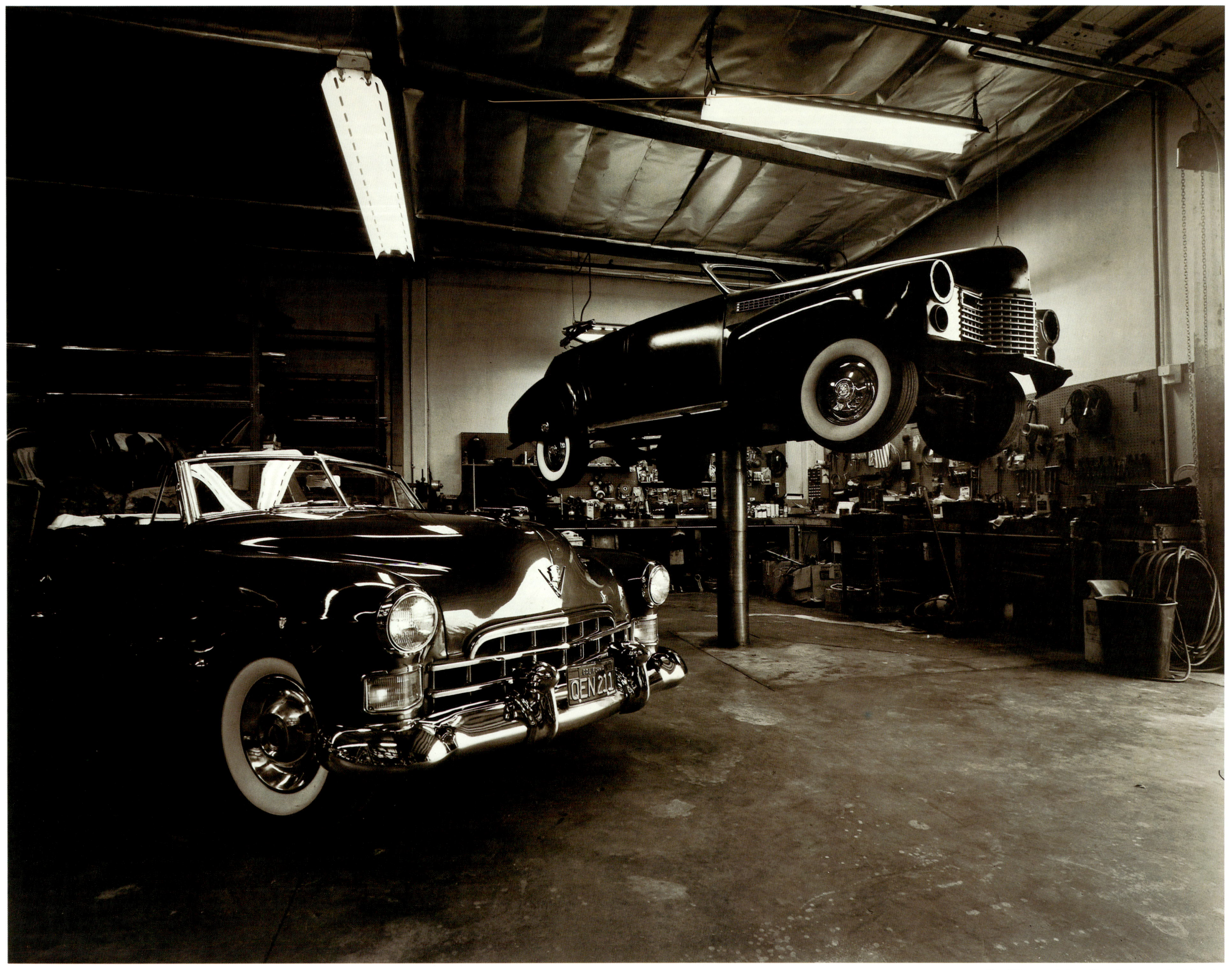

Cadillacs of the 40s; Sylmar, California

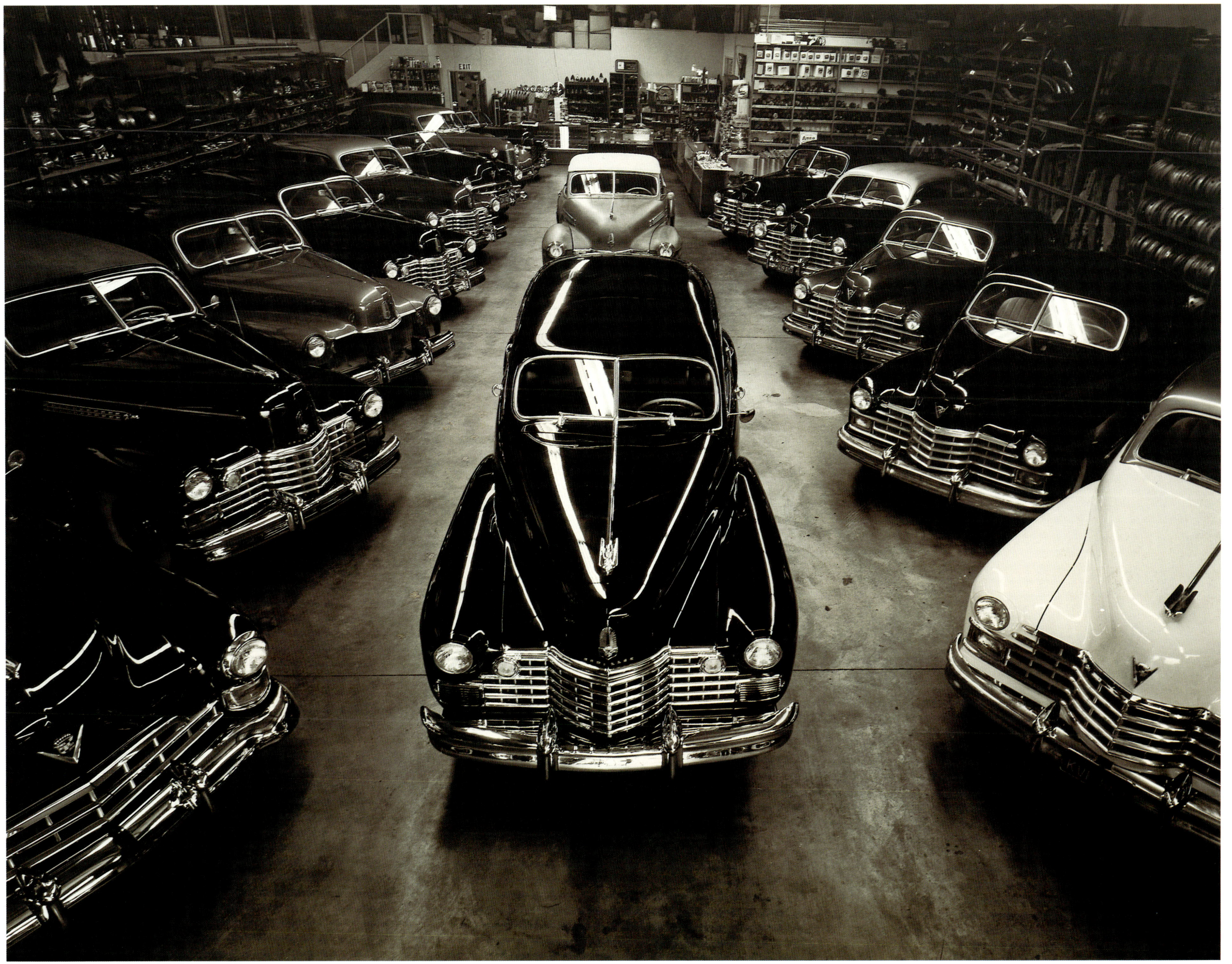

Cadillacs of the 40s; Sylmar, California

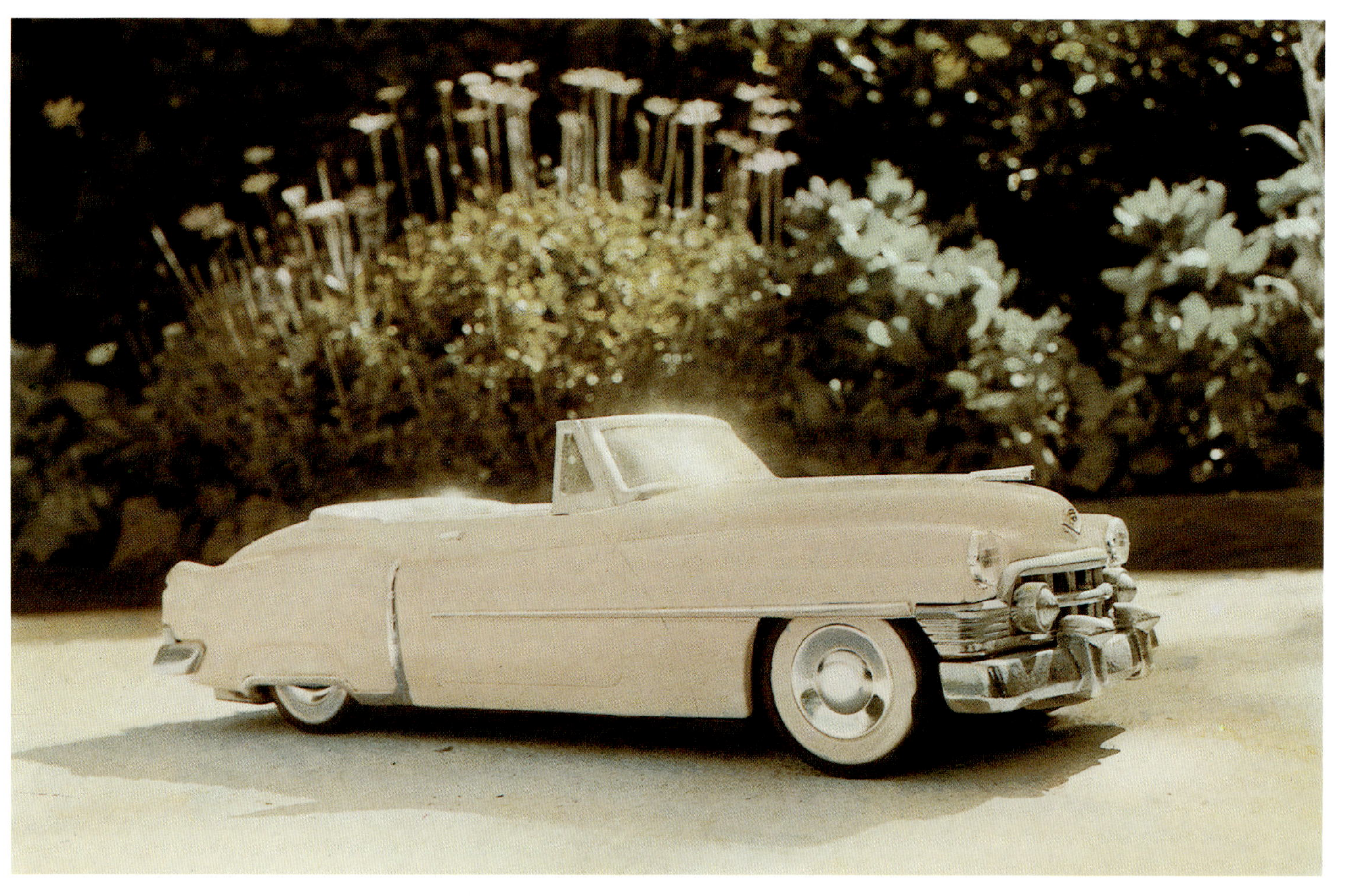

1953 Convertible; Venice, California

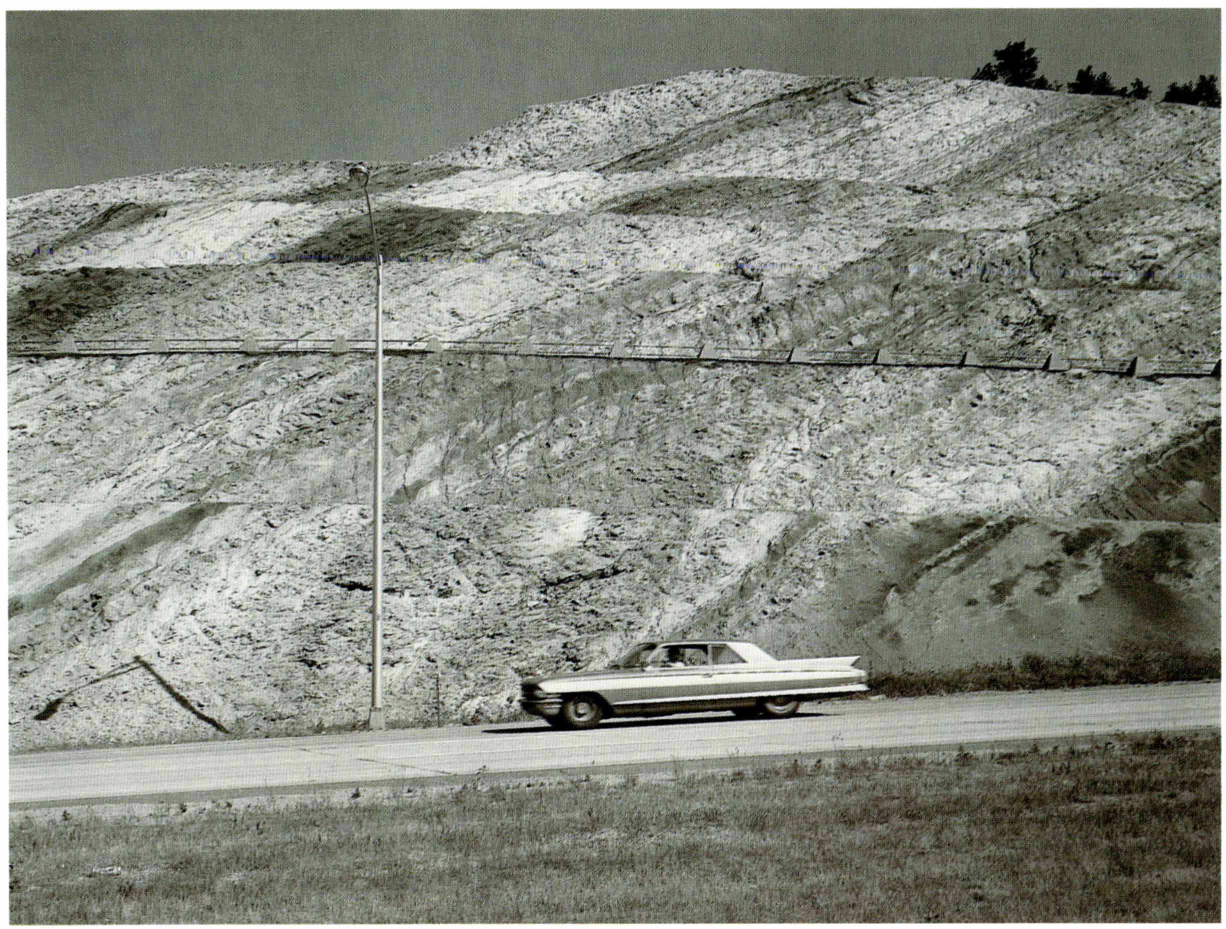

1962 Coupe; Utah

1941 Coupe; New York

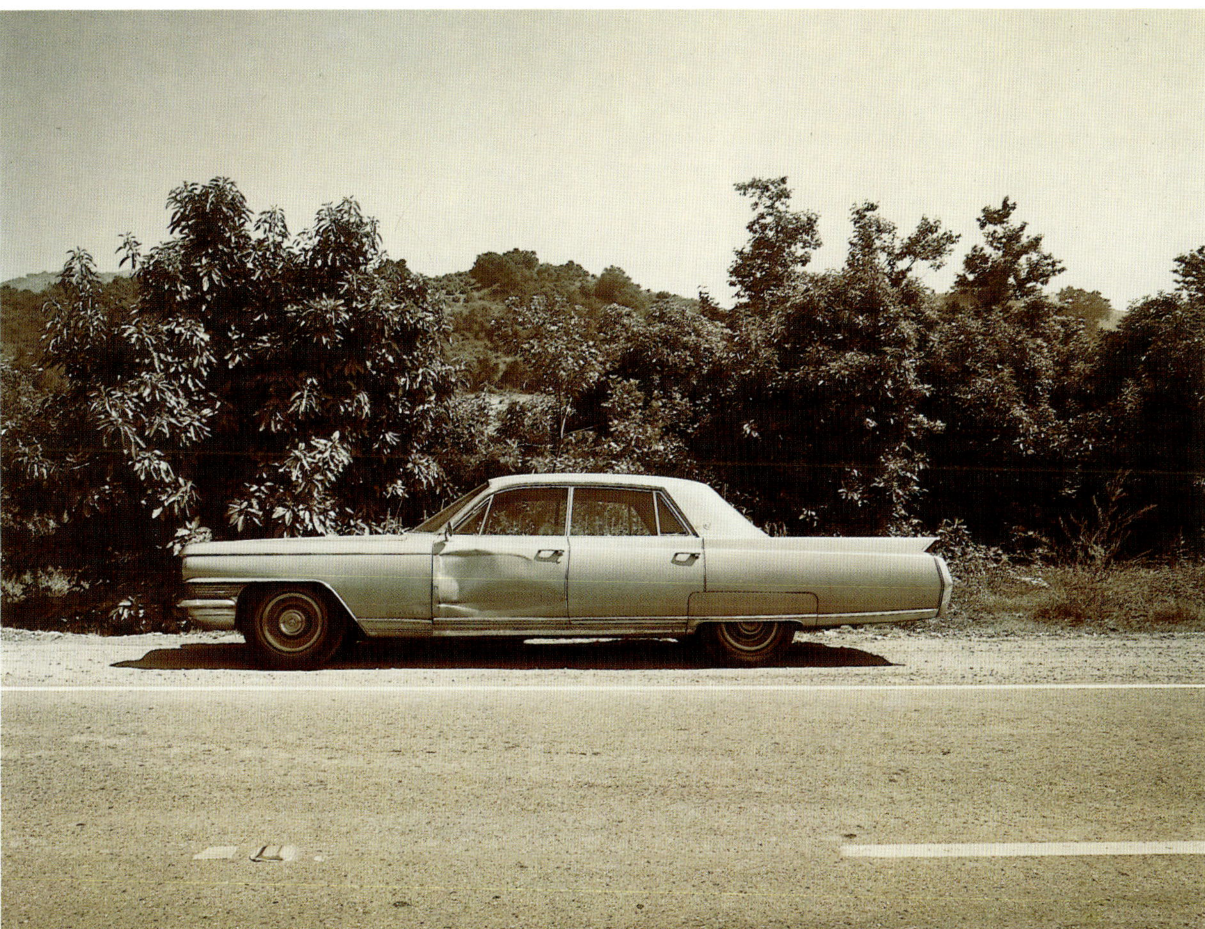

1964 60 Special Fleetwood Sedan; Nebraska

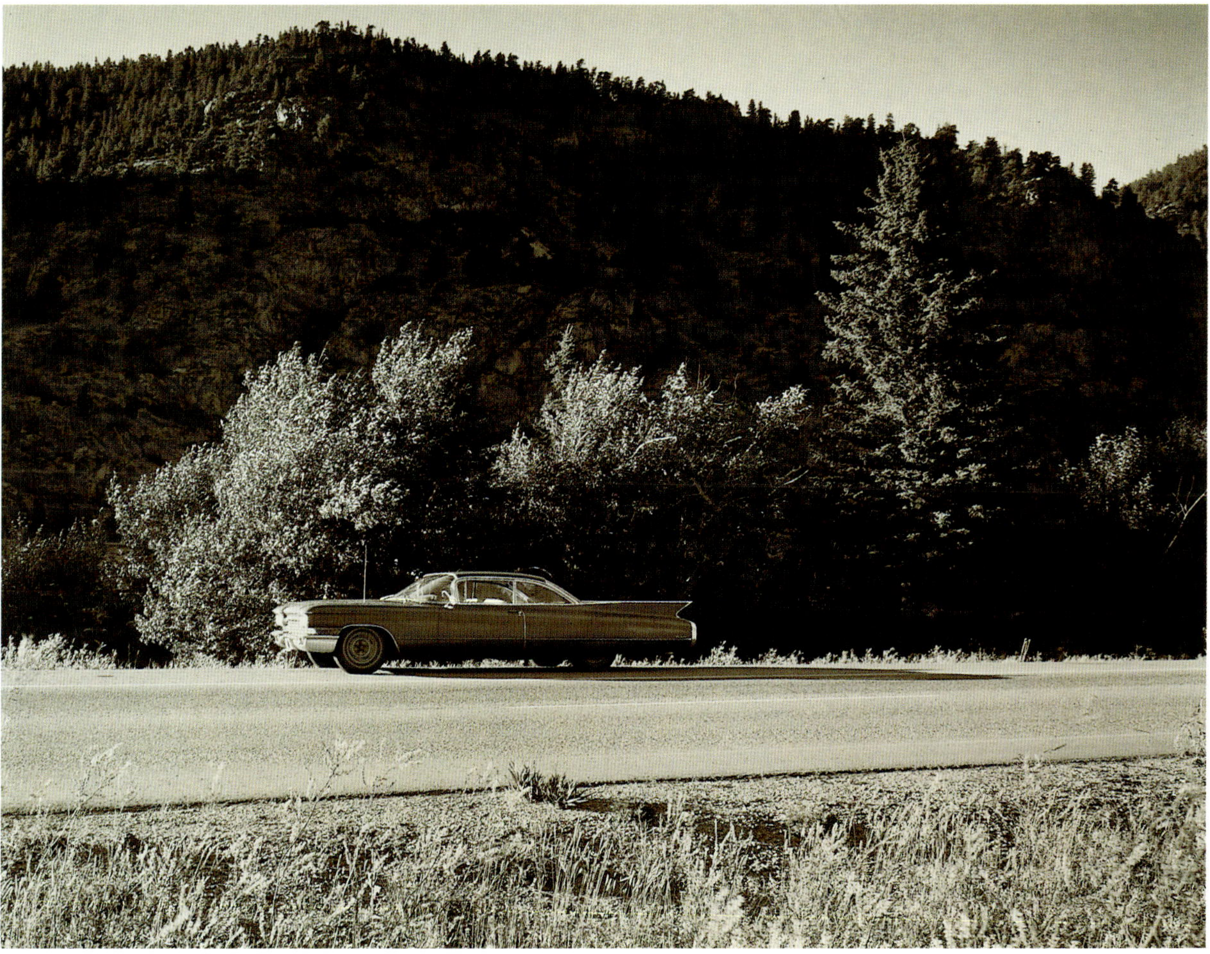

1960 Coupe; Colorado

Yet the Cadillac mystique goes on, despite the sea change. For Americans by the millions, the name alone can conjure up a heady mix of emotions, and the virus that bit Stephen Salmieri is surprisingly infectious. Salmieri's images can raise the Cadillac-consciousness even among infidels not previously enlightened. Once you begin thinking again about the Cadillac in its great, unabashed form, the primeval Caddy of daddies, once you spend time with Salmieri's resonant portraits, then the machine dreams they evoke are constantly coming to life before your eyes. . . .

At a high point on Mulholland Drive, on a parking aerie looking down on the vast car-worn plain of Los Angeles, I come upon a dazzling white '59 convertible, truly the last convertible, empty and alone, as if left there to stand forever as the Stonehenge of our age.

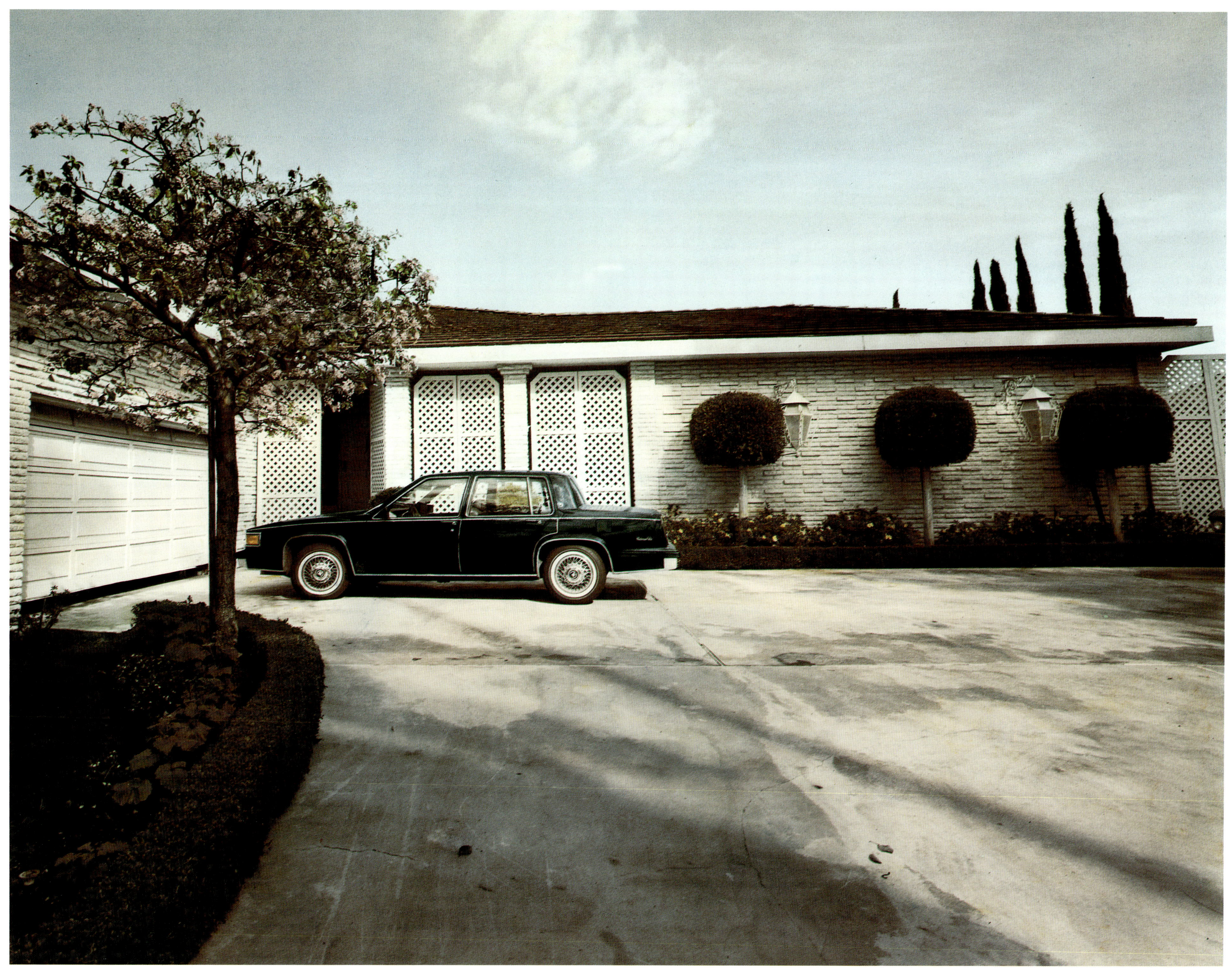

1985 Sedan de Ville; Beverly Hills, California

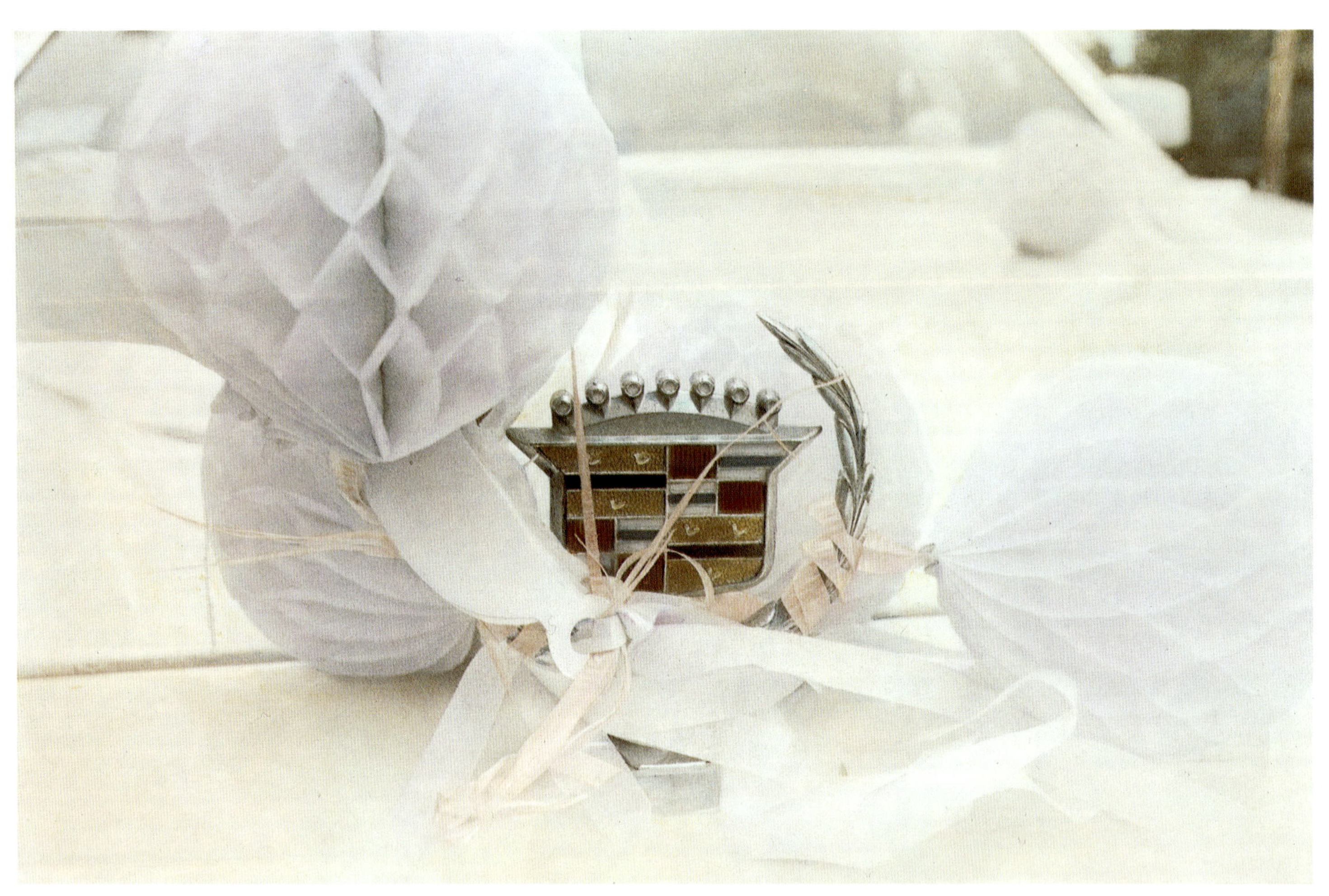

1980 Hood Ornament; Beverly Hills, California

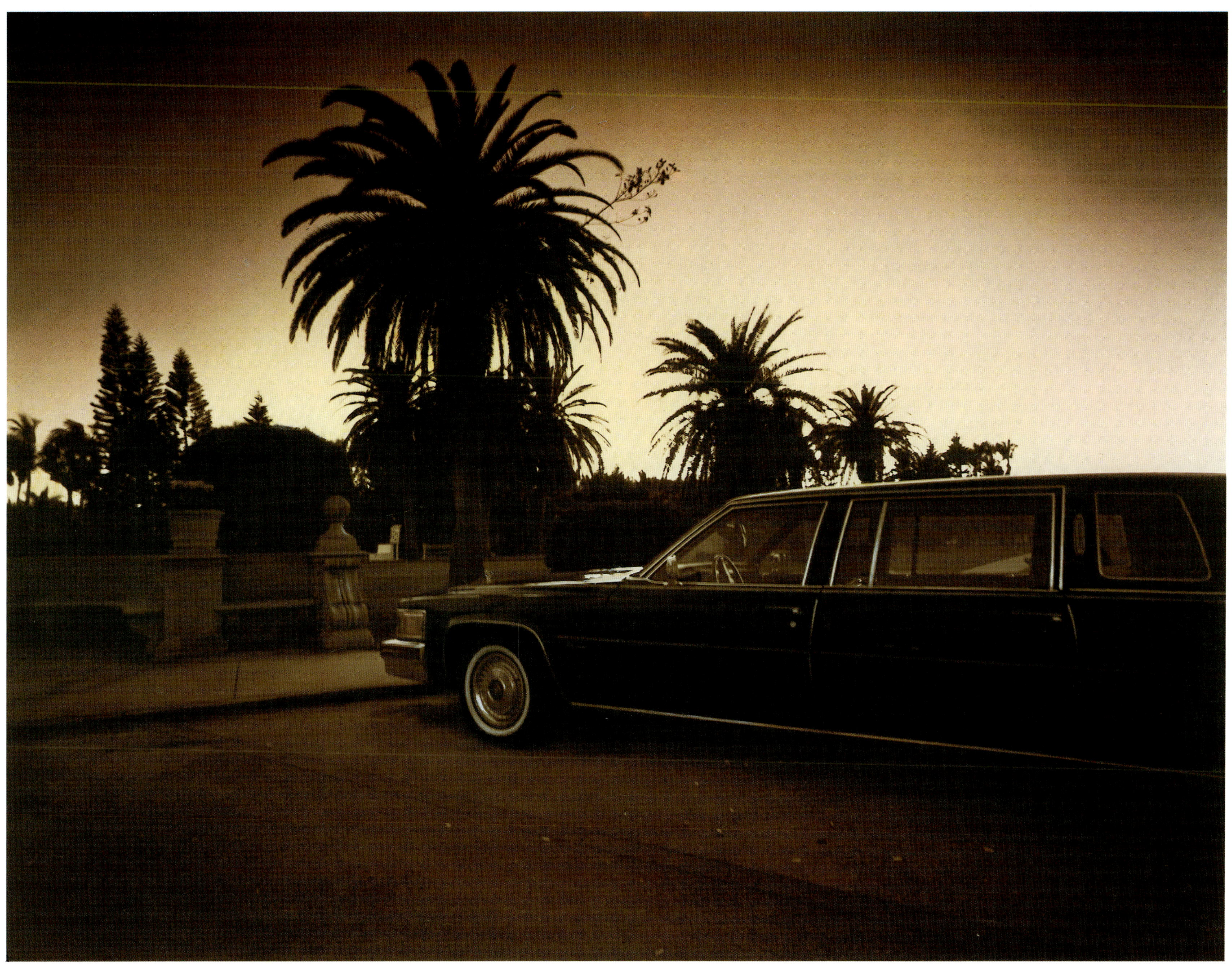

1985 Fleetwood; Palm Beach, Florida

In Detroit, enjoying a brief moment of celebrity on a book publicity tour, I crisscross Motor City in the appropriate conveyance, a black stretch Cadillac limousine. Despite the low-decibel modesty of the modern limo, with its featureless chassis and darkened windows (purdah as privilege), and the standard amenities that homogenize fame, letting anyone with fifty dollars spend an hour in the style of movie stars and diet doctors, the soft machine is still a treat. I lounge in the back seat, eight luxurious feet from the window that seals the driver off from my daydream, watching the soaps on a color television, drinking Grolsch from the built-in fridge, and fighting the urgent impulse to ask the driver to take me home to New York. There are stretch Mercedeses, of course, and even stretch Volvos (*very* downscale upscale), but for *my* fifteen minutes in the klieg lights only the Caddy will do.

Señor Fangio, salud!

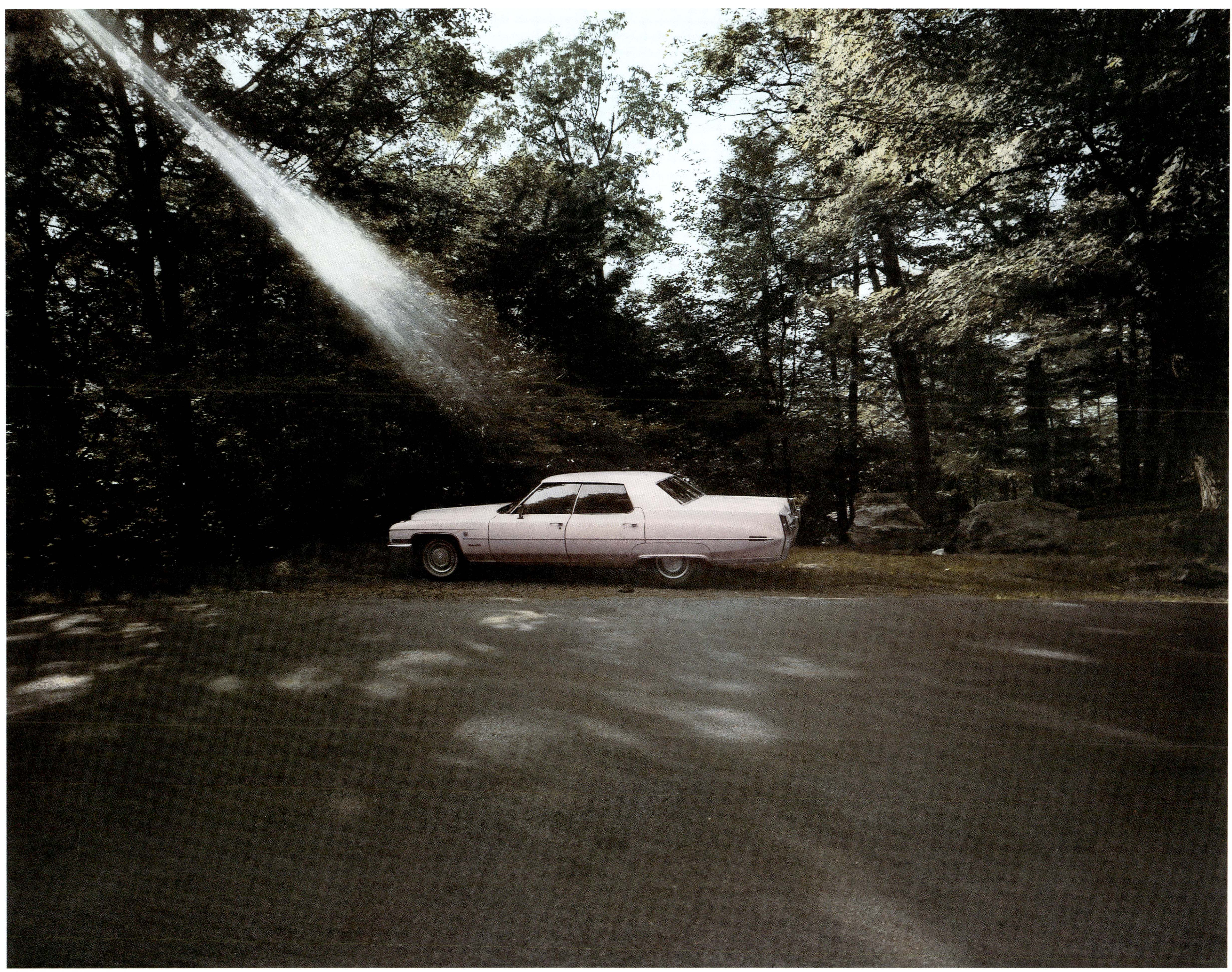

1972 Sedan; Stowe, Vermont

ACKNOWLEDGEMENTS

This project took twelve years, during which I learned a lot about Cadillacs, and even more about relationships. One night, in back of a taxicab in New York City, I said to my friend and now wife Sydnie Michele, "What do you think about photographing Cadillacs across America?" Her response was immediate, and electrically positive. She said, "Let's go." Since then, she has been involved in the project in every way, including her essential role as a colorist. It could not have been done, and I would not have done it, without her.

For the realization of the book, it was my editor Bill Dworkin at Rizzoli International Publications who responded to my vision and brought it to his publisher, Gianfranco Monacelli. It was only with their support that I was able to complete the project. This book is exactly the way I had envisioned it. There was no compromise. Rizzoli truly became my partner in creating a piece of art. I am grateful.

Owen Edwards asked the right questions about Cadillacs. Incredibly remembering it all, he meshed his own experience with mine, selected only the most salient facts and poignant experience, and recreated the tone of my pictures in prose. It was an amazing collaboration.

Milton Glaser and Walter Bernard, designers of the book, generously contributed their creativity, coupled with an enormous knowledge of book design. They and their staff are truly committed to excellence for which I am indebted.

It is no exaggeration to say that if there had been no Harley Earl, there would have been no Cadillac as we know it. In a very real sense, he was a constant presence in this project and a powerful collaborator.

Finally, what makes someone travel in search of one particular car for a dozen years? For a kid from Brooklyn, the Cadillac was the ultimate symbol of success. Photographing Cadillacs probably made me feel successful, which may explain why I spent so long doing it. It is the special nature of the Cadillac that as I began to make pictures, and began to understand the car better, Cadillac owners began to respond to me, and I to them, in an increasingly supportive and genuinely friendly way. I discovered that I had become part of an incredible network of owners and lovers of this car which is as close to a true psychic bond as we are likely to find this side of a Tibetan monastery.

A CADILLAC BESTIARY

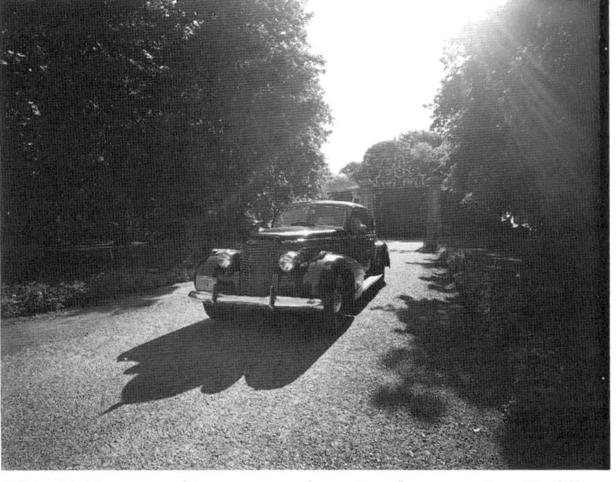

13 In 1940, many things were changing forever. For Cadillac, the end came for the venerable V-16, sidemount spares, and running boards, that last romantic vestige of carriage days.

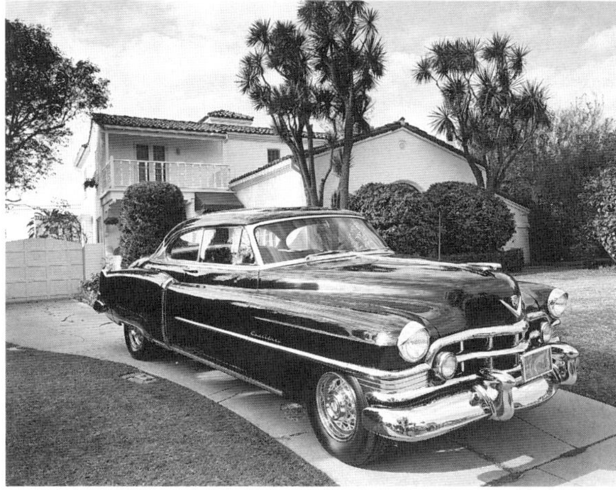

15 The combination of might, mass, and fluidity was never more elegantly evident than in this 1950 Coupe de Ville, reflecting the opulent effect of Earl's self-acknowledged greatest influence, Cecil B. De Mille.

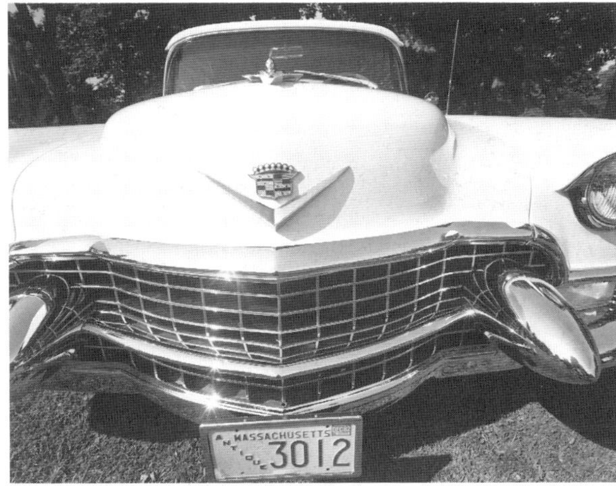

16 Cars don't have faces any more, but in 1955, Cadillac owners could still bask in the benevolent smiles of their zoomorphic machines.

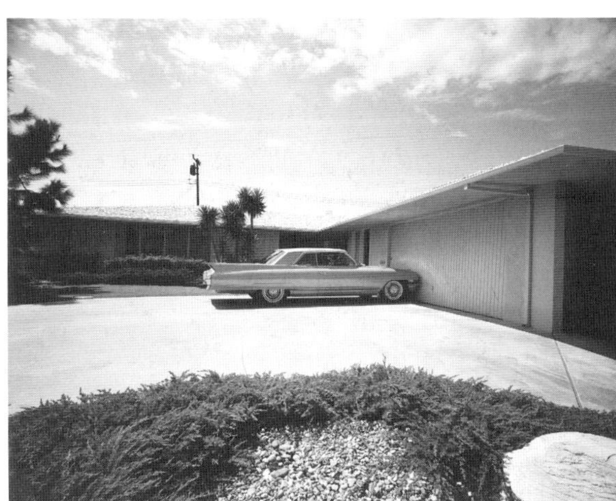

17 Not even Cadillac was immune to the influence of the International Style on the looks of things. By 1962, when purity of form was creating glass box architecture, the style of this toned-down coupe might almost—but not quite—be described as functional.

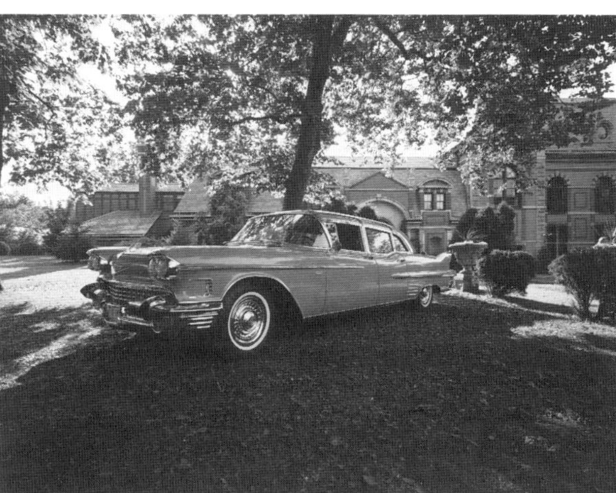

19 Cadillac celebrated General Motor's fiftieth anniversary in 1958 by producing cars like the Fleetwood Seventy-Five Sedan which, if a bit on the grandiose side, were clearly to the manor born.

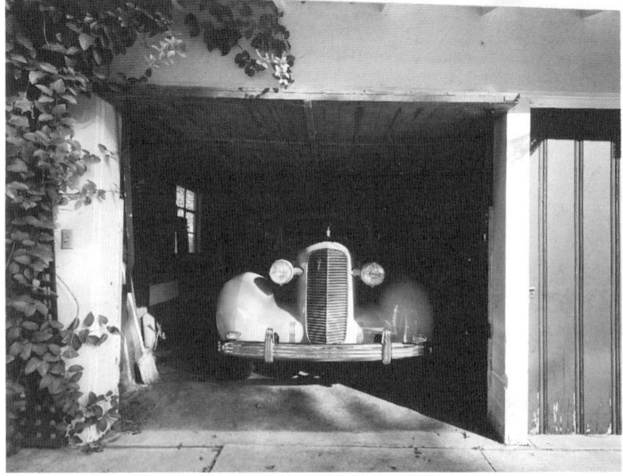

20 Perhaps it is the aquiline grille, or the wide-staring headlights, or the imposing fenders, but the 1936 Caddy had an undeniable hauteur. This one, subject of much admiration, even disdained to come out of the garage.

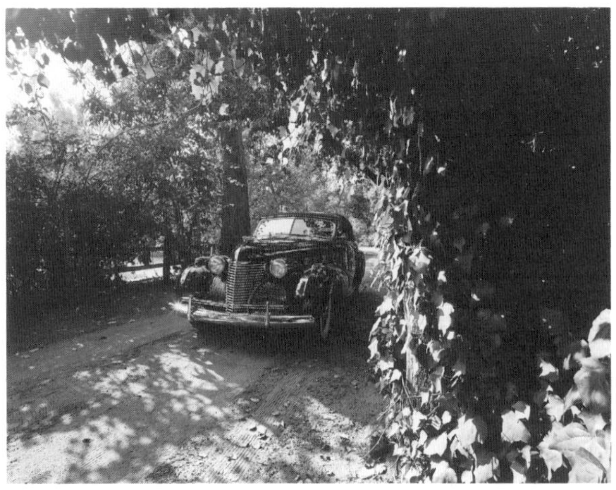

21 In the shade of obsolescence, the 1940 nevertheless prefigured the lower, horizontal look of postwar cars, without losing aristocratic élan.

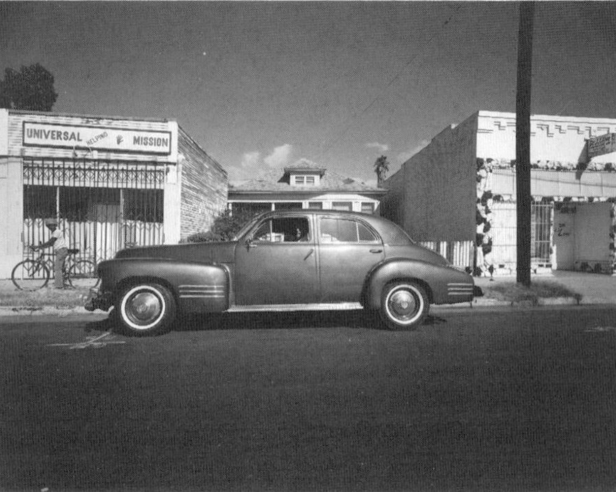

23 Not all Cadillacs bespoke glamour, power, or pretension. This 1941 Series 62, just one of an incredible outpouring of styles—nineteen models in six series—has the unshowy demeanor of a good citizen facing difficult times.

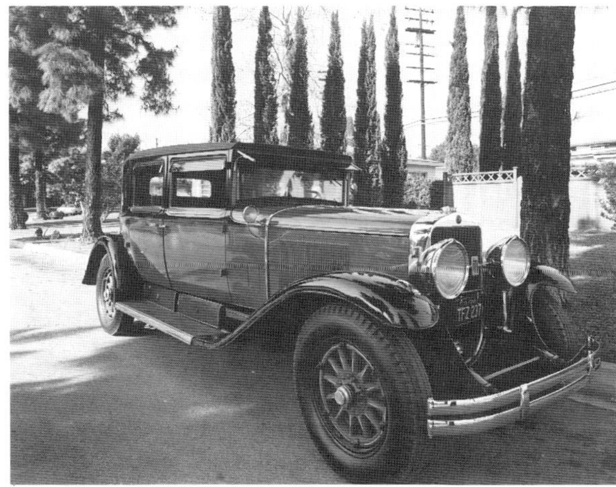

25 The singular flair of Harley Earl first shaped Cadillac in 1928, visible in the sweep of this Fleetwood's fender, the long, crisp line from front to rear, and sheer architectural integrity.

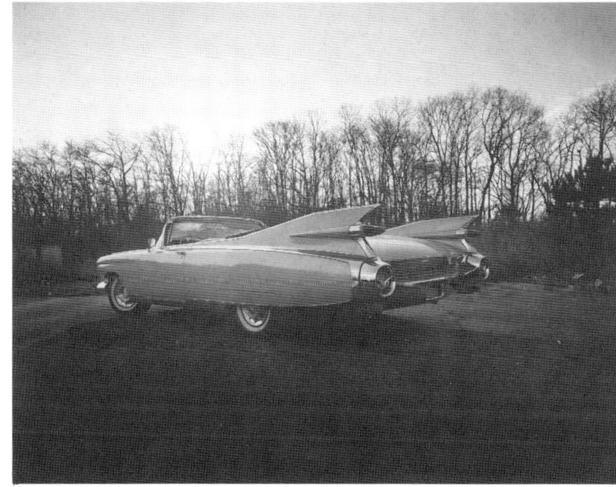

27 Earl's beginnings as a car customizer fabulously reasserted themselves in the rhapsodic 1959 Eldorado convertible, truly the American Dream in sheet steel and chrome.

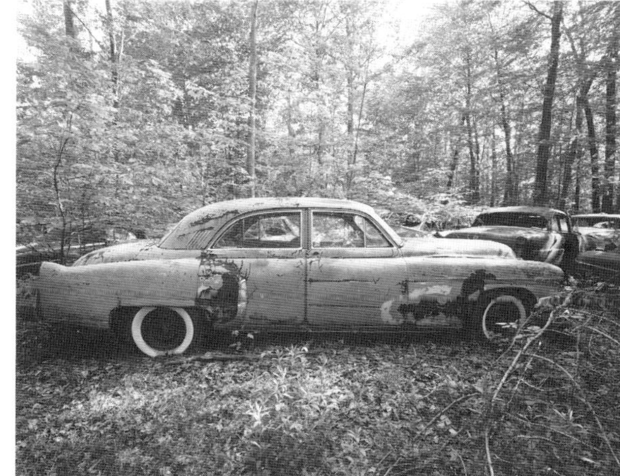

28 The very same entropy that will some day collapse the universe consumes a 1949 Fleetwood Sixty Special in a wooded auto graveyard.

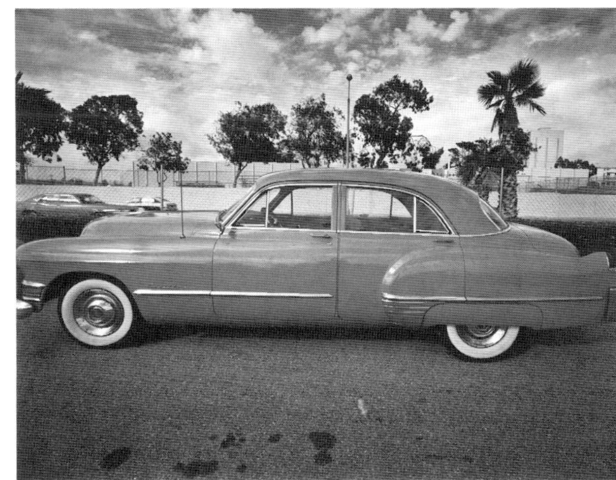

29 A series 61 of the same vintage with a longer lease on life handsomely indicates why 1949 was Harley Earl's favorite year. The first subtle use of the tail fin and the soft sleekness of the near-perfect lines made this Motor Trend Magazine's first "Car of the Year."

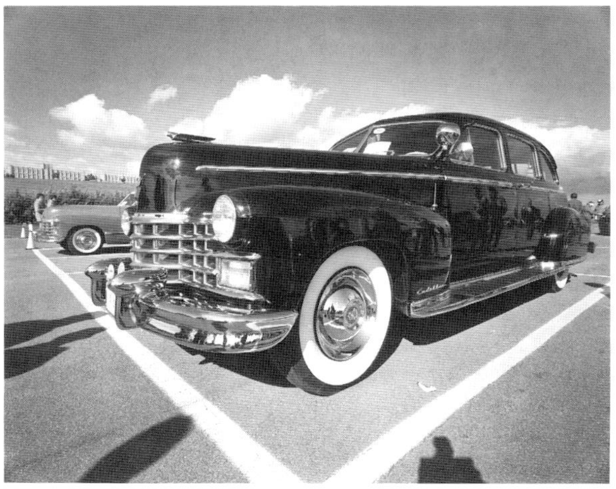

31 Two months after Cadillac Motors made its last tank, the 1946 Caddies began rolling off the line. This stately Fleetwood Seventy Five sedan, one of only 150 built, with its arch-traditional steel running boards and massive bumpers, has more than a little of the M-24 tank's formidable integrity.

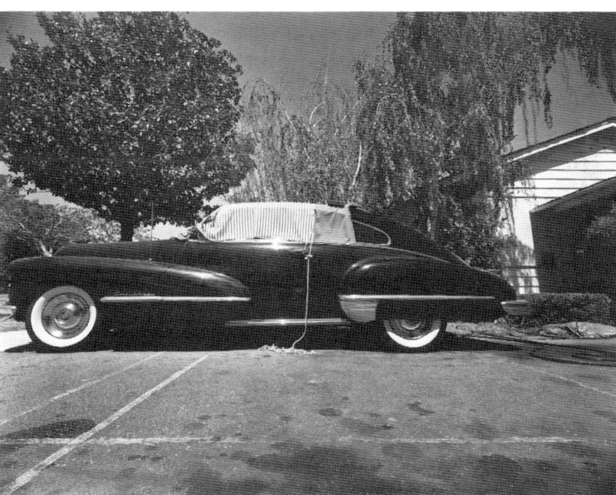

33 Not even tacky drapes can hide the brilliant combination of sleekness and substance that characterize this 1947 Series 62 Sedan, a holdover of a prewar design that defines the streamline ideal.

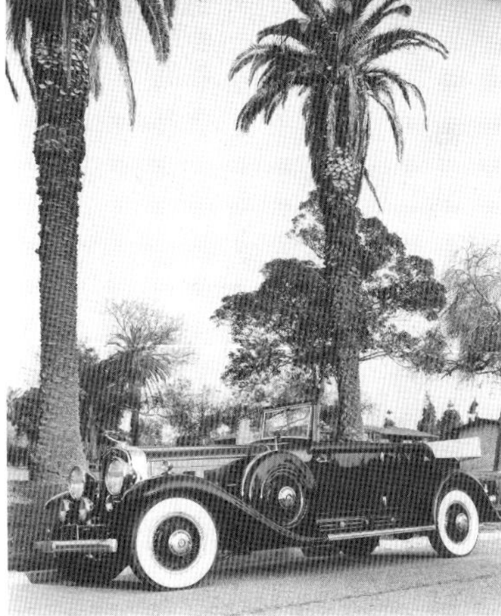

34 Like a Fred Astaire musical or a mansion in Newport, the mighty 1930 V-16 Convertible Sedan was an impeccably appropriate way of treating the Depression with stylish disdain.

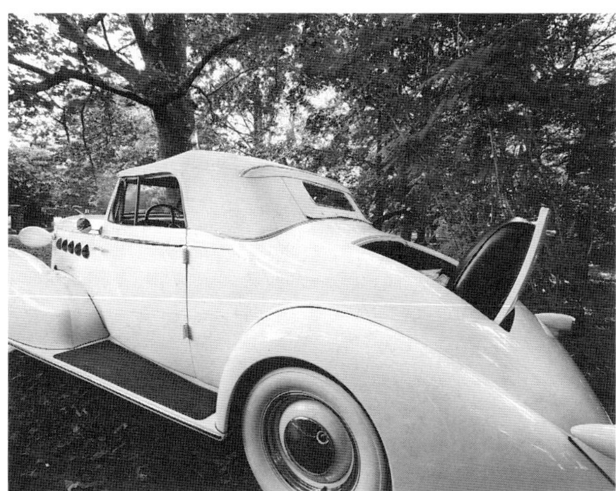

35 No one who ever had the good luck to ride in that wondrous invention, the rumble seat, can help but mourn its demise. On the 1935 La Salle convertible, it was delight with perfection.

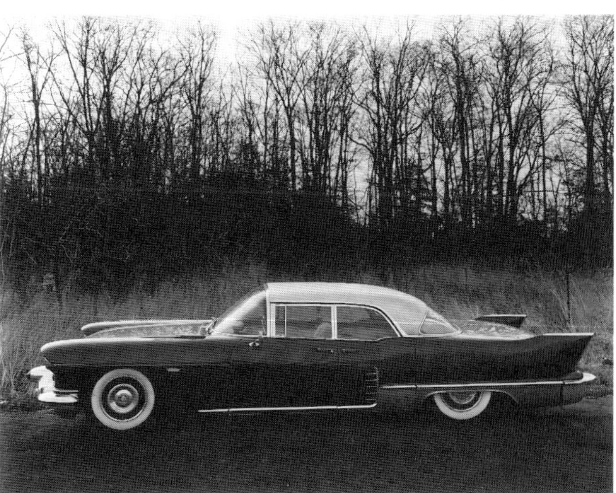

37 Only 400 of the 1957 Eldorado Brougham were built. With a price of 13,074 uninflated dollars, and a look derived in part from Harley Earl's early fifties experimental Le Sabre, the car was determinedly luxurious, but not quite a Cadillac.

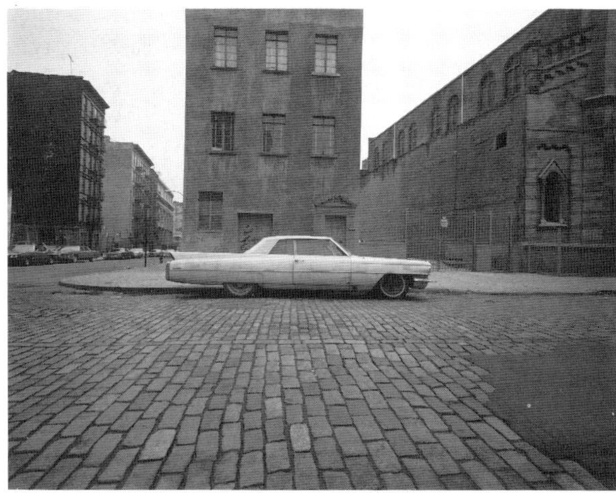

38 The remembered discomfort of GM's management over the flamboyant '59s plus a sobering recession in the auto industry had a dour effect on sixties models. The Baroque splendor of the Earl style was history by the time the 1963 Coupe de Ville was built. . . .

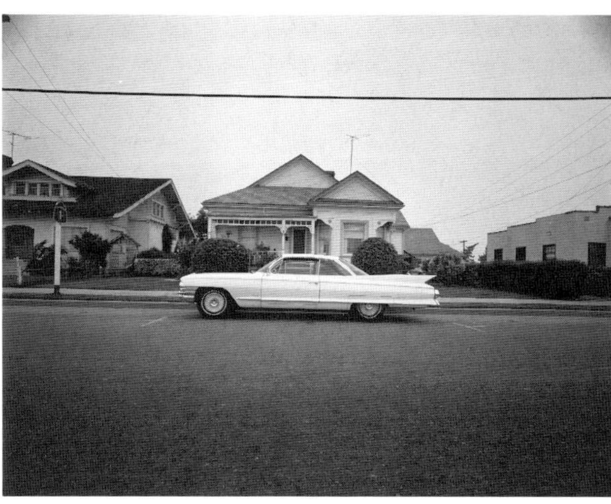

39 . . . but a well-turned-out '61 can still make a man's home his castle.

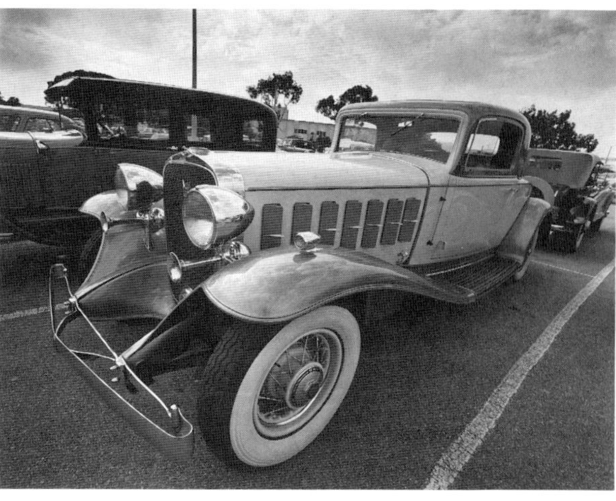

41 There are fenders, and there are fenders, but it's hard to imagine a more sensuous warp of metal than that which swooped up over the whitewall tires of the 1932 coupe sculpted by Fisher.

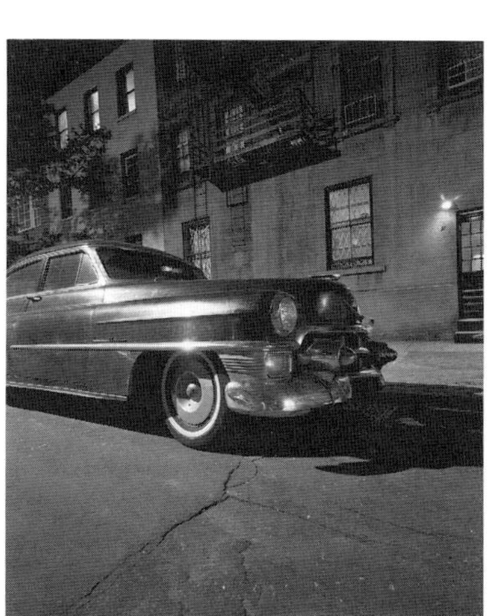

42 In 1953, Dwight Eisenhower rode in an Eldorado convertible in his inaugural parade. Six presidents later, a series 62 sedan parked on a New York street can make time seem to have stood still.

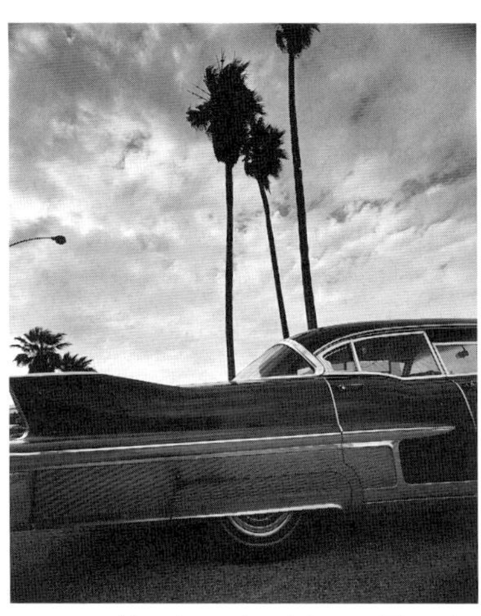

43 The place: a parking lot in Las Vegas. The player: a 1958 Fleetwood. The plot: bullet holes in a rear window? A play without words about power and downfall, leverage and loss.

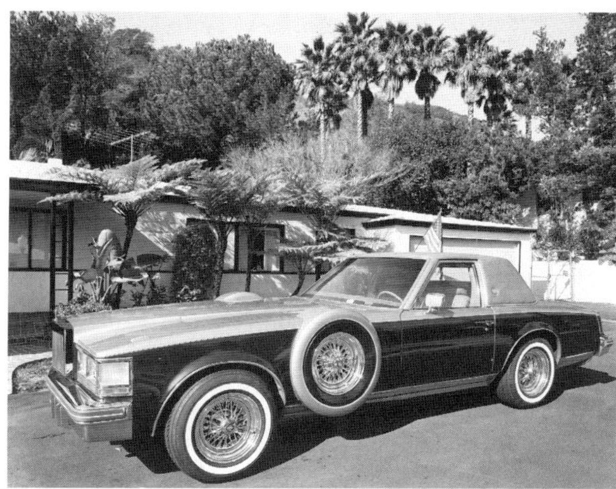

45 Judges ought to be sober, but they need not be drab. At least not in California, where one not-too-august presence on the bench drives this Grandeur Opera Coupe, a 1978 Seville customized by a shop in Pompano Beach, Florida.

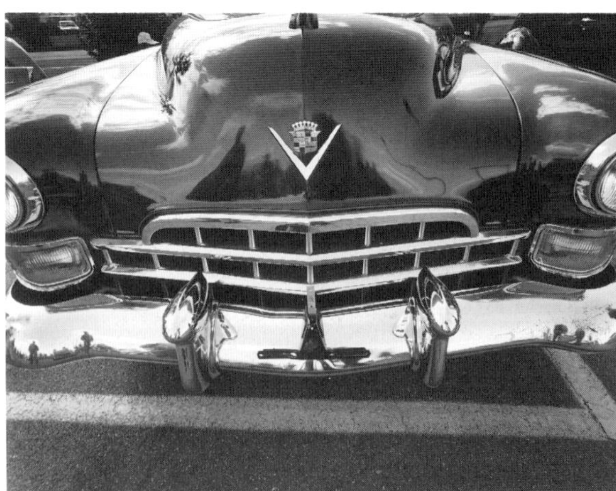

46 The alluring hint of fins on the 1948 models diverted attention from a grille that managed to be at once simple and sophisticated.

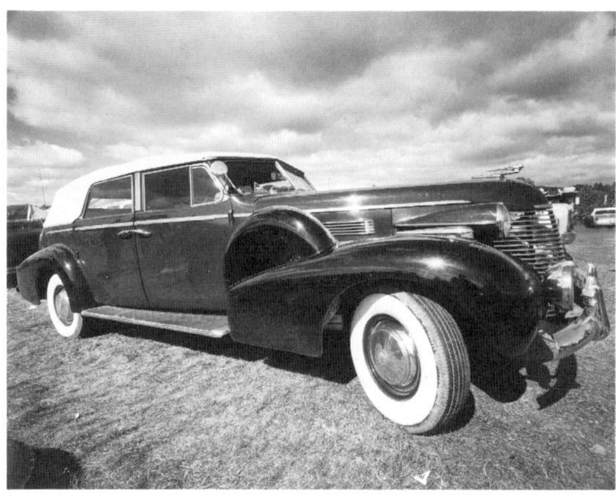

47 Running boards, side mounted spares, a rag top and four doors gave owners of the rare few 1940 series 75 convertible sedans everything a car lover could want, except, perhaps, Claudette Colbert looking for a ride.

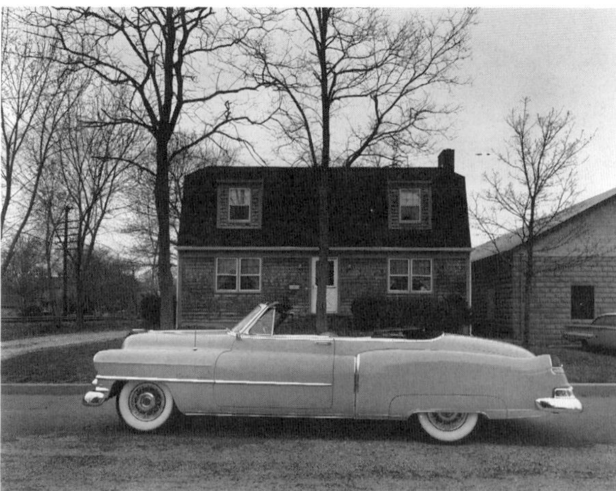

49 In 1951 the good life was pretty well defined by a house in the suburbs, a weekend golf match at the country club, and a Cadillac convertible. In the sweet dreams of this recent past, of course, the top is always down.

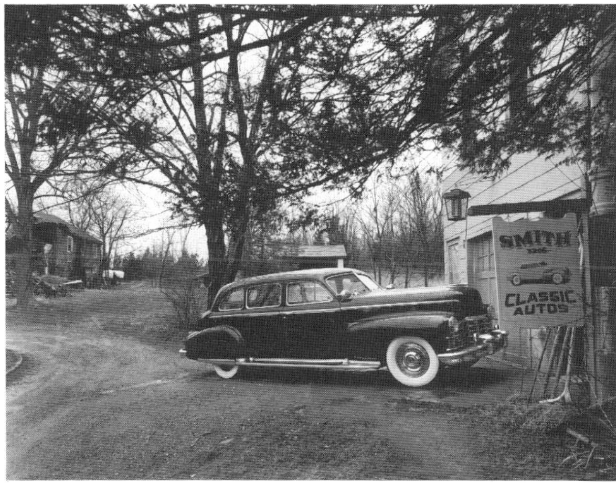

51 The 1946 models were hardly different from the last of the prewar Cadillacs, but the big Fleetwood sedans seemed especially determined to hold on to the swaggering glories of the past.

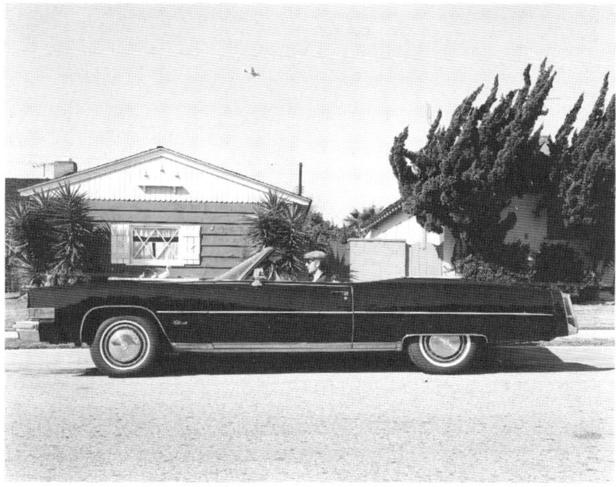

53 The last convertible—at least the last to emerge from the era of limitless hope—was the 1974 Fleetwood Eldorado, a leather-trimmed vision of glory that can wonderfully focus the mind despite low flying planes, the L.A. sun, the hallucinatory trees, and ducks on parade.

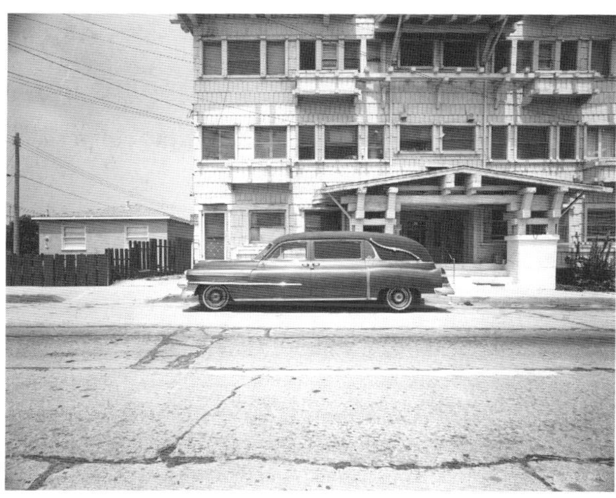

54 Everyone has to go, and the odds are that most of us will take our last ride in a Caddie. Retired to civilian duty in Venice, California, this 1953 Superior-Cadillac Automatic Side-Serving Landaulet no doubt added a final touch of class to many an ordinary career.

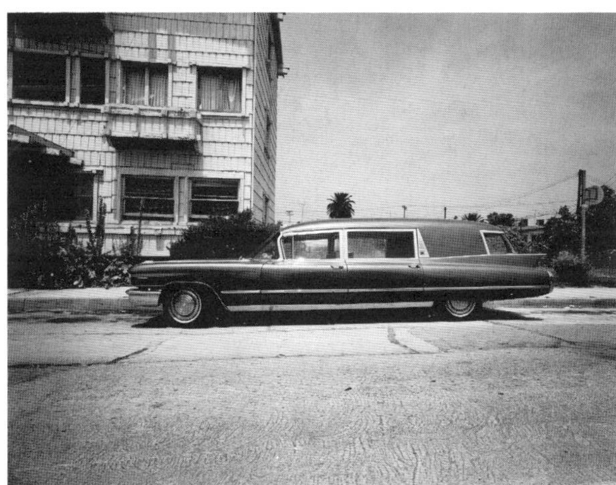

55 The funereal mood of this sunny neighborhood is emphasized further by a 1960 Landau, with a somewhat unnecessary capacious rear view for the presumably uncaring occupant.

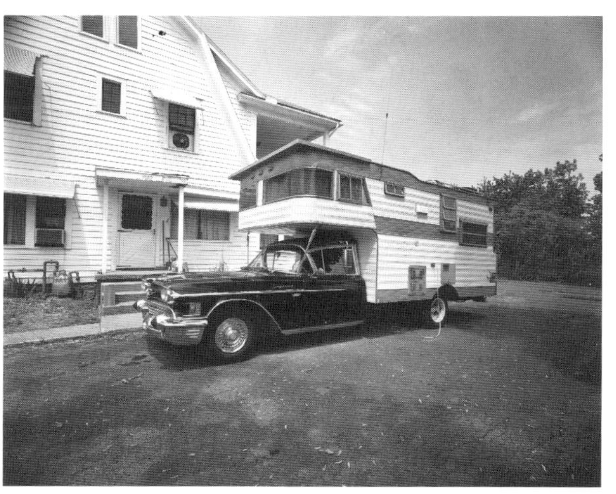

57 There are, perhaps, some things even the dauntless Cadillac shouldn't be asked to do, and this much put-upon 1958 had had to trade its shark fins for a turtle's life.

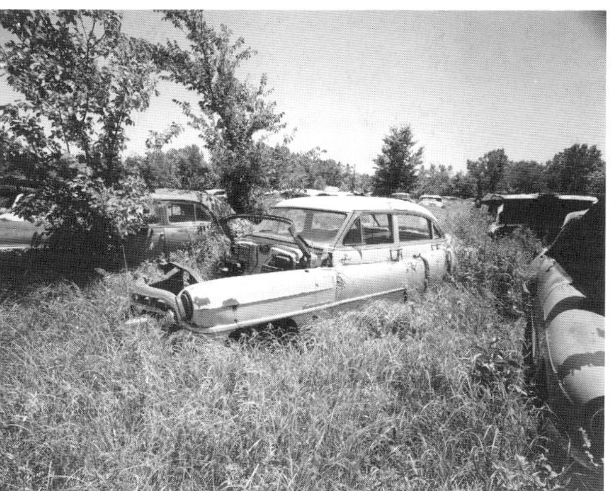

58 In the long gone summer of '52, this Sixty Special had 190 horsepower, a four-barrel carburetor, power steering, and at $4,269 cost a bit more than a dollar a pound. Yet all paths of glory . . .

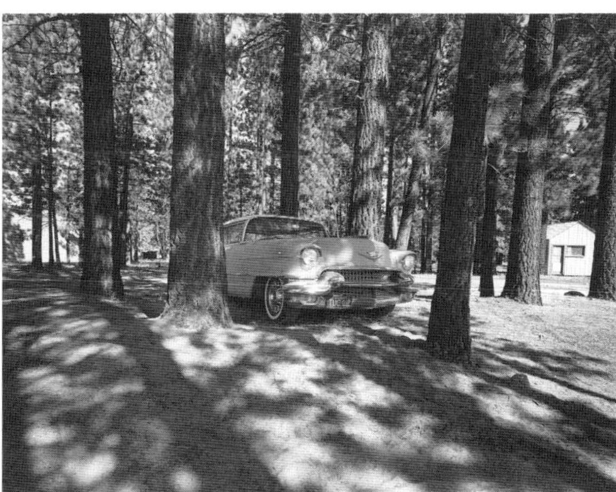

59 As if emerging from a wrinkle in time, this 1956 Coupe de Ville recalls an era of Bill Haley, Fats Domino, the French in Indochina, all the gas in the world, the Giants vs. the Colts, and the driver in the grey flannel suit.

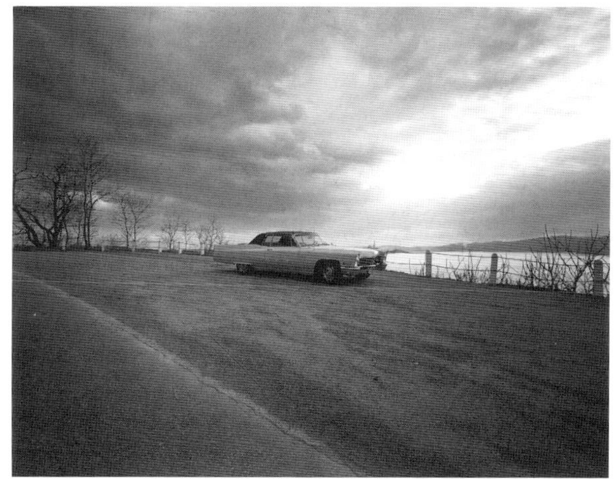

61 In 1967, the Coupe de Ville sold a record 63,935 units. But looking back, the sun was setting on the absolute hegemony of the Cadillac empire.

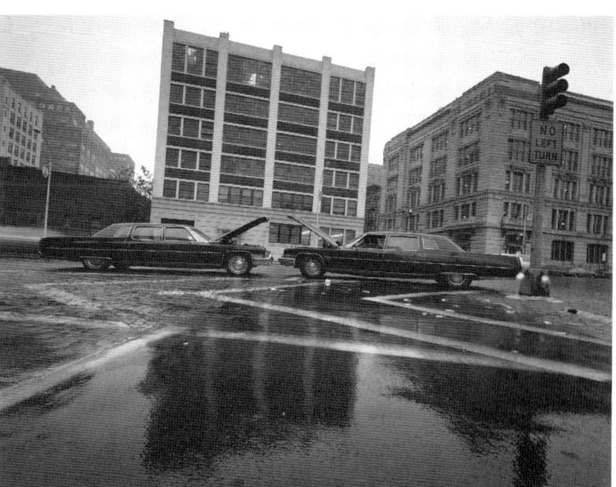

63 A rare view of 1973 Fleetwoods mating, in an unusual tête-a-tête manner once regarded as unlikely by knowledgeable observers of the breed. With this picture, the Cadillac book was born.

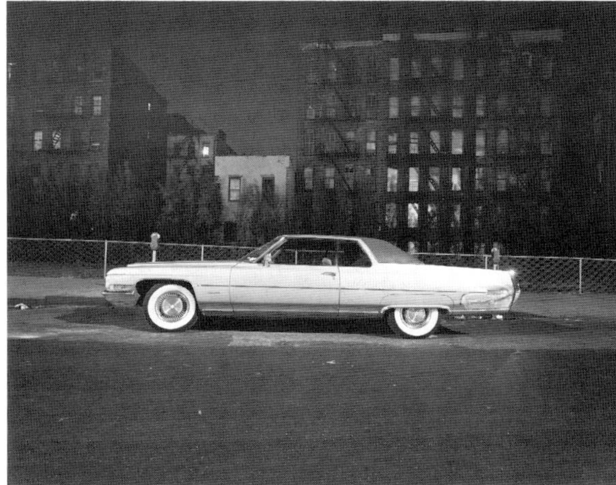

65 A slightly battered 1971 Coupe de Ville, with its subdued, almost anonymous style, seems to prove that not even a low profile can guarantee a quiet life.

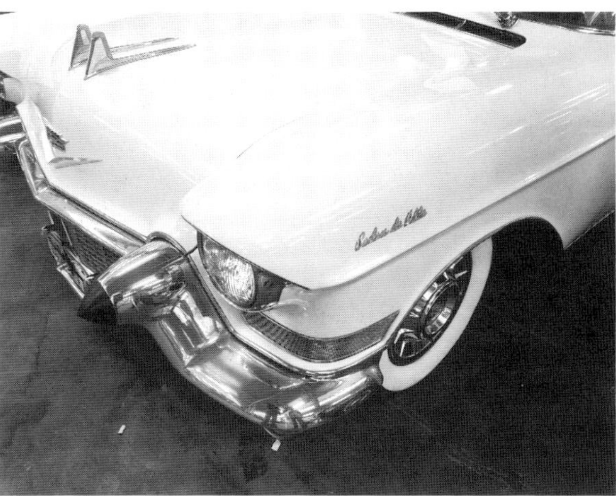

66 Early one morning in 1942, at an air field near Detroit, Harley Earl stood for a few minutes staring at a P-38 pursuit plane, a revolutionary design with twin engines and twin tail booms. Years later, the effect of that moment would surface in the front end of the 1957 Cadillacs . . .

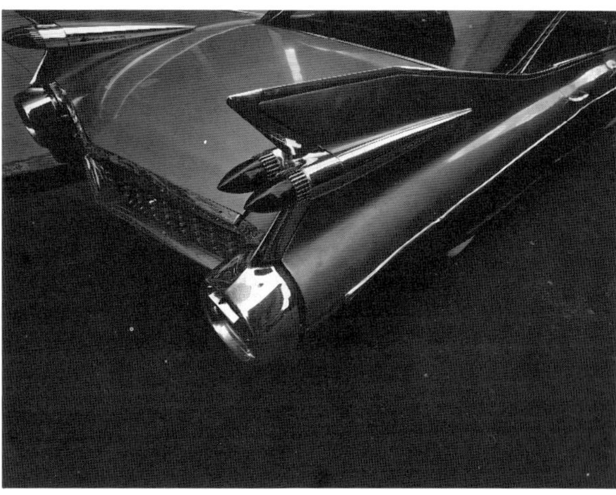

67 . . . and the monumental rear of the '59s.

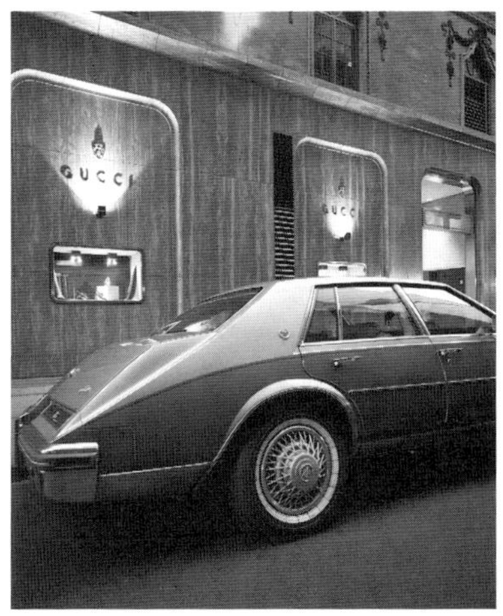

69 If status is an imitation of style, and Gucci is a name synonymous with instant status, what better place to appraise the Rolls-ish rear deck of a 1982 Seville Elegante?

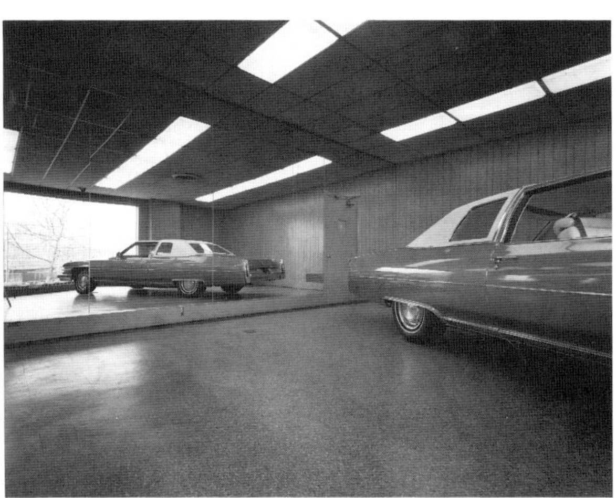

70 By the time this 1974 Coupe de Ville stood in cool, reflective assurance, the Arabs had sent the first tremors of discontent with "heavy metal" through the car-buying public.

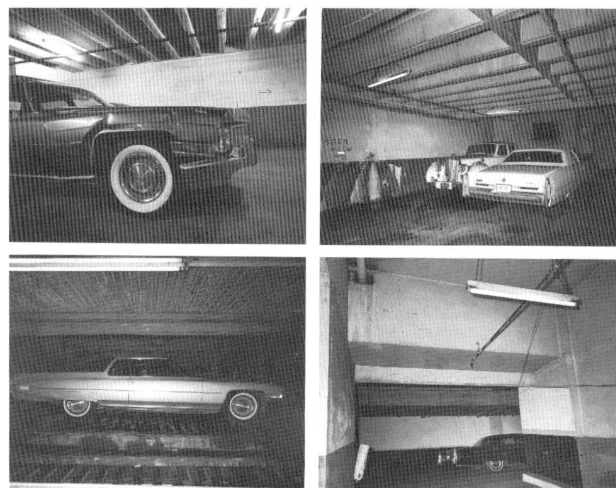

71 In the hellish environment of city parking, one solid Caddie gets the bends, the rich tend to stick together, a '72 Coupe de Ville takes an elevator ride, while another, Garbo-like, just wants to be left alone.

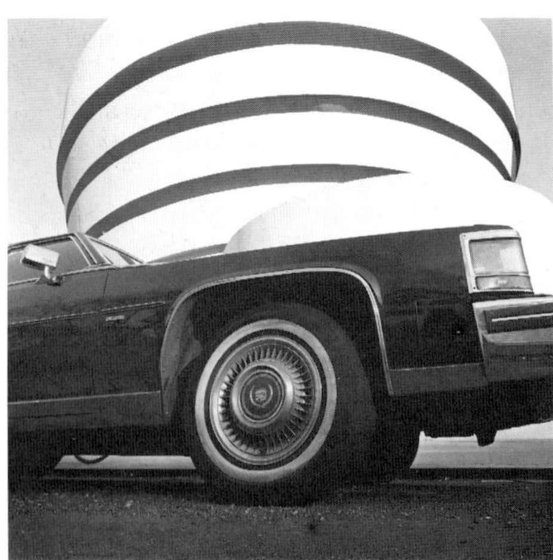

73 Had Ezekiel seen the wheel of a Sedan de Ville, would his vision have looked something like this 1980 at Frank Lloyd Wright's Guggenheim Museum?

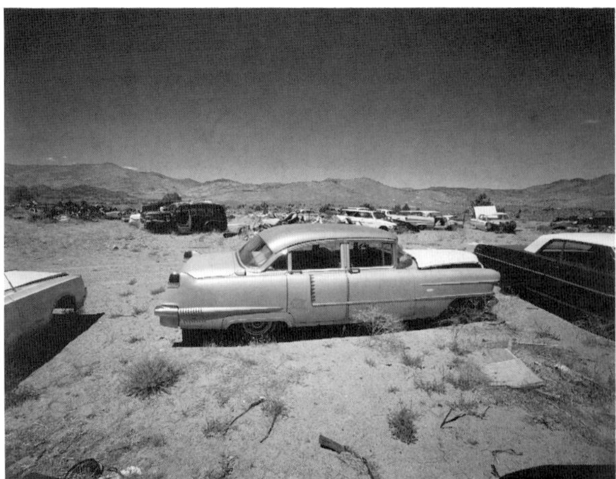

75 The 1956 Cadillacs took more features of Earl's dream of highway airplanes, complete with streamlined air intakes and streamlined fairings on the rear fender. Some of these machines crashed in the desert.

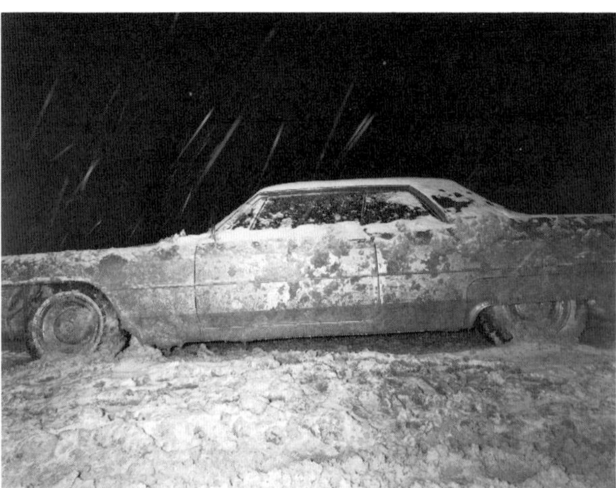

77 In the classic owner's dream, the Cadillac sits on a spotless macadam driveway, being curried by a happy and adoring family. Sometimes, reality fails to cooperate.

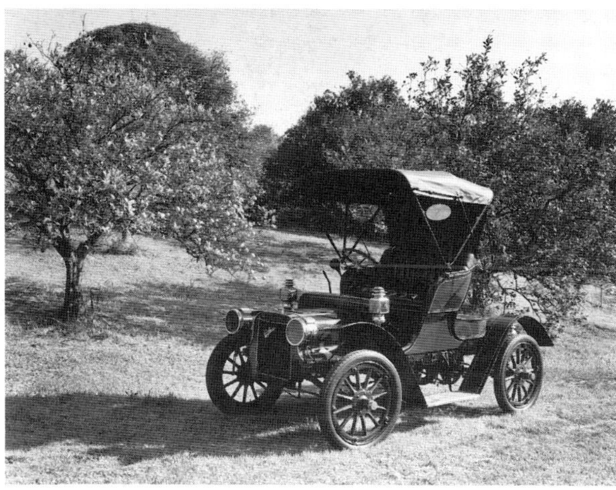

78 Though fragile-looking, the 1908 Cadillac managed to win its class in a 2000-mile Royal Automobile Club endurance race.

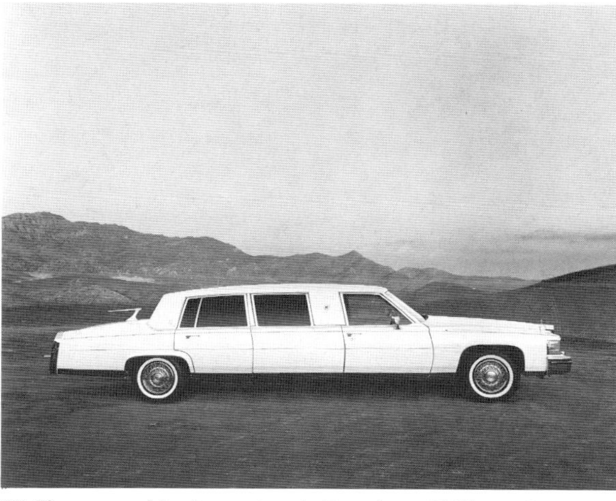

79 The now ubiquitous stretch limo in a 1985 version produced by O'Gara Coachworks in southern California, where folks rent these to go next door to borrow a cup of caviar.

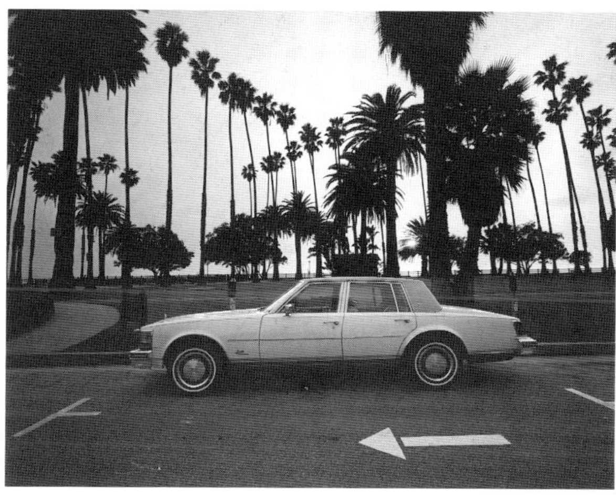

81 In 1976, the new Seville set the standard for little more than indecision. Was it a novel approach, or just a humbled Cadillac? Not even mad pinball surroundings can save it from ignominy.

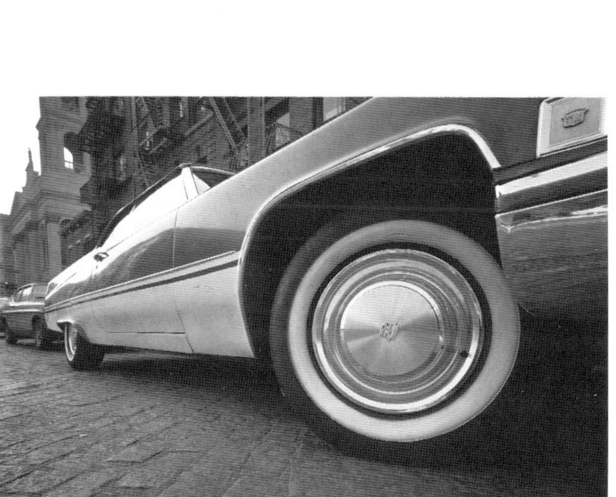

83 The Coupe de Ville convertible, out of production since spring of 1969, still has no equal for declaring the simple joys of possession.

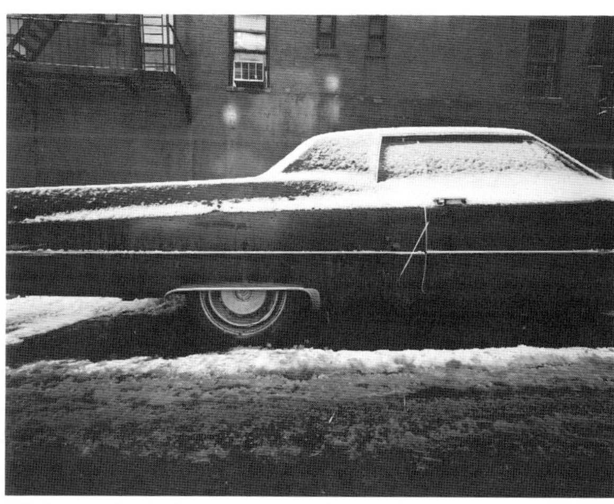

85 As smoke is the measurer of aerodynamics in wind tunnels, snow is the measurer of line on the streets. Under a light dusting of revelation, the '67 coupe holds up well.

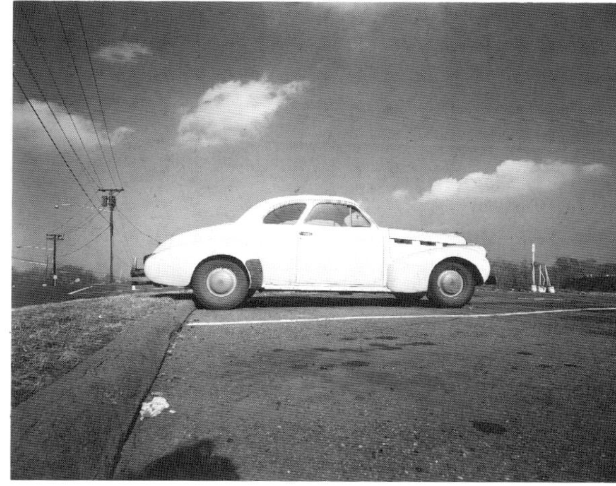

87 The 1940 La Salle was nearly the end of a spirited line that had long let people who couldn't afford Cadillacs, or didn't want Cadillacs, to have Cadillacs.

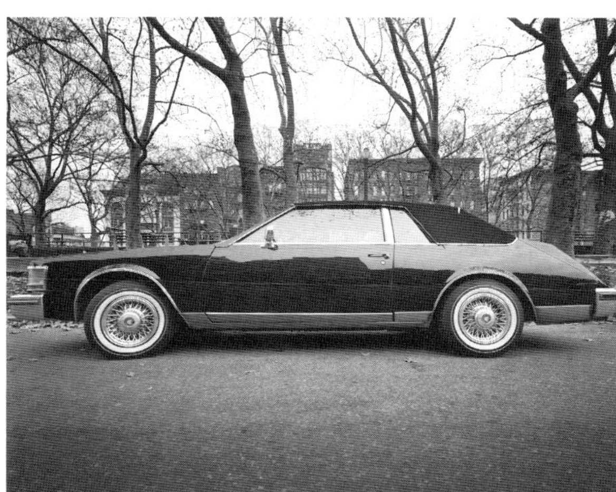

89 Call it a "Full Cabriolet Roof" or the worst kind of fakery, the convertible top that doesn't convert makes this 1982 Seville more faux than friend.

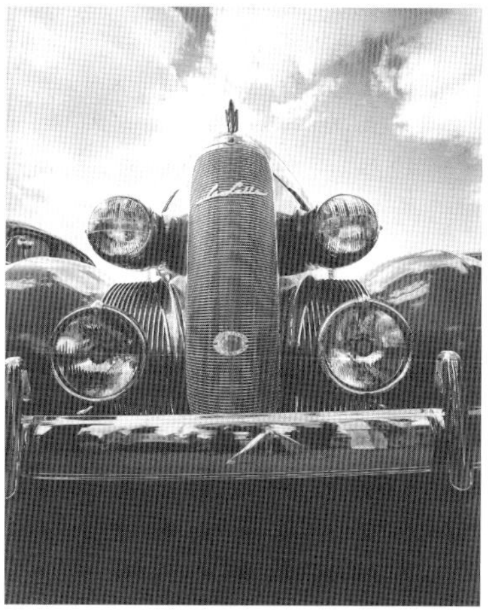

91 The extraordinary front end of the '39 La Salle, with road lights added by an unwise owner, may be one of the finest examples of prewar industrial design produced in America.

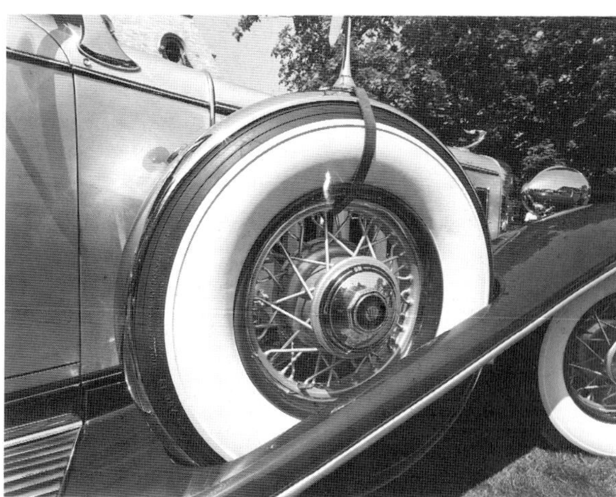

93 On the 1932 Fleetwood the necessity of a spare was the mother of adornment. The Fleetwood line this year included eighteen body styles built by no fewer than fourteen coachworks.

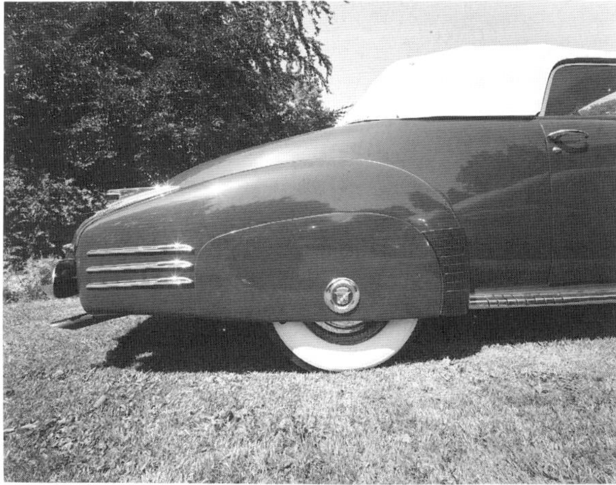

95 As we know too well, progress doesn't invariably entail improvement; looking at this 1941 convertible, one can appreciate the tragedy of the fender's demise.

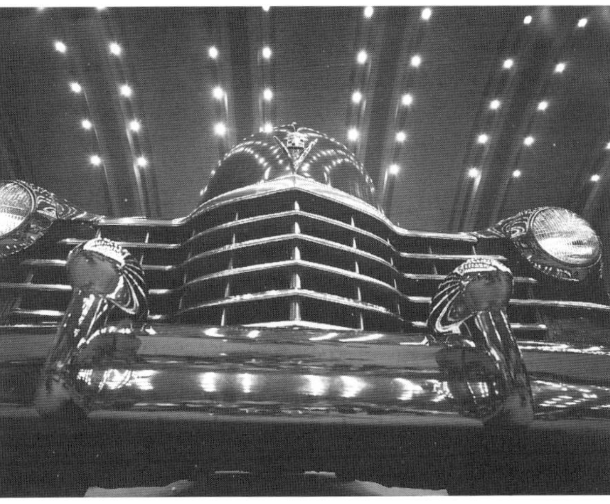

97 Harley Earl had always been ahead of his time, so the fact that this 1946 model was unchanged from the 1942 line mattered little to a car hungry public. The wide, horizontal grille spoke of things to come.

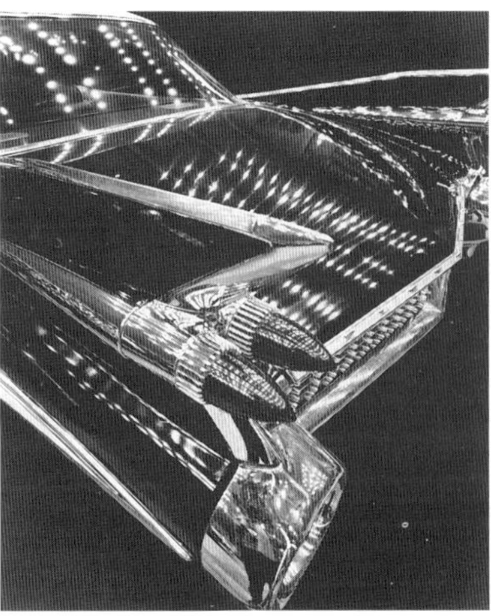

98 Words like "inimitable," "unprecedented," and "extragalactic" seem scarcely adequate to describe the rear end treatment of the 1959 zany classics. In mirror–bright chrome surfaces, the design seemed to vie with Versailles.

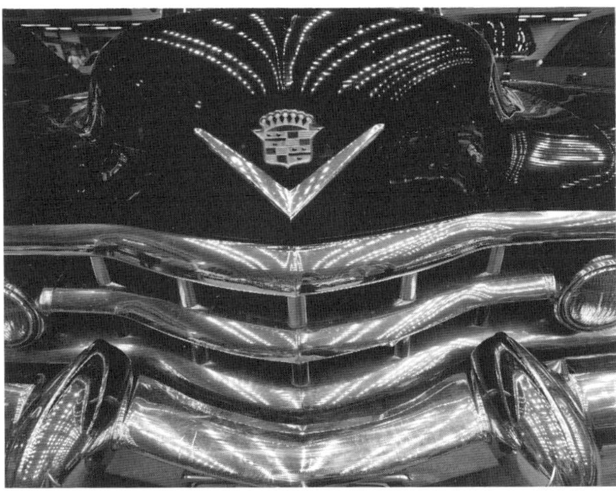

99 The Vee, of course, stands for V-8. The crest, with its heraldic ducks in a row, is the escutcheon of Le Sieur Antoine de la Mothe Cadillac, a noble Gascon explorer and military commander who in the late Seventeenth Century founded Detroit.

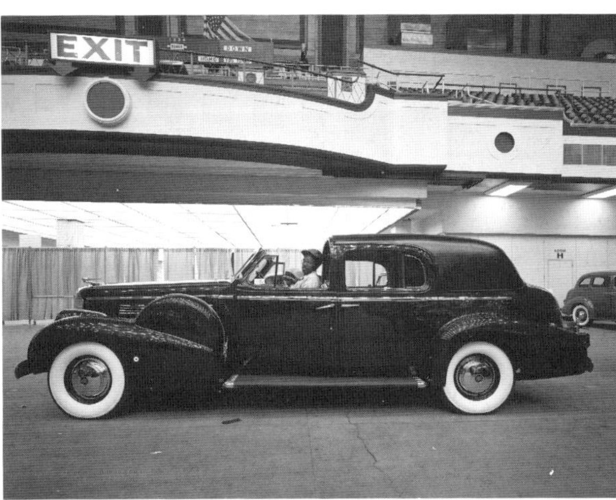

101 The perverse joy of the town car series, like this 1938 version, was that they so emphatically separated the haves from the have-nots. While the chauffeur got wet and cold, his employers could discuss his well–being in comfort. Happily, some of the former have-nots ended up having.

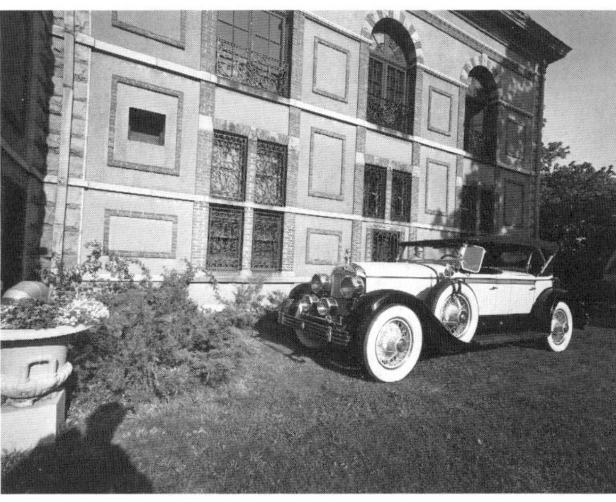

102 Though hired to design the La Salle, customizer Harley Earl's influence was visible in the two-tone paint on this 1927 Cadillac Roadster.

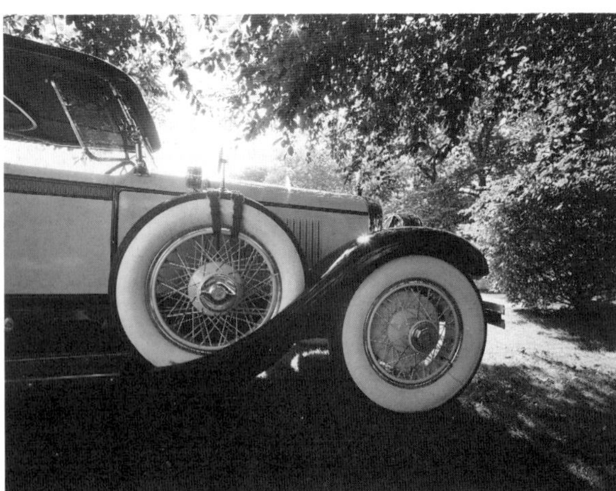

103 If the paint job, bright whitewall tires, and rakish wing windows weren't enough for the demanding swell, Earl added just a touch of wicker to the doors.

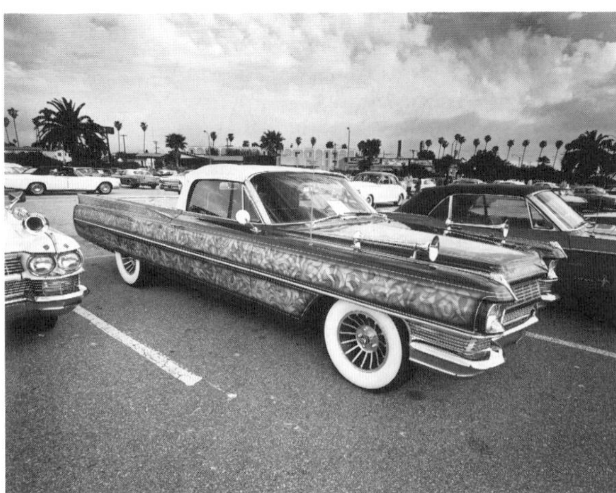

105 What Cadillac took away from its cars, some determined aesthetes put back, with a vengeance! This madly inspired reworking of a 1964 Custom Ranch Wagon is nothing less than a street car named Desire.

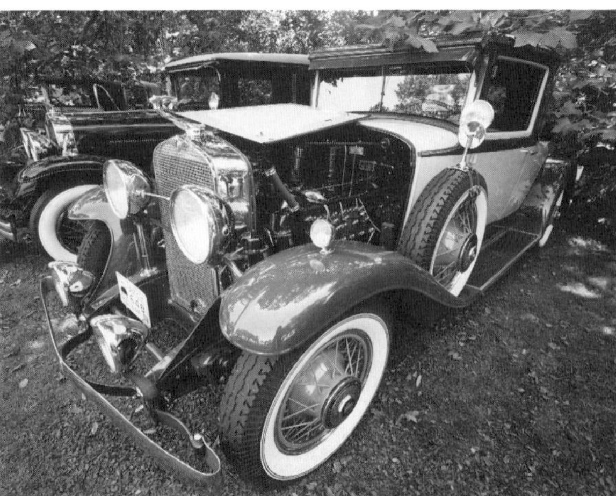

106 Not the least of the '31 La Salle's charms was perhaps the most graceful radiator ornament ever sculpted. Rolls Royce, eat your heart out!

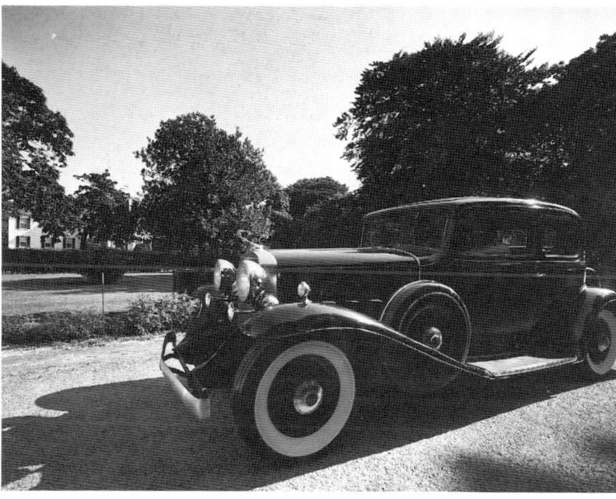

107 The ventilator doors on this 1932 La Salle Town Coupe quickly became a standard feature of luxury cars, ending up years later in vestigial form as a Buick stylistic trademark.

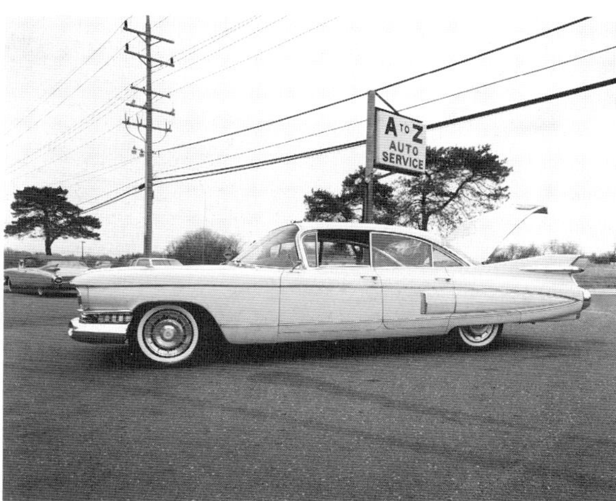

109 There were giants in the earth then, and you could fit several of them in the yawning trunk of a '59 Fleetwood.

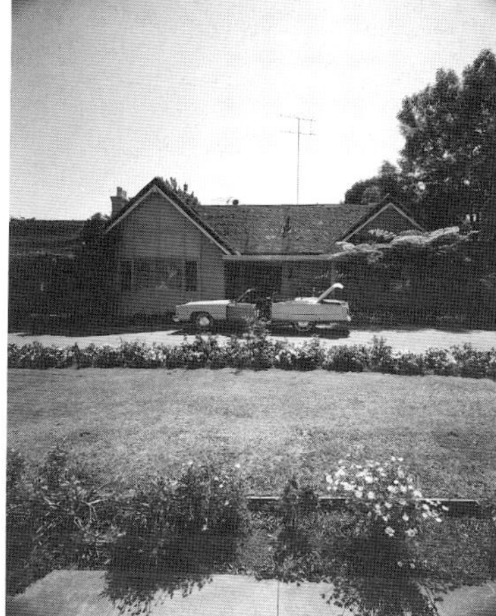

110 In 1974, the Eldorado line was 20 years old and as fabled as the city it was named after. More than any other car, the Eldorado convertible exemplified a way of life in which crabgrass and bad breath were major problems.

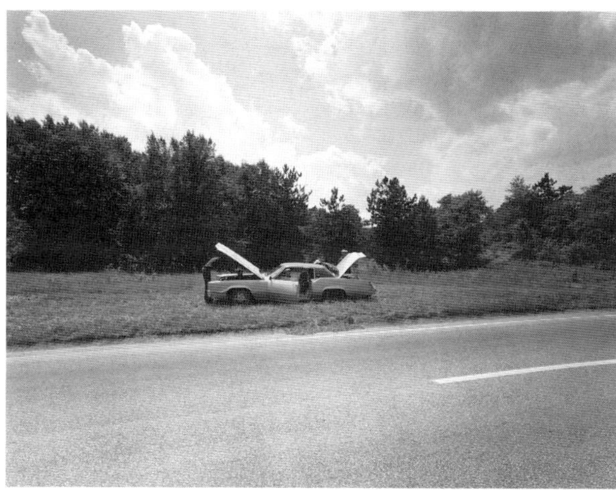

111 Sometimes, when a vacation starts wrong, the best thing a man can do is stick his head in the mouth of his ailing car and hope for the best.

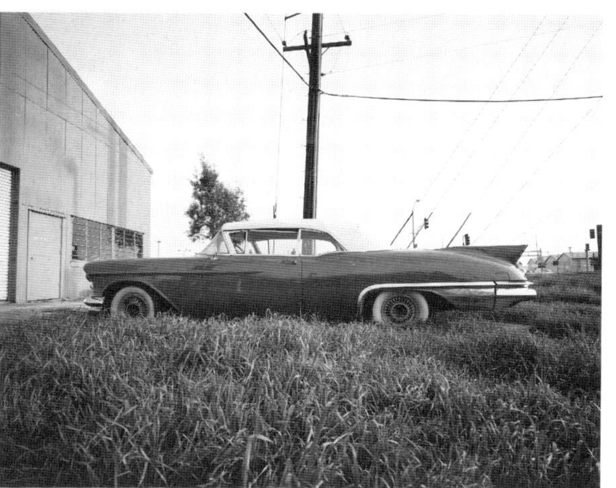

113 The 1957 Eldorado Biarritz convertible, a rare bird with only 1800 produced, reflected more than any other Cadillac the stylistic effects of Harley Earl's eccentric and imaginative experimental models like the '54 Bonneville show car.

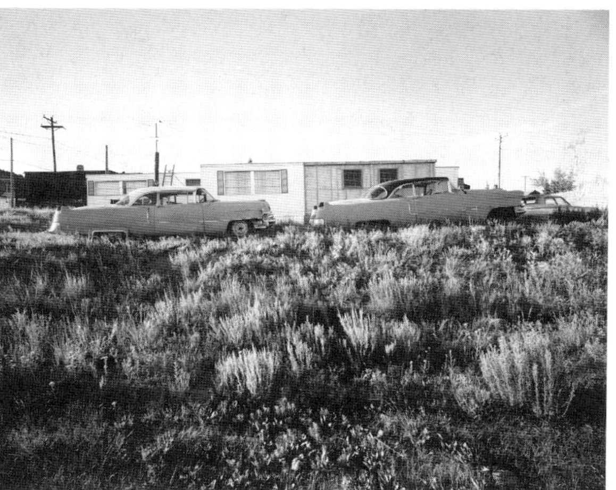

115 No matter how many things have failed to work out, a brace of '55 Coupe de Villes waiting at the front door can have a lifting effect on the neighborhood.

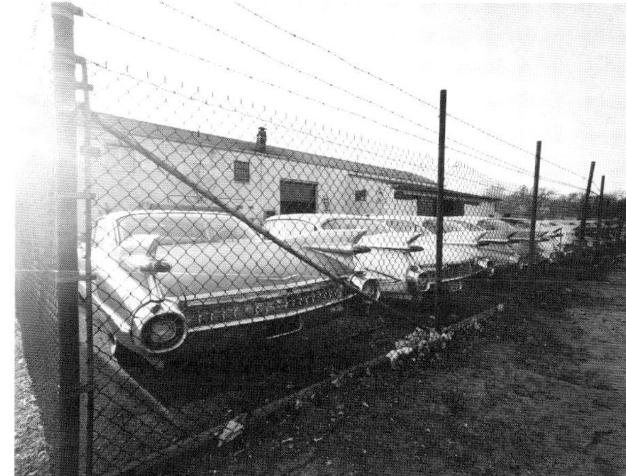

116 In a far-off galaxy called Long Island there is a man who has taken as his task in life the collecting of every model Cadillac made in the watershed year of 1959. He keeps them healthy and well-guarded, the way Anheuser–Busch keeps his Clydesdales.

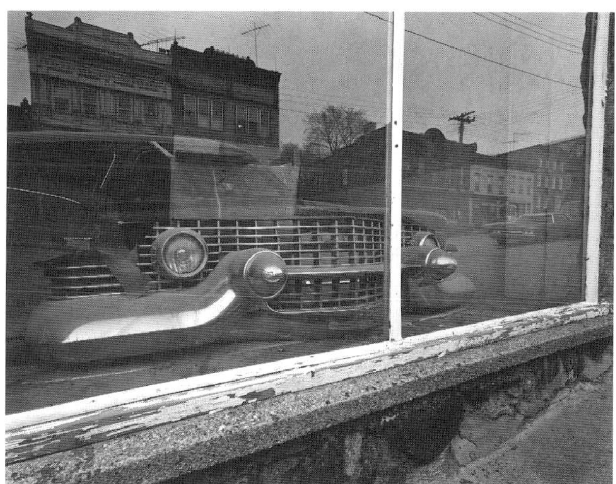

117 It seems quite possible that the buxom front bumper of the 1954 models weighed as much as the entire body of the Honda CRX.

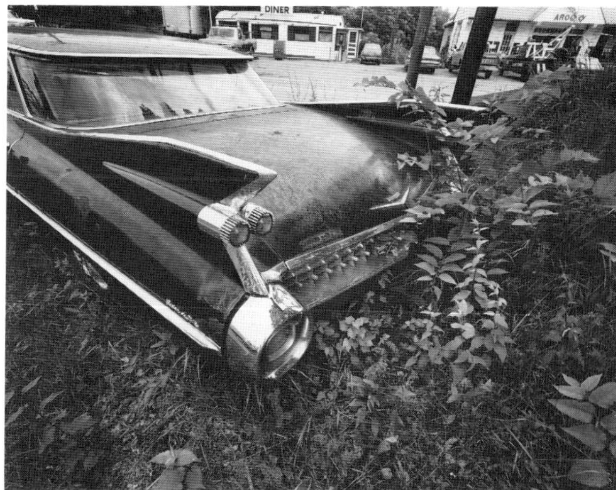

119 In the fifties, the P-38–inspired Caddies soared into the stratosphere, where they became jets, and finally, rocketships. After the crescendo of 1959—like diners and gas stations with free roadmaps—the vision became part of history.

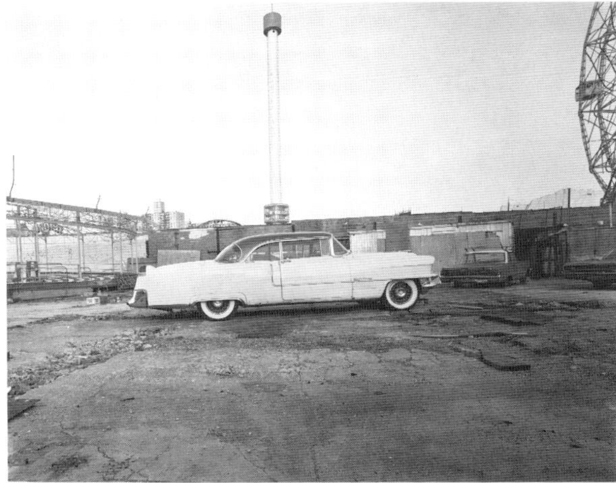

121 1955 was a great year for Cadillac and a great year for Coney Island. Of the two, this Coupe de Ville seems to have held up better.

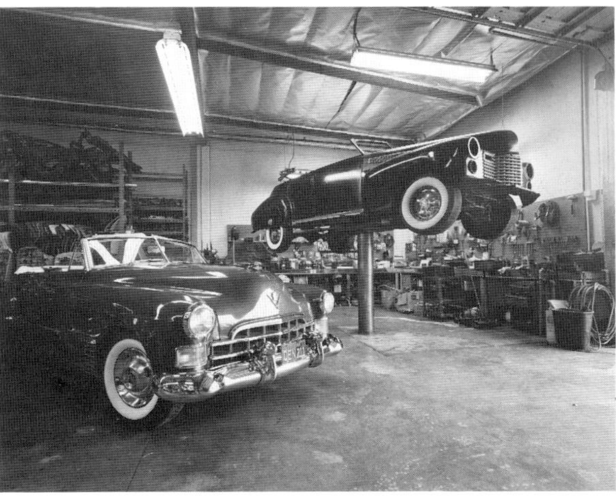

122 A certain subgroup of Cadillac cognoscenti favor only those cars made in the forties, like the '48 ragtop on the floor, or the '41 levitated on the right . . .

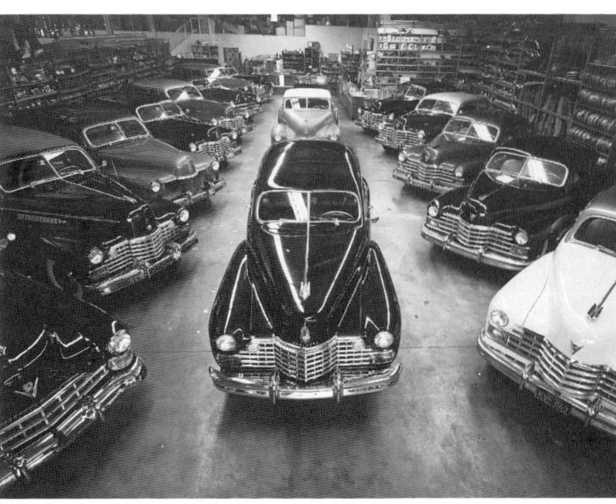

123 . . . an auto erotic paradise where anything is possible, someone has made those pre-and post-warriors his profitable specialty.

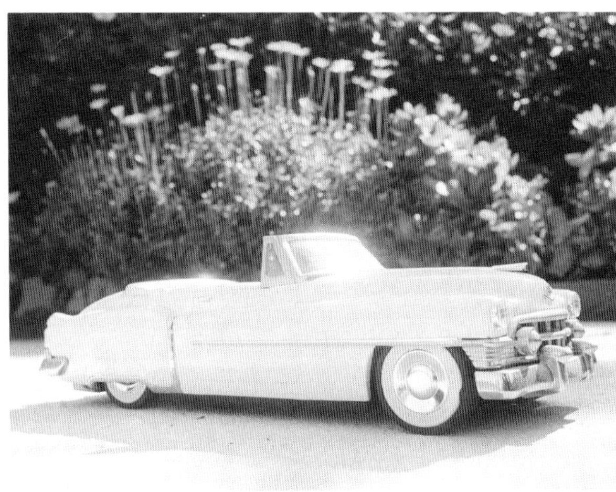

124 Even a toy Caddy retains the larger-than-life numinosity of the real thing.

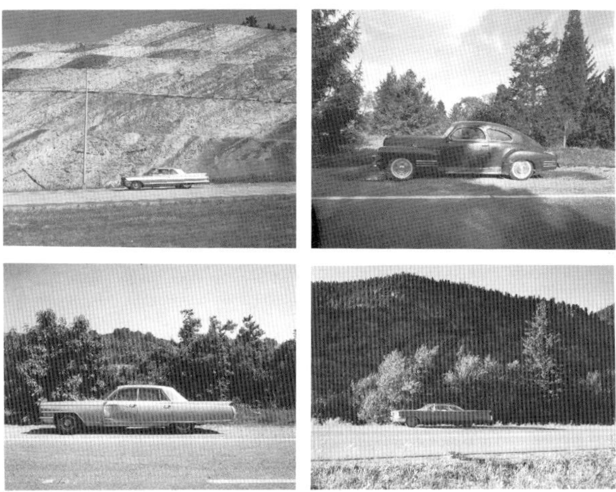

125 There is life in the fast lane, and life in the slow lane. But life just off the road, a possibility for any Cadillac, be it a shiny '62, a faded '41, a dented '64, or a stately '60, may be just a stop along the way, or the beginning of the end.

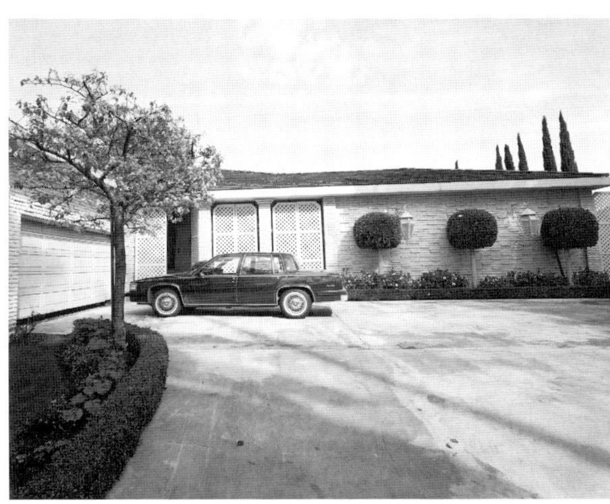

127 Pruned, clipped and neatly reigned in, the front wheel drive 1985 Sedan de Ville is a drastically diminished reminder that nothing lasts for ever.

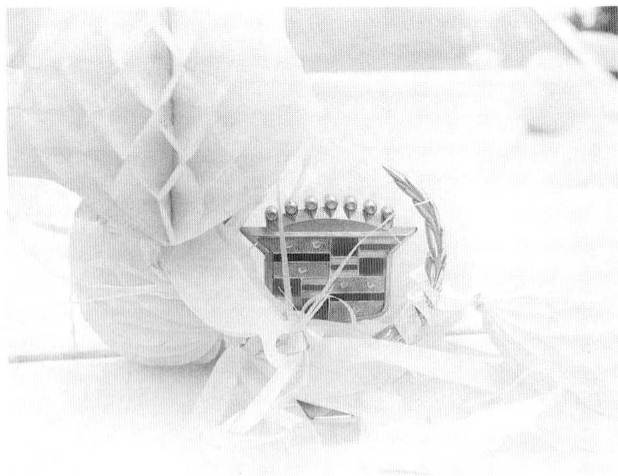

128 Cadillac has long been the real thing. Whatever the future holds for it, the trademark and its resonant meaning are part of the American psyche.

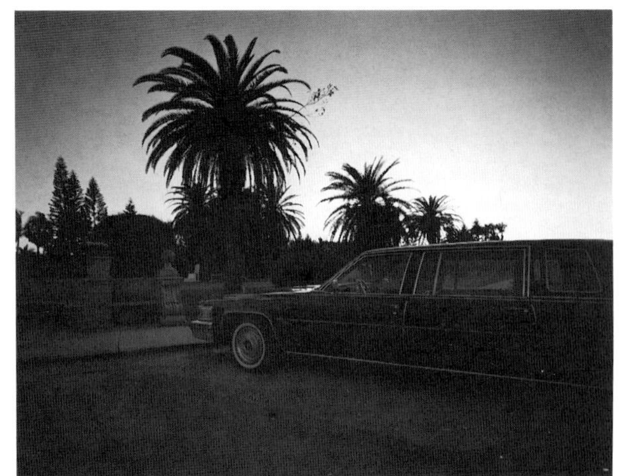

129 A 1985 limousine, a formal Floridian garden, and thou beside me in the wilderness. The sweetest dreams never die.

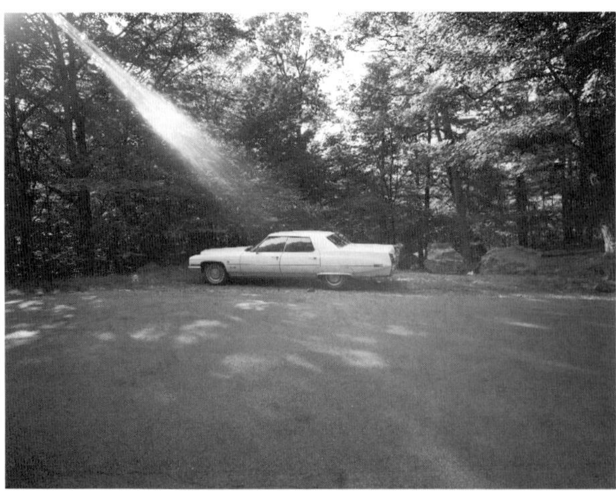

131 And God said, "Let there be Cadillac . . ."

FIN